iPhone Game Blueprints

Develop amazing games, visual charts, plots, and graphics for your iPhone

Igor Uduslivii

BIRMINGHAM - MUMBAI

iPhone Game Blueprints

First published: December 2013

Production Reference: 1191213

Published by Packt Publishing Ltd.
Livery Place
35 Livery Street
Birmingham B3 2PB, UK.

ISBN 978-1-84969-026-3

www.packtpub.com

Cover Image by Rogix (info@icoeye.com)

Credits

Author
Igor Uduslivii

Reviewers
Robbyn Blumenschein
Zbigniew Kominek
Clifford Matthew Roche

Acquisition Editors
David Barnes
Joanne Fitzpatrick

Lead Technical Editor
Anila Vincent

Technical Editors
Pragnesh Bilimoria
Veena Pagare
Ankita Thakur

Proofreaders
Ameesha Green
Paul Hindle
Stephen Swaney

Copy Editors
Alisha Aranha
Brandt D'Mello
Tanvi Gaitonde
Gladson Monteiro
Karuna Narayanan
Kirti Pai
Shambhavi Pai
Alfida Paiva

Project Coordinator
Shiksha Chaturvedi

Indexer
Mehreen Deshmukh

Production Coordinator
Manu Joseph

Cover Work
Manu Joseph

About the Author

Igor Uduslivii is a freelance illustrator and graphic designer with more than a decade's experience in this domain. He specializes in artwork for mobile games and UI graphics such as icons and buttons. Currently, he cooperates with Spooky House Studios UG (haftungsbeschränkt), a game development company that has created popular puzzle titles such as Bubble Explode and Rail Maze.

Right from his early years, he was passionate about drawing, computers, and video games. As a child, he liked to create illustrations by traditional painting methods as well as designing simple 8-bit games. After completing his studies from the Republican Colegiul de Informatica in Chisinau, Moldova, he began his career as an editor at Electronic Office publishing house, writing articles about new technologies and particularly, computer graphics. In parallel, he started studying Flash technology and animation. After that, he began actively working as a media designer, creating promo animations and Flash games. Igor also worked on the graphical look of software products, designing visual identities and UI elements. Among his clients were Kaspersky Lab, Reasoft, LemonStand, and many others. By now, most of his time is taken up by games. He is working on a full bunch of graphics, such as the application icon, characters, background art, props, textures, and animations.

He is fond of design as an art form and pursues it as a hobby, developing various concepts in the domain of print and simple industrial design elements. In fact, all the images (except the screenshots for games and the photos) that appear in this book are designed by him. He also worked as the main graphic artist for mobile games such as Blueprint3D, Rail Maze, and Bubble Explode. One of his projects called Jackets and Bookmarks was showcased at the Kleinefabriek exhibition at Amsterdam in 2010.

I would like to thank my family for their patience and endorsements during the process of creating this book. I would also like to thank Andrei Gradinari, Pavel Carpov, and Kostya Stankevych for their help and support.

About the Reviewers

Robbyn Blumenschein has a Bachelor of Science degree in Game Art and Design. She has done an internship at IPlay, a mobile game company, and has worked as a freelancer since graduation. She is recently working on a project (developing and designing) that is a cross platform for funding startup companies She received second place for the first competition for Z-place Technologies Inc.

Zbigniew Kominek is an experienced software developer who loves pure and tested code. He started his professional experience with client/server applications. After a few years, he made his dream come true and started working as an iOS game developer. One of the titles he worked on is the award-winning Bridgy Jones game. Now, he continues to pursue his passion for game development with Unity.

Dawid Szczepaniak (Executive Creative Director and Partner at VML Poland) says, "Zbigniew is one of the best iOS developers I've ever met. He is highly skilled and most of all, a mature and reliable person."

Gogula Gupta (Principal Software Engineer at Sabre) says "Zbyszek is a very talented and passionate developer. He has extremely good technical knowledge and ability to learn quickly. He delivers work with amazing speed and excellent quality. He has very good personal skills too. It is very valuable to have him in the team."

Artur Staszczyk (Programmer at CD Projekt Red) says "Zbigniew is a very skilled developer. Despite that his knowledge about design patterns and iOS programming is enormous, he is always willing to learn new techniques. It was a pleasure working with such experienced developer; he was a valuable member of our team."

I would like to thank my wife Ola. Her patience and support during tough moments gave me the strength to work hard and accomplish everything I wanted to do.

Clifford Matthew Roche is a self-taught game programmer who has been working on AAA projects since 2008, focusing on engine development, performance, and animation. He is credited on several games including NHL 09, FIFA 10, and MotionSports: Adrenaline.

Recently, he started his own game development company, Firestarter Games, where he works to bring high-quality games to mobile devices and consoles with Unity 3D. The company's first project, Globulous, was nominated for Best Audio (Casual/Indie) at the Audio Network Guild Music Awards.

www.PacktPub.com

Support files, eBooks, discount offers and more

You might want to visit www.PacktPub.com for support files and downloads related to your book.

Did you know that Packt offers eBook versions of every book published, with PDF and ePub files available? You can upgrade to the eBook version at www.PacktPub.com and as a print book customer, you are entitled to a discount on the eBook copy. Get in touch with us at service@packtpub.com for more details.

At www.PacktPub.com, you can also read a collection of free technical articles, sign up for a range of free newsletters and receive exclusive discounts and offers on Packt books and eBooks.

http://PacktLib.PacktPub.com

Do you need instant solutions to your IT questions? PacktLib is Packt's online digital book library. Here, you can access, read and search across Packt's entire library of books.

Why Subscribe?
- Fully searchable across every book published by Packt
- Copy and paste, print and bookmark content
- On demand and accessible via web browser

Free Access for Packt account holders

If you have an account with Packt at www.PacktPub.com, you can use this to access PacktLib today and view nine entirely free books. Simply use your login credentials for immediate access.

Table of Contents

Preface

The main objective of this book is to inspire the audience to begin creating more interesting games. Game development is a magical process, but the magic has some rules that should be determined and followed. All elements, principles, and methods are connected; one thing arises from another and it is very interesting to note such links. As soon as you see and feel a game as a system of events and factors, where even a tiny cogwheel is very important to the whole mechanism for operating like clockwork, you can control and tune it properly to get amazing results in the form of remarkable products. The entirety is one of the most import features. This book is a collection of blueprints that will show you how the mechanism works by demonstrating some vivid examples. It tries to note and explain many details, including the tiny ones.

What this book covers

Chapter 1, *Starting the Game*, helps to plan your very first game title, beginning with a plot and story. Some interesting ways to work with the plot are exposed, including plot squares, allowing generating various situations on a fly. Specific attention has been given to game identity as right naming and an application icon, which can help to appear on an app store in the best form. The second part of the chapter comprises useful information about game artwork: backgrounds, tile-textures, animation sheets, achievement graphics, and promo graphics.

Chapter 2, *Ergonomics*, is fully dedicated to a player's comfort when he is playing a game. Sometimes that is an issue, especially if a gameplay is complex. The chapter starts with **user interface** (**UI**) design and moves on to optimal screen dimensions of buttons, reliable logic of elements, and so on. The second part of the chapter gives information about increasing the accessibility of games. In an ideal case, a game product should be for many people, including those with some disabilities. Some advice is given on how to make the application color-blind friendly, how to try preventing possible problems with **photosensitive epilepsy** (**PSE**), and so on.

Chapter 3, *Gesture Games*, demonstrates that strictly functional mechanics as input processes on touchscreen devices can be easily transformed into a game. It is worth starting your very first game taking such an approach; the experience can be used for creating advanced controls for future games. The principles of gesture games are simple. An application asks a player to make a specific gesture if the objective is achieved, since the player will get some points. Though this doesn't sound much, with the help of good graphic ornamentation and a good game idea, the gameplay can be very interesting. There are several vivid design ideas in the chapter.

Chapter 4, *Card and Board Games*, explores the world of digital interpretations of traditional board games. It introduces some general elements of games that humans have played for centuries: a gameboard, gamepieces symbolizing various objects or characters, bonuses, pitfalls, and so on. The process itself is usually a war or a race. These principles, in some symbolic form, can be seen in modern games, including the most advanced ones. The chapter describes the concept of a virtual card game with RPG mechanics, a story of opposition between a group of robots on a small asteroid. Players may construct their own robots by upgrading their abilities, fighting monsters, collecting bonuses, and so on.

Chapter 5, *Puzzles*, tries to answer the question: is it possible to create very addictive gameplay by using a minimum amount of game pieces? The answer is affirmative. Puzzles need only few elements with a pretty plain simple design, but game developers should define smart rules very accurately. If the job is done well, it will be very difficult to stop playing the game. Moreover, it is usually easy to generate a lot of variations of gameplay based on a fixed number of elements. The chapter illustrates this thesis by exploring boundaries of the match-three puzzle paradigm. Several game modes have been described, including the exotic ones such as a match-three RPG game.

Chapter 6, *Platformer*, takes the next step; it increases the complexity and realism of games. They are not made of abstract elements any more. From now there is an interesting plot to follow and admit several objectives, large sceneries, and of course, characters (both a protagonist and antagonists). The chapter tells us how to create a charismatic main hero, how to develop a scary enemy, and what the uncanny valley is. Several aspects of animation have been referred to, including some psychological aspects of perception of motion on the screen and walking cycle animation details. All this is implemented into the description of a platformer game with some match-three puzzle logics. Its plot is about a planet where all robots, except one, have become crazy and hostile.

Chapter 7, *Adventure*, sends you into an engrossing journey by introducing various types of interactive and non-linear storytelling. Adventure games are novels where a plot can be controlled and changed by a player's actions or will; they are "The Garden of Forking Paths", storing many possible alterations of events and situations. The chapter portrays a concept of point-and-click adventure games. It takes place in a fictional diesel-punk universe where very long trains are used. They look like small towns constantly moving. The main protagonist is Anna-Amelia, a girl who wants to be a pilot. Some plot technicals are described, a portion of text is given to a conversation tree, inventory system, and, of course, puzzles.

Chapter 8, *Action Games*, introduces some popular genres such as shooters, which are one of the most dynamic and advanced classes of games. They are an eclectic mix of different genres, technologies, and story approaches, since they can be considered as an apogee for each game developer, a top everyone dreams to climb up to. This chapter exposes some conceptual ideas of a simple action game, where a player controls an astronaut lost in space. The story can be expressed in the best way by using 3D engine (however the game can be 2D as well), so there is some reference to low poly modeling, texturing, and so on. Special attention has been given to control issues, a controversial point of mobile devices when 3D games are involved.

Chapter 9, *Games with Reality*, starts with principles and definitions of mixed realities, both augmented reality and augmented virtuality, so that they can be turned into a game experience. The image of the technologies is pretty deliberate and honest, both unique advantages and obvious disadvantages are fully listed. The main interest is contributed to applications based on graphical tracking markers. There are several examples of popular designs. Few words are given to location-based games. The last sections of the chapter are dedicated to unusual practices, such as controlling of remote control toys with some video game logics in mind. There is some reference to gamification, a method where an everyday routine is turned into a game process, motivating people for some achievement and even helping to resolve some needful problems; by playing this game, players assist scientists.

What you need for this book

You will need some SDK you are familiar with. However, there is no special preference. The content of the book is pretty universal since there is no code accompanying the description of logic and graphic content. The book is mainly oriented to 2D games rather than 3D products; only the two last chapters describe games that are better to be done in 3D. You can use Cocos2D, Corona SDK, Unity, and so on.

For creating and managing graphics, it is good to have Adobe Illustrator; Adobe Photoshop is good as well, but it is better to use it only for additional raster operations that Illustrator cannot afford. Because there is a great variety of screen resolutions and games are usually ported on dozens of platforms, artwork should be vector based (with raster effects turned on), so Adobe Illustrator is a very efficient and handy solution.

3D graphics can be created in Blender, a very popular and free cross-platform editor with a huge fan base.

Who this book is for

The content of the book can be fascinating for all who are interested in game development, both for novices and professionals who can get some extra additions for their skills. The general audience is people who are dreaming to start creating games, but do not have an idea or plan to start with. The book might help them because they only have to take some concepts, customize them a little bit, and begin to design interesting products. The book can also help graphic designers who create artwork for mobile games, since they can begin to understand many processes in depth.

Conventions

In this book, you will find a number of styles of text that distinguish between different kinds of information. Here are some examples of these styles, and an explanation of their meaning.

Code words in text, database table names, folder names, filenames, file extensions, pathnames, dummy URLs, user input, and Twitter handles are shown as follows: "`Icon.png`: This is the name for the app icon on the iPhone"

New terms and **important words** are shown in bold. Words that you see on the screen, in menus or dialog boxes for example, appear in the text like this: "An element of the game's comfort is associated with the **Continue** button".

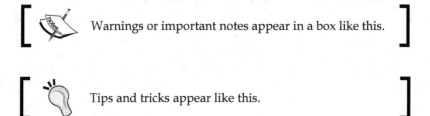

Warnings or important notes appear in a box like this.

Tips and tricks appear like this.

Reader feedback

Feedback from our readers is always welcome. Let us know what you think about this book—what you liked or may have disliked. Reader feedback is important for us to develop titles that you really get the most out of.

To send us general feedback, simply send an e-mail to feedback@packtpub.com, and mention the book title via the subject of your message.

If there is a topic that you have expertise in and you are interested in either writing or contributing to a book, see our author guide on www.packtpub.com/authors.

Customer support

Now that you are the proud owner of a Packt book, we have a number of things to help you to get the most from your purchase.

Downloading the color images of this book

We also provide you with a PDF file that has color images of the screenshots used in this book. You can download this file from https://www.packtpub.com/sites/default/files/downloads/0263OT_Images.pdf.

Errata

Although we have taken every care to ensure the accuracy of our content, mistakes do happen. If you find a mistake in one of our books—maybe a mistake in the text or the code—we would be grateful if you would report this to us. By doing so, you can save other readers from frustration and help us improve subsequent versions of this book. If you find any errata, please report them by visiting http://www.packtpub.com/submit-errata, selecting your book, clicking on the **errata submission form** link, and entering the details of your errata. Once your errata are verified, your submission will be accepted and the errata will be uploaded on our website, or added to any list of existing errata, under the Errata section of that title. Any existing errata can be viewed by selecting your title from http://www.packtpub.com/support.

Piracy

Piracy of copyright material on the Internet is an ongoing problem across all media. At Packt, we take the protection of our copyright and licenses very seriously. If you come across any illegal copies of our works, in any form, on the Internet, please provide us with the location address or website name immediately so that we can pursue a remedy.

Please contact us at copyright@packtpub.com with a link to the suspected pirated material.

We appreciate your help in protecting our authors, and our ability to bring you valuable content.

Questions

You can contact us at questions@packtpub.com if you are having a problem with any aspect of the book, and we will do our best to address it.

1
Starting the Game

We live in an amazing time. Not just groups of professionals working in large companies but even ordinary people have access to technical tools that give them the ability to create many wonderful things: they can shoot movies, record sounds, compose music, draw pictures, create stories and poetry, and communicate with people all over the world using procurable devices. The only thing that is needed is an idea and some aspiration. Games are not an exception; in fact, they are the quintessence of all creative intentions: they are stories told with the help of various interactive tools, graphics, music, and animation. And one of those could be your story.

Telling a story

The following figure shows the underlying mechanics of how a game tells a story:

Idea/Synopsis:

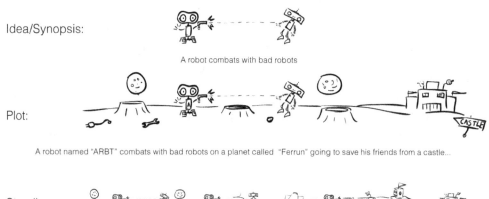

A robot combats with bad robots

Plot:

A robot named "ARBT" combats with bad robots on a planet called "Ferrun" going to save his friends from a castle...

Storyline :

| level 1 | level 2 | level 3 |

The preceding figure has the following three important parts:

- **Synopsis**: This is the game idea. It conveys the essence of the game.
- **Plot**: It is the description of the protagonist, their goals, conflicts, weapons, prizes, enemies, game settings, and many other things.
- **Storyline**: It decides the game levels.

A game is not a novel or a play, so the story is not the most important part of it. But the game idea or synopsis is. Your game should have clear and obvious principles that can be described in a few words. This is the keystone of your game; it must be solid and constant.

Try to start with something simple; you are not a big studio about to produce a new AAA title. Be modest. Use simple rules, graphics, and media.

It is important to remember that a game idea is not always unique. There are tons of games with identical principles and rules: to match-three elements in a row, to save a princess, to defend a base, to shoot enemies, and to win a race (the only exceptions are unique titles with revolutionary new principles of gameplay, but such games appear once in a blue moon as it is very hard to think a new type of reliable and addictive gameplay). To stand out from the crowd, the game needs a plot (or **semantic ornamentation**). The volume of information it conveys can differ; games with a complex gameplay (packed with adventure and RPG components) feature screenplays made of hundreds of pages and thousands of lines of text. This includes the main storyline, various side quests, alternative variants of the same events, subplots, and so on. There is an interesting list on gaming at `http://gaming.wikia.com/wiki/List_of_longest_video_game_scripts`, showing descriptions of some of the longest scripts for modern video games; for instance, *Fallout 3* from *Bethesda Game Studios* has a screenplay made up of 40, 000 lines. But some visual novel games have scripts with more than 1,00,000 lines. This is more than in the movie industry (a traditional film screenplay has about 120 pages (one page per minute) and around 50 to 55 lines of text per page, since the overall number of lines is something close to 6,500). This is not only because the games are longer, but also because they are non-linear. At the same time, simple games, which are reasonable to begin a game developer career with, may have very short plots, barely longer than the synopsis. For instance, it can describe a game setting and some minor notations: an underwater bubble match-three game with a few unique bonus elements. Such type of plot is perfect for small puzzle games because the game's mechanics are clear enough that you only need to describe its graphics—the look and feel.

Stronger efforts on the plot are needed when the figure of the protagonist (the main character) is introduced. In this case, some classic dramatic principles are turned on. The player needs to know something about the character: his motivation, goals, and strong and weak points. Maybe the character's past is unclear (this is a good way to create intrigue), but he should have a recognizable pattern of behavior and some principles and characteristics; in other words, he should have some spirit. In this case, the player would feel as if he/she is with the protagonist. A well-written character needs an appropriate framework in the form of a good story that should be interesting to follow. It is important to note that any genre can have a deep and exciting plot. One of the wonderful examples of great storytelling is a critically acclaimed indie game, *Braid* (`http://braid-game.com/`), designed by *Jonathan Blow*. It features an interesting plot, gameplay and story-driven design as a platformer game with puzzle elements.

It is good to demonstrate *the evolution of narrative species* in the game. The very first level must start with the synopsis, that is, it should demonstrate the keystone rule of the game: the player should make a single and simple action in one step. Then he/she should be able to see some plot elements, for instance, some bonuses or should meet somebody. And after that, he/she should face the story: game shows him/her the next level.

There is an interesting indie-game project called *Storyteller* (`http://www.storyteller-game.com`). It is a puzzle game with a unique main concept: a player needs to create a specific story. He has some plot elements—characters, situations, secrets, and state of mind—and the player's objective is to combine generating dramatic conflicts and climaxes and creating the story. An amazing idea, isn't it? The plot of the game is to create a plot:

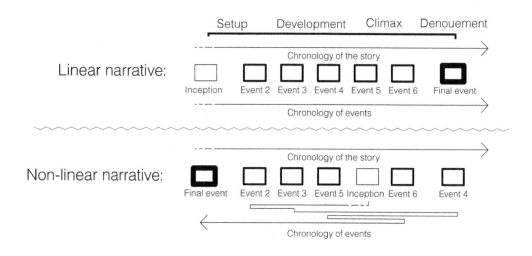

Your main enemy is monotony—players don't like routine repetition of identical elements over and over again. Therefore, there must be progress of game elements, either evolutionary or revolutionary. For example, the game should become faster, puzzles should become harder, opponents should get more strength, and so on. This is an extensive way to solve the problem. But the more intensive it becomes, the more attractive it is.

The game should be changed more widely, by introducing new settings, props, characters, enemies, and obstacles. The main goal is to not let the player get bored. If he gets the hang of a specific tool, tactic, or weapon, turning the game process into a mechanical routine, the game should change the conditions a little bit to force the player to find some new ways. You should explore the range of abilities your game elements have and use them creatively, surprising the player very often. What will happen if we begin to use the element of the puzzle a bit differently? What will happen if gravity were suddenly turned off? Will the weapon be effective under water? How will element A interact with element B? It is great when a game item has more than one scope. The story becomes more flexible and pleasantly unexpected. People like to be pleasantly surprised.

But try to avoid bad examples of the unexpected things: various forms of *deus ex machina*. Each twist in the story should be natural and slightly predictable in various premises in the plot. Look at the movies; directors always show a specific object in advance before it is used in a corresponding scene. For example, in the *Alfred Hitchcock* classic, *North by Northwest* (1959), the main character played by brilliant *Cary Grant* first sees an airplane far afield, and then he almost forgets about it. Suddenly, the airplane begins to attack. So, the scheme is simple: drop a hint and only after that initiate some action. It is very important to convince players that a game world is solid, every tiny detail matters, and links between elements are well thought out and designed. A good game is a complex organization of dozens of components working together. They don't create a single event, but a sequence of well-connected situations letting players experience some specific emotions. This is an attempt to create a model of life rather than a calculator with few binary triggers. As it is very important to try to think globally while working with a script, there should be an evolution of events and obvious logical connections between the stages of a story.

A vital issue is realism in games. There is a lot of debate about this by now, mainly because power capacities of CPUs and video chips have increased, and as a result, many more variables and factors can be introduced in gameplay. The question is not only about the graphics, rather about other components of virtual worlds. For instance, 3D objects might have not only an external shell but some naturalistic structure inside; by breaking them into pieces, players might expose some new features of internal materials.

Another example is NPCs, whose psychology and behavior can be more realistic or a player's avatar which has all the features of a human body including weaknesses. The truth is simple; a portion of realism is needed only if it helps to improve gameplay, if it can create some interesting situations, and add some specific experience. In other cases, it may turn a game into a series of boring procedures and events players run away from in real life. In casual and arcade games, an action should not become more complex only because it would become more realistic (simulators are another case).

Video games are more about entertainment than documentary. Since the degree of realism is under the control of game designers, they decide what proportion to choose for better playability. Such a characteristic is not unique for video games only; most of the arts manage reality very freely. Painting, sculpture, music, literature, and movies are not realistic, even if they pretend to be; it is always an interpretation whose main objective is better expression of some authors' intents. Elements of reality are always being changed (within reasonable limits) if it would help to describe or display some things better. Such practice is known as **artistic license** (also known as **poetic license**, **dramatic license**, and so forth). Moreover, the audience is already familiar with and prepared for such tricks, as if they are watching the performance of a magician. Everybody knows that all his actions are tricks and he is not a real mage; they simply want to see a show. Ignoring some simplification and distortion of realistic rules in favor of more attractive quality of a piece of art is known as **willing suspension of disbelief** or in short, **suspension of disbelief**. Because of it, players overlook a lot of roughness on screen menu, such as avatars who are capable of carrying tons of weapons in their pockets, cars with infinite fuel supply, indestructible walls, and so on. The only point to note is that the suspension of disbelief is a matter of a delicate concern; any simplification must be compensated with something vivid, or a disappointed audience will be very critical. The following is an example of the plot squares chart.

There is an interesting way to explore the plot and to invent some original situations. I call it **plot squares chart**. It is based on illustration (or text description) of the basic plot element. For example, it includes the character and its weapon. Then a list of different circumstances should be composed — the more unusual and abstract they are, the better — rotation, showing half of the square, absence of gravity, strong wind, legs instead of arms, entropy, and so forth. There can be dozens of them in the list. After that, you need to put the plot square in each circumstance, fixing what could happen with the character.

There are only a few circumstances shown in the following figure but their list can be longer:

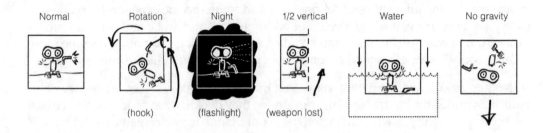

| Normal | Rotation | Night | 1/2 vertical | Water | No gravity |
| | (hook) | (flashlight) | (weapon lost) | | |

How would he adapt to a new condition? It will let you invent some new details for the story.

More complex plots must be explained in a proper way. Normally, players don't like to read a lot of text in the video games, they don't like long introductions and cut-screens, so it is better to use contextual narration—telling the story while the player is playing the game. The storyline should be cut into small pieces scattered on the game levels. It should not be textual; all the game elements must tell their stories: gameplay mood, character's design, backgrounds, and props. For example, you can display a large portion of text about a spaceship crashed on a planet, or just show an image of the crash at the game background, displaying all the aspects graphically. Not words but the behavior and image of a character can show the fact that it is a negative character. Some cracks on the surface of game object can drop a hint that the object is breakable. Design is an important part of a narrative system.

Dialogues are a good part of the storyline, especially for games with some RPG elements or for adventure quests. They must be short and clear. A small portion of humor can increase their attractiveness. The main problem with dialogues is the necessity of a voiceover; the game needs professionally recorded and mixed voices to sound cogent enough. This problem can be solved by introducing graphic speech bubbles with some text instead of real voices. This can make localization easier too. A sound effect with some balderdash and indecipherable syllables can be added, and sometimes that approach can be very funny. The dialogue system will be expressed better in *Chapter 7, Adventure,* of this book dedicated to adventure games.

Game development is a knotty process, so you have to accept the fact that the plot, and particularly the story, will be in a state of constant transformation. Some ideas will be dropped for a variety of reasons (for example, they can be unrealizable from a technical point of view or test players will not like them) or your experiments with the game will reward you with new ideas. It is important to know that the gameplay is usually more important than the story; bad game mechanics can ruin a perfect story, so don't worry about some ideas if they do not work well. Try to find new ones instead.

The funny part of the storytelling is the inside jokes or Easter eggs. Sometimes, this is a way to resolve tiny problems with the story. For instance, there is a bunker in the game that needs a name written on a wall. The name can be constructed from your name or it can be an allusion on your favorite movie (remember the *Lost* TV series, for example), popular Internet memes (recall the famous phrase, a phrase in broken English, "All your base are belong to us"), and so on. Not only can small text be a tribute to something but also level compositions, a character's name or look, and even a sound design.

There is a very popular in-joke in the movie and video game industry; when a character dies screaming, a special sound effect is used known as the **Wilhelm scream**. Few people know this, but the same scream is used in more than 200 movies. Don't forget that it is always pleasant to make hidden references to other game projects you've done before, for instance, characters from previous games can be turned into props as toys or posters.

Characters

The following are the various components in a game:

- **Protagonist**: This is the main game character, the persona the player associates himself with. In most cases, it is under direct control of the player.

- **Game trigger**: These are the various interactive elements (switches, buttons, and so on) that the player can operate; they may have an effect on the game world or on states of characters.

- **Enemy**: These are the characters (or situations or events at abstract level, for example, time can be the enemy too) that are hostile to the main character and its progress in the game. Their main objective is to hinder the player.

- **Friendly/neutral character**: This is any persona that has no aggressive plans towards the main character. Usually, this is something extra, walking the game level. Sometimes, they should be protected by the protagonist or they can be player's companions helping to perform some specific tasks.

Some games can be handled without any characters. Most of the puzzle games, for instance, the match-three games, have no persona. Are various color bubbles characters? I don't think so. They are game triggers, I would call them "precharacters" or "character ancestors" because they do interact with the player and perform some actions but their personality, both functional and graphical, is minimal. Their digital soul is small. But there can be the exceptions too, for example, tile-matching game *Chuzzle* by *PopCap Games* uses not soulless color triggers but real characters named *Chuzzles* — shaggy balls with eyes and some personality that are very cute.

A main character is the representation of the player in the game universe; this is his avatar, so he should like its appearance and behavior. This does not mean that the character must be perfect, but he must have some charisma to be attractive. In other words, he should have some unique features.

Frequently, there are characters in the game but no a protagonist. In this case, the game operates with the characters, enemies, and triggers, but the main character is the player himself; he plays the role of an abstract demiurge controlling the game world. For example, most puzzle, tactical, and strategic games do not have any player representation. In this case, the player empathizes with not only one person but the whole game world. The following figure shows a character and its components:

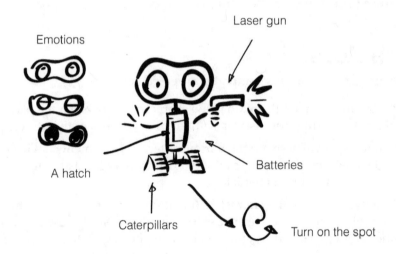

"ARBT" robot

Emotions

Laser gun

A hatch

Batteries

Caterpillars

Turn on the spot

Before designing any type of characters you should think about its graphic look and functionality. Try to create a list of the actions it would perform, starting with the basic ones: walking, jumping, shooting, and so on. This will help you to determine the character's anatomy and dimensions. For example, if he has to collect some items from the ground, he should have arms of a proper length and should be able to bend. If there are going to be ladders in your game, the character should have a constitution letting him climb up and not being stuck by the ladder. The world outside the character must be proportional to him and vice versa.

To design the character right, you need some concept art or sketches to determine its look. Of course, big game studios feature every breathtaking example of concept art and real states of art; everyone wants to buy such images and put them on the wall. But at the first step of development, they are not necessary at all. The sketches can look like some doodles, more important are the ideas that can be written there. Usually every interesting concept is born from a scrawl, sometimes made on a table napkin. So, don't worry about the graphic quality for now; you will need it later, when the working process on sprite or 3D models starts.

Levels

The levels are your story and express the plot; they are chapters in your novel told via the game mechanics. So, pay attention to each of them, especially the first ones, because that is the place where the player meets the game. The players should like the beginning to continue playing.

You can start planning the levels on paper, making different notes and sketches. Then it is better to switch to a more flexible tool. For example, it is good to use spreadsheets tools (Microsoft Excel or Calc from the OpenOffice.org package) to create a sketch of a level. That is unusual, but let's break stereotypes because spreadsheets can be very efficient: you can add various colors to cells, copy, paste, and cut them, move some sections of the level, and make some grouping operations. Moreover, you may find the way to save the spreadsheet document in a form that can be recognized by your game, so you will have not a sketch tool, but an improvised level editor!

The following is an example of the level sketched in the spreadsheet application:

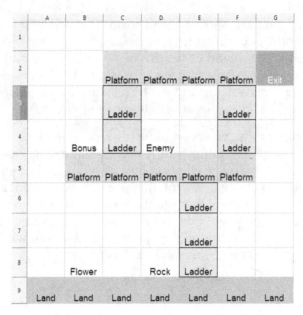

Of course, a special level editor is better, especially if it has a test/preview option. This means that the editor should be based on your game engine. Try to make it practical, so that not only you but other people could use it too. Initially, all the level designers can be from your team, but then you can try to offer level creation features to a wider audience. Projects that let users generate content are always in fashion.

Naming

It is no secret that the name of a game should be unique, easy to remember and reproduce, and also should be short. Ideally, it must reflect the game's idea and have an emotional tone very close to the game's mood. This is your brand, so pay the maximum attention to it.

The name can be based on the plot of your game and include either the description of the game's situation or one of the character's names. It can include some hints on the game's genre or mechanics. Try not to overthink the name and avoid including various semantic games and rebuses in it (in exceptional cases they are really genius). Try to recall the *Tom Hanks* movie, *That thing you do!* (1996), in which there was a pop band that called itself *The Oneders*, thinking that the audience would know to pronounce it "one-ders". The word was supposed to be wonders, but they thought it was smarter to spell it this way. Of course, they were wrong because all around called them "oh-need-ers".

It is highly possible that all the single-word names will already be taken, but do not get discouraged, because with a double-worded name you have more chances. But try to avoid too-long names. In *iTunes Connect Developer Guide*, in the chapter *Adding New Apps*, there is a phrase:

> *"The app name cannot be longer than 255 bytes and can be no fewer than two characters."*

So, 255 bytes is the maximum length of the app name, but most people do not reach that limit. Practically, there is a more important point: the length of a text label situated below the application icon. Subjectively, the title looks more attractive and professional if it can be written in a single row of text (different subtitles and functional words can fill in the second row). The following screenshot illustrates various text labels. Some of them have only one row of text, some use two, and the last one fills up all the lines and features some symbols truncated:

The length of the text label is measured in pixels, not in text characters. Usually it is equal to dozens of letters. If your name includes narrow letters such as I, L, and J, there will be many more characters in the text label (for example, up to 16). In contradistinction, the words with wide letters W, O, and so on would take more space. So, always experiment with various words. The hyphenation algorithm used on the App Store works with phrases, so it breaks down not words into letters, but phrases into single words, this is why it is sometimes difficult to write a few long words in a single line. If the name is longer than both text rows, the name will be truncated, the system will replace some letters with an ellipsis. iOS in its turn writes names of applications in one line without hyphenation. So, if a text label is long, it has been broken off and has got the ellipsis, which looks very unattractive, like a torn dress. That is why some developers try to use abbreviation or short forms of their titles on devices. For example, *PopCap* had to use a shorter alias for *Plants vs. Zombies 2*, which was overly long for iOS, so *PvZ 2* was used instead. When talking about names for mobile games, the old phrase *"less is more"* rings true.

Having invented the name, try to check its availability. This can be done by searching for it on Google, App Store, and other popular locations. It is worth checking whether or not your chosen name is already a trademark. Otherwise, if the title (or some of its parts—for example, the term "Tower Defense" is copyrighted) and belongs to somebody, but your published game used it widely, there can be some unpleasant consequences: because of trademark disputes, the application can be removed from App Store. There was a buzz about the puzzle game *Edge* by *Mobigame*; despite being a critically acclaimed product, it was removed from App Store a few times because of disputes about the word "Edge" used in the title (`http://en.wikipedia.org/wiki/Edge_by_Mobigame`).

The availability of a name can be checked via various official online services, for instance, **United States Patent and Trademark Office (USPTO)** has **Trademark Electronic Search System (TESS)** on their website `http://www.uspto.gov/trademarks/index.jsp`. There is a similar system in the United Kingdom, the Intellectual Property Office has search trademarks option on their website `http://www.ipo.gov.uk/types/tm.htm`. There is also The Office for Harmonization in the Internal Market, which is the registry of trademarks within the European Union. It has a database search on its website too (`http://oami.europa.eu/ows/rw/pages/QPLUS/databases/searchCTM.en.do`).

You must be prepared for the name to already be taken (there are thousands of games in the world, so many good-looking titles are already used), so always have some alternatives. It is always better to check the name before development, because the name can be introduced in the plot and the story.

If your name is free and you can use, it is necessary to secure it; you must register the Internet domain name (it is better to use the `.com` address) and create topical accounts on communities on social networking sites. For example, you will need a Facebook page for your game, a YouTube page, a Twitter account, a Tumblr page, and so on. Of course, the main marketplace is the App Store (Google Play, BlackBerry World, and so on too if the game is ported on new platforms); nevertheless, an official website and social media should not be underestimated; they may help the game with additional marketing. On the website, we can embed some YouTube videos: a trailer or some gameplay demonstrations, some descriptions, and examples of artwork, and a blog can be made of developer diaries. Many players like such information very much, especially if they are familiar with previous titles of a developer. Additionally, some extra plot information can be placed on the website to expand the world of the game; this can include image maps of the in-game universe, special web episodes, simple comics, or short novels related to the title. Another good idea is to have small goodies for the audience: wallpapers (both for handheld devices and desktop computers), some images that can be printed as stickers, and some papercraft maybe.

The main idea is to convince current and potential players that you love them a lot. The design of the official page should be simple and clean, concentrating all attention to a central table with the game logo, video, and some text description; an App Store Badge with a link to iTunes is mandatory. The social networking sites are much easier to manage; they only require you to update status periodically to keep the audience up. Various likeable screenshots and illustrations from the game are good. To properly decorate the account, you only need to choose proper avatars and title backgrounds.

Working with graphic assets

Strong visual style is one of the important components of a game's success, but it is not the primary component because without a good game idea and its proper implementation, the game would be only a graphical cover. On the other hand, a game with great mechanics and good gameplay but with indifferent artwork may expect only partial success or even failure. Ideally, the graphics is not an ordinary set of beautiful pictures but a tool to establish communication between the game and the player; it tells him the story and demonstrates how the game world works.

The number and types of graphics depend on the game's genre and its complexity. In most simple cases, the game can operate only the graphics rendered by itself. All geometric shapes and even 3D forms are drawn by programming codes, but most modern games use pre-rendered artwork in a form of raster images.

There are several basic types of 2D graphics the games use, which are as follows:

- **Sprites**: These are small images being used as different components of the game process. They can display game characters, weaponry, landscape elements, various props, and bonuses. They can also be an integral part of special effects, such as smoke or fire.
- **Animated sprites**: These are special form of sprites that help to create an animation. These are series of still images, each of which is displaying a specific phase of an object's movement. Together they are collected into one image sheet. The game plays a particular type of file and the player sees the animation associated with this file.
- **Tiles**: This is a special case of ordinary sprites. Tiles are special graphic *bricks* helping to draw up the game scene. They can be both functional and decorative. In contradistinction to the sprites, the tiles sometimes are only *construction material*; they do not include any game character. They are collected in tile sheets—files with all the image elements for a certain game level or scene.
- **Textures**: These are images that are used as textures for 3D models or for screen backgrounds.

- **Backgrounds**: These are images that are used as backdrops for game scenes. Often they are pretty large.

- **GUI elements**: This includes all the graphics that are used like a control inside the game. Buttons of different size, switches, radio-buttons, and various panels to display alerts and text are gathered into GUI sheets.

- **Icons**: These are GUI icons, achievements, and trophies.

The main principle of a good artwork is simple: **solidity**. All the elements of graphics must have equal style and quality and should have identical principles of formation. Each of them can have his own color, texture, and details, but all these characteristics must obey the general rule you've designed for your game. Think about the music, a melody (for example, the famous *James Bond* theme) can be mixed in a hundred ways, can be played faster or slower, or can be rearranged for new genres, but it will still be recognizable because the core is always appreciated. This analogy helps to illustrate that each element made out of the general rule may look fake. The audience will notice that unconsciously and this will reduce the perception of the product's quality.

In the authorized biography by *Walter Isaacson* of *Steve Jobs*, there is a wonderful quote by *Jobs*:

> *"When you're a carpenter making a beautiful chest of drawers, you're not going to use a piece of plywood on the back, even though it faces the wall and nobody will ever see it."*

It is pity, but some developers or designers try to ignore such philosophy; their products have a pretty beautiful facade but ugly backyards; for example, menu pages and some secondary-class game graphics are made slovenly, without any love and attention to the details, as though such components "are facing the wall and nobody sees them". This approach is wrong because your game is not only one game screen but a product with many edges, each of which must be done thoroughly. Otherwise, it shows that you don't like and don't respect your audience, and the product is not professional.

I recommend using a vector-based graphic editor to work with artwork for games. It is a much more flexible and secure way to provide graphics for different resolutions and situations. My favorite tool is Adobe Illustrator, which lets you draw complicated illustrations using graphic tablets; it supports both vector instruments and some useful raster effects. There is truly direct manipulation philosophy, not like the layered one in Photoshop, which lets you edit objects more easily. It has multiple artboards, which is very good for exporting routines (especially together with slices). There are symbols (if you know Flash, you will understand their potential efficiency) and dozens of other pleasant tools.

Sprites and tiles

One of the most important characteristics of a sprite image is transparency (also called the **alpha channel**). The image must be combined with underlying graphics (with backgrounds or other sprites) at the game screen, creating an appearance of a solid picture. Some decades ago, when computers had no such advanced calculating power, the sprites were small, and the simplest form of transparency was used. Each pixel could be turned on or off, so the images featured so called **hard edges**; there was no soft transition between a transparent pixel and an opaque one. To mark a zone in the image which would be transparent, a special color was used; usually, it was a color never featured in the drawn artwork, for example, magenta (sometimes developers called it **magic pink**). The sprites with such transparency had sharp contour and worked well only on graphic video systems with a small resolution.

Nowadays, most platforms, including mobile devices, support a more complex type of transparency called **alpha channel** that supports shades of opacity. With this, smooth transitions and translucent elements can be displayed. In most cases, the PNG file format is used for sprites. It is lossless, no pixels will be lost after exporting the image, and by default, the image editing tools create PNGs with a straight (non-premultiplied) alpha channel. The term *straight* means that pixels have no precalculated data for compositing, the only information is the exact RGB value and the alpha channel (colors and alpha are not interconnected; a value of transparency cannot distort values in color channels). On the other hand, premultiplied type of transparency (color and alpha channels are interconnected and by changing alpha information you also change the RGB values) is in demand, because of its efficiency, natural behavior, and being compression friendly, but PNG by default cannot work with it. This is why some developers try to choose TGA or TIFF, which support both types of alpha channels, or try to find third-party tools to convert the straight alpha channel type of transparency in PNG to premultiplied. Besides normal transparency, game engines can also offer some additional modes when creating the final scene is a bit more complex, which let us create interesting visual effects. For instance, the Multiply mode, where dark pixels of foreground images are added to the background but white ones are ignored, helps to create shadows. A Screen mode is the opposite of Multiply; it lets us light up some elements, creating the illusion of reflections, hotspots, and so on.

iOS devices also support a specific type of texture compression called **PowerVR Texture Compression** (**PVRTC**), created especially for effective storing and using of raster images; the files themselves are frequently referred to simply as PVRs. The file format is native for the PowerVR GPU used in iOS devices (and some other platforms, so the format is pretty universal), so it is accurately optimized for graphic hardware and uses advanced methods of data compression (up to 8:1).

PVRTC does not required software-based decompression, images take less volume of memory, there are lesser amounts of data to be transferred, and is managed by the hardware; therefore, the files are rendered much faster than traditional PNG. The performance and thrifty usage of memory resources are the main advantages of the format. But there some disadvantages; first of all, the compression algorithm is lossy, so some portion of graphical information is lost and there can be some visual artifacts. This can be critical for elements that require some pixel accuracy, for instance, UI elements. In this connection, it is wise to strike a compromise and use PNG for static elements with a lot of small fragments but PVRTC for texturing fast objects where the ideal quality is not an issue.

Another problem with PVRTC is some lack of support from popular graphics software; there is no native support for it by default; special plug-ins are needed. Nevertheless, the issue can be solved by compressing tools with the official cross-platform software suite *PVRTexTool* (`http://www.imgtec.com/powervr/insider/powervr-pvrtextool.asp`). There are also some specific requirements for images: they should be square and their dimensions must be in the power of two, but in most cases that is not onerous at all. The following screenshot shows the tile sheet from a puzzle game *Rail Maze* developed by *Spooky House Studios UG (haftungsbeschränkt)*:

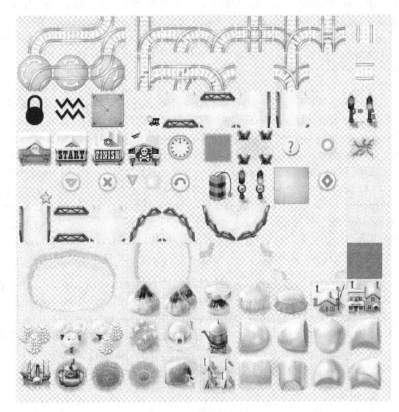

The sprites and tiles are not usually stored as single images because there are dozens of sprites in games and the content folder would be crowded with image files. It is more convenient to collate them in special graphic sheets stored in large image files. The sprite sheet (alternatively, **texture atlas**) is divided into small fragments in which each sprite fits. The size of the fragment depends on the game ; usually, sprite width and height are multiples of eight—something like 64 x 64 pixels or 128 x 64 pixels, 128 x 128 pixels, and so on. The sprite sheets in turn are much larger; their maximum dimensions depend on the specifications of a device as shown in the following table:

Device	Dimensions
iPhone 2G, iPhone 3G	1024 x 1024 pixels
iPhone 3GS, iPhone 4, iPad 1	2048 x 2048 pixels
iPhone 5/5S/5C, iPhone 4, iPad 3, iPad 4, iPad mini	4096 x 4096 pixels

To calculate how much space a sprite sheet in PNG format will occupy in graphics memory, a simple formula can be constructed. Standard bitmaps are used in uncompressed form, so the content is irrelevant; only dimensions matter. It is known that there are four channels in PNG, colors and alpha, each one is described by a byte of data. The formula is as follows:

$$(Height \times Width \times 4)/(1024 \times 1024) = space\ in\ megabytes$$

For example, a texture of 512 x 512 pixels occupies 1 MB of memory, 1024 x 1024 pixels in turn occupies 4 MB, and so on. To get an idea of hardware resources, including the amount of RAM for iOS devices, it is good to look at the special table published at `http://docs.unity3d.com/Documentation/Manual/iphone-Hardware.html`.

There are special applications that can help to create and manage sprite sheets, for instance, a very popular tool Texture Packer (`http://www.codeandweb.com/texturepacker`) designed by *Andreas Löw*. It supports many compression algorithms, including PVRTC, and works with many actual game engines, such as *Cocos 2d*, *Corona SDK*, *Sparrow*, *Unity*, and so on. Texture Packer also features a handy drag-and-drop interface, as well as a bunch of various settings for texture sheets, letting us tune them deeply. The great advantage of this application is the ability to convert default PNGs into their analogs with a premultiplied alpha channel.

Alternatively, sheets can be developed in standard graphics editors, such as Adobe Illustrator. The only point to note is that some routine operations are performed manually. According to my experience, it is better to draw and export the sprites (or tiles) one-by-one, and then collect the exported images in the sheet file. In other words, you need to have some files only for drawing sprites (let's call them **canvases**) and one file to organize the final illustration in the sheet (let's call it a **sprite collector**). First of all, this speeds up the exporting routine: if the source file for the sprite sheet consisted not of linked raster files but real vector illustrations, it would make exporting the final file a much longer process. Secondly, it offers protection from *shadow artifacts*: images are the sprite sheets that stay tight, so some elements of one illustration would overlap the illustration nearby a little bit for sure. Usually, the edges of soft shadows lean out of the sprite's frames; as a result, some sprites or tiles get unnecessary dark lines. In the sprite collector, there won't be such a problem, because each sprite is already an exported image and has appropriate dimensions.

The dimensions and position of tiles inside sprite sheets should be chosen properly; otherwise, there is some risk of visual artifacts such as thin faded lines at edges caused by compression. They look ugly and are easy noticeable even on Retina displays. Remember that OpenGL likes fours—sizes of texture elements should be multiples of four to achieve better results (this is because, at the time of encoding, an image is split into blocks of 4 x 4 pixels). Some examples of the sizes of texture elements are 64, 128, 256, and so on. It is obligatory to have a grid system in the sheet file. It will help you to determine the exact position and borders of each sprite. The grid should be made of translucent rectangles arranged in chess-board order. This is a much more precise way than a grid based on guides. The rectangles must be placed on a separate layer; this lets you to switch them on and off. One of the advantages of this type of grid is an opportunity to export it with the sprites for testing purposes; for example, to check how the game engine cuts out the sprites from the sprite sheet or how the graphic proportions work in the application. Tools such as Texture Packer successfully automate such procedures.

The basic design rules of good sprites are simple: the illustration should be contrasting and perceptible, and its details should express the element's functions in an unambiguous manner. The player should not have to conjecture what is in front of him. If an element has few states—for example, it is a switch—that means that each state should be thoroughly indicated. The artwork must be most descriptive; don't be afraid to over-describe. The following screenshot shows the grid system used in the Rail Maze game; it helps to determine the borders of tiles and to connect central parts of the tiles properly:

Preparing animation

It is impossible to imagine a modern game without animation. The game world should be alive to compel attention. There are two major types of animation: based on programming code and frame based stored in animation sprites. The first type requires some programming algorithm to move or transform a graphic object; in most cases, this is a linear process. An object is moved from location A to location B with predetermined speed, its size is increased, and its alpha channel is changed. Such type of the animation with automatic incrimination is called **motion tween** in Adobe Flash. At a more complex level, the object has curved trajectories and moves with some acceleration and there is inertia in its movement; the games in which such interpretation is used require advanced control on an element's dynamics; first of all, I'm talking about various physics puzzles.

Frame-based animation on the other hand is a way to beautify the motion. Besides the automatic animation successfully moving a sprite around the screen, the illustration inside the sprite would be still; for example, a character would not step. Several images to illustrate the walking cycle are needed so that the game can form animation sprites. This is a bunch of images, portraying various phases of motion. Modern SDKs usually have rich collections of methods to work with the animation sprites. They can be played in the order in which they are stored in the animation sheet, or they can be organized by using an array with a custom order, which is very useful because more complicated animation sequences can be created with a minimum number of images.

Here are some tricks: if there is a portion of opposing movements (for example, a character is showing up from a hatch and then hides back), the animation sheet can include only half the frames, displaying the motion in one direction; the other part would be constructed from the same frames but played backward. A pause in an animation of given duration can be organized by simple repetition of one of the sprites. Another interesting option of non-linear frames are *extra frames*, which helps to deal with sameness of animation cycles. Each gesture and movement an object makes in the real world is pretty unique. Take for example a passerby walking in the street, his legs make steps in cycles; the cycles are pretty similar, but not quite the same. There is a beautiful metaphor:

> *"Sometimes a butterfly lands on the shoulder, so step at this moment is a little bit different."*

So, it is good to add the unexpected touch to the animation frame sometimes. It can be done by replacing an ordinary frame with one differing frame that has some small unique detail. There can be several extra frames; the game would choose them randomly.

It is good to animate characters in Adobe Flash and then to export the result as separate still images, finally collecting them into one Adobe Illustrator document and exporting it as an animation sheet. It is worth mentioning about a very interesting tool for creating smooth and natural character animation called Spine (http://esotericsoftware.com/). Its general advantage is that it is a 2D skeletal system with various fragments of a character (head, body, legs, feet, and so on) attached. Positions of bones and their angles are calculated in real time and interpolations are very smooth and correlated with the frame rate; therefore, the motion is very smooth. Moreover, because animation is not tied to strictly defined frames, the system is very flexible; this means that some combination of motions can be easily introduced without redrawing a full sequence of frames. For example, by default in traditional frame-by-frame animation, a character running and the same character running and shooting are two separate sequences, which increases consumption of memory resources and makes animation exporting a bit complex. A skeletal animation has no such complications; various gestures of the character can be combined more easily with minimum memory costs. Of course, this is possible only if a game did not use a raster output of Spine in the form of video files or sprites, but used binary data of virtual bone positions and keyframes stored in special documents instead.

Different special effects are based on animation too. For example, smoke can be created by using a translucent and blurry circle being duplicated around the screen; the opacity of each circle should be reduced softly, but their sizes should be increased.

Background

Backgrounds are the essential part of every game without reference to their genres. In order to express game elements in the best possible way, they should have a graphic background. There are two types of backgrounds: static and dynamic. The first ones have a fixed position at the screen, being changeless. The second ones consist of several separate image layers, being mobile to each other. This helps to create various effects; foremost is the illusion of parallax. In this case, each image layer has its own horizontal speed depending upon its imaginary z axis position. Such a type of background is usually used in games with dynamic gameplay: platform games, arcades, actions, racing, and so on. The following is a chart showing screen resolutions of the iPhone/iPad family:

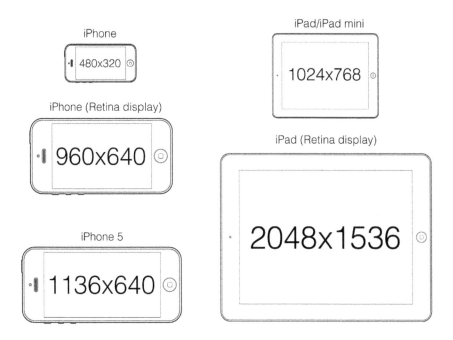

The main difficulty with the backgrounds is their dependence on the screen resolution. There is a wide range of screen dimensions in iOS devices, starting with the legacy of the first generations of the iPhone and finishing with the iPad featuring Retina display. Your game should try to take into consideration all of them (this will be much more problematic if you would want to make an Android port of your game because there are many types of resolutions).

There is a very useful website, http://screensiz.es/, that displays a table with all popular screen sizes (including both iOS devices and Android ones).

As an option, you can try to prepare all the backgrounds you need in advance, letting the game check the current device and choose the proper image file. This is very simple from the programming point of view because the portion of code working with the background is not complicated; it is only needed to display one static image at specific screen coordinates. But that can be a real challenge from the graphic design point of view because a dozen versions of each background should be prepared. Having made minor changes in the backgrounds, you're required to re-export all the versions again. Such an approach also needs some additional disk space for all the backgrounds (however, this is not so problematic; iOS games now can be pretty big). The source file for a background used in the *Blueprint 3D* game is very wide; it includes extra parts to cover all possible widescreen ratios. The following screenshot shows the background used in Blueprint 3D:

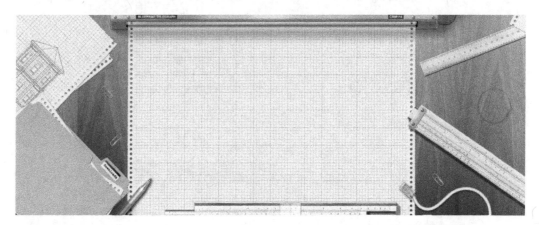

However, if you choose this type of background for your game, try to optimize the process as much as possible. First of all, try to design the background with some reserve. Its canvas can be a little bit larger than the actual screen resolution; it is good to mark it like a 16:9 (or even 21:9) frame, which will save you from all possible shocks the new generation of devices will bring. All the types of backgrounds can be stored in one AI file with several artboards. The first artboard serves iPad; it has resolution of 1024 x 768 pixels (in this example, the landscape orientation of the canvas is used). Being exported in double resolution, this artboard will provide the background for a Retina-based iPad (2048 x 1536 pixels).

The second artboard is placed at exactly the same position at which the first one has but features another height: it is not 768 pixels, but 683 pixels. Are you confused a little bit? You are right: there is no such screen size in the specifications. The secret is simple: this is a graphic billet for the iPhone with screen ratio 3:2 (first four generations of the device). You should export the background by navigating to **File | Save for web** and entering the correct dimensions — 960 x 640 (or 480x320 for pre-Retina models) — in the **Image size** tab; in other words, 960 x 640 pixels is 93.75 percent of 1024 x 683 pixels. Voilà! An export process becomes a bit easier because you need nearly one illustration to create a background both for iPad and classic iPhone. Starting with iPhone 5, the new type of resolution is used: 1136 x 640 with a rare aspect ratio 71:40. You can try to use the same width of the artboard, introducing the billet with the size 1024 x 577, but such canvas is too narrow, and large parts of the background illustration will be truncated. It is better to create a new artboard with a height equal to 683 pixels but with a larger width equal to 1212 pixels. The exporting routine is still the same: in the **Image size** tab, the correct dimensions should be specified: 1136 x 640. And don't forget about the potential reserve: a 16:9 screen ratio. I would suggest something like 1360 x 768 or 1366 x 768; the exact accuracy is not important yet. The image would have gigantic width, but it could have a practical purpose too: various promo materials, for example, website promotional blocks often require a wide background. The following screenshot shows the artboard scheme for solid backgrounds:

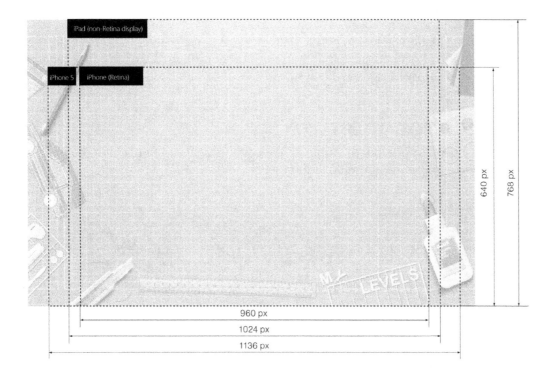

There is another way to operate the backgrounds, much more flexible and resolution independent. In this case, the background is not a solid image but a collage made from several graphic elements. The game itself manages their position and behavior. Some elements are tiles and let you cover some space with specific texture (the tiles can be real big, about 512 x 512 pixels to fill large rooms without noticeable repetition). A few elements are created to be stretched at the screen; for example, some gradients to create a sky. There are sprites with various props too; each of them has a position proportional to the screen's height and width. Overall, each element has its specific rule to calculate its x and y coordinate. This approach is a little bit harder than the static backgrounds, but it gets rid of bulky and clumsy background files and lets you to implement some dynamic mechanics to the backgrounds and even to make them a little bit interactive.

From an illustration perspective, there should be several varied backgrounds in the game: one for the main menu, special backgrounds for options and about the screen, and so on. But the most important of course are the images for game levels. Try to add a personal touch to each of them. The background should be contrasting enough to make the details on the foreground well marked; the background helps to express all the game elements in an appropriate way. Its color and texture must not dominate because it is only a scene, not a character; the viewer's visual comfort is a primary goal. Try to use decorations and props that are related to the game's plot. This is an additional way to include some narrative in the images. They may not translate direct messages but create some specific mood. Moreover, it is easier to come up with some idea of ornamentation by looking back at the story. What should I put there: a unicorn or a barrel with oil remembering that the game is about robots? Of course the unicorn is perfect! Some sense of irony is always good too.

Application icon

The following is a screenshot of Apple's iTunes with a dozen of app icons. The images, not text titles, compel the attention of the viewer:

It is hard to overestimate the value of an application icon for the mobile application, especially for the game. This is one of the most powerful elements of its identity. Generally, people don't read the name of the application on the App Store; they set their eyes on the icon. It has to tell a whole story to them: what is the genre the game based on? Does the game have beautiful graphics? What is the main element of the gameplay? Who is the main character? Is it funny? Many more questions are answered by small graphic images. As the Chinese proverb says:

"One picture is worth ten thousand words."

In our case, we can paraphrase: one app icon is worth dozens of letters in the application name.

Some people try to steal graphic ideas of famous and popular titles trying to ride on someone else's success. That's a pathetic concept. First of all, that is not right from an ethical point of view (don't forget about copyright issues too); also, that behavior can play a nasty trick on your game, because it would look like a secondary class product with a lack of any new and original idea not worth spending money on. Nobody loves copycats. So, that can be a hard strike on your image.

Nevertheless, you may or even have to learn from successful examples. Nobody can stop you from adopting some ideas, but you have to interpret them by yourself. Even a simple story can be told in a thousand ways. Your intonation is very important. Borrowing of some graphic trends can help to embed your game into App Store universe easily and will not make you look like a white crow. Although it is good to be pretty trendy, is bad to be a copy. For example, if there are many applications with glossy graphics and bright colors, you can use that approach, but if there are many icons with the same composition or main element (for example, many match-three applications are using a large image of a crystal or color ball, racing games are using finish flags or wheels, and so on), it is always better to introduce something unique. Otherwise, your icon will sink into the ocean of identical images. So, the application icon can be based on trendy methods (graphic style and colors), but you must pay more attention to details. If everyone around is putting one image of a bubble or ball, you have to put two, three, or add unique and bright special effects (fire, sparkles, and so on). Are there many images of car wheels in racing arcades? You should put an image of a front light of a car. Are all games about zombies using an image of zombie head? Not a problem, use a leg with a caricature bone or an arm! You need to have your own voice. Wherein, you do not to use too unusual tone in order to sound overly original.

To choose the main element of the icon, you need to ask yourself: "what (or who) is your game about?" The answer should be short and clear; otherwise the answer is wrong. It is good to break your game into the logical fragments and try to reflect some of them in icons, searching for good combinations. Use the main gameplay element first, one of the bonuses after that. Does one of the bonuses look great in the game? If the answer is yes, try to use that fragment of the artwork in the icon.

It's desirable to use a graphic style related to the artwork of your game in the icon. If the game is using the cartoon style for images, the app icon is cartoonish too; more realistic game graphics need a photo—a realistic icon.

There is an interesting trend in icon design for iOS: designers trying to compose the image in the peculiar shape of the icon. Its rounded corners are used as a natural contour of a drawn object, so the final result looks like a truly 3D image. Such icons are amazing; they are real works of art. Most appreciated works on Dribbble are usually the icons in such graphic style. They have a giant potential to inspire you. The only problem is the fact that many of those icons were created for portfolios only, they look great, but they are not commercial examples serving real applications. Partly, it can be explained by the fact that such icons usually are only object based; they illustrate a thing, for example, a treasure box or a piece of cake (there are tons of icons portraying sweets), so they are very static. But application icons often need to display a simple scene, to illustrate some motion and interaction of elements or simply to show more than one object. This is why such wonderful pieces of pixel art become dismissed and turn into decorations of portfolios. However, it would still be great to use such an icon for your game if conditions were appropriate. The following are two examples of such graphics:

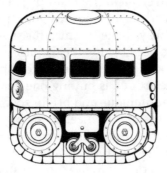 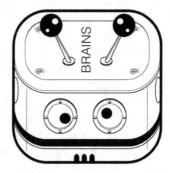

iOS 7 brings some new aesthetics into application icon design—graphics became flat, there is more interest in simple and smooth shapes and clean colors rather than in photo-realistic illustrations, rich textures, and so on. Most artworks look like vector graphics with solid fill or delicate gradients—the main color accent is made on a bright background; central element of compositions are emphasized by the so-called *diagonal shadows*; they are pretty long, tilted by 45 degrees, and have no blur effect (or its volume is minimum). Such elements can be generated in Adobe Illustrator by using Blend Tool. You only need to create a primary shape of the shadow, then it should be cloned and its copies are shifted right and down by diagonal trajectory. The opacity level of the copy must be defined as zero; after that, it can be connected with the primary shape by Blend Tool; the number of interpolations can be adjusted via the tool's menu. Another important approach is color; a palette used in iOS 7 is a bit different from the previous era, it is clean and usually has ambivalent visual characteristics; for instance, shades can lie between red and orange, or green and blue.

You should try to avoid including any large portions of text in the icon, particularly the name of the game itself or it will be a sign of bad taste. The application name inside the icon looks silly, because there is an actual name below the icon at the home screen displayed by the system, and together they form a visual tautology. There is another reason too: the long text will be unreadable, being scaled down, notably on pre-Retina devices (don't forget that icons for the first iPhone had a width of 60 pixels).

The only exceptions to the text inside the icon are short service words (up to 4 to 6 letters in length) helping to differentiate one version of the same application from another. I'm talking about such designations such as:

- **HD**: This is the high-resolution edition for Retina iPad.
- **Free/Lite**: This is the gratis version of the application.
- **PRO/Lux**: Usually, this is a denotation for the ad-free version of a free application. It may include extra content too.

If your game is a sequel, its index number can be included in the application icon too; people need to know that this is something new, not the game they've already played before. Furthermore, several icons with indexes on them make it clear that this is not a single game, but a small franchise. This can increase the attractiveness of your title.

Some developers think global and design special graphic elements, uniting app icons of all their applications. They get something like a corporate rule for all the images they produce. That can be a unique background, an element of composition, or a special frame for the application icon. The frame is one of the most common ways to make your game unique, it is easy to create and use, and it can hold the text designations.

You need to think deep about the colors you will use in your app icon. Each color has its own power and psychological meaning. One of the pioneers of abstract art, an art theorist and Russian painter, *Wassily Kandinsky*, in his book *Concerning the Spiritual in Art (1911)* notes that cool colors (blue or violet ones, for example) are concentric, they are directed inside an object and move away from a viewer, but warm colors are eccentric; they are directed outside, moving to the viewer:

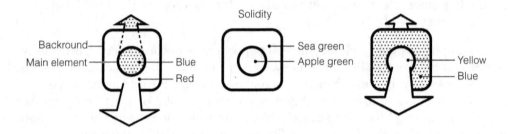

At the practical level, this means that a main element, painted a bright and warm color, can create a feeling being jumped up from the icon frame (now remember the app icon of the illustrious Angry birds, displaying a red bird). It is an extroverted type of graphic, so it is ideal for games with a pretty fast gameplay, with a lot of action, characters and game elements, in other words it serves various types of arcades, action-oriented puzzles, shooters, races, and so on. Whereas cool and dark colors being used as backgrounds help the main element to shine and be more attractive (roughly speaking, cool backgrounds move away from the viewer, but the warm main elements move toward the viewer, so their speeds are added together resulting in a vivid image). The icon can have only cool and dark colors too; this is good for more static and solitary games with more complicated rules. Blue is an intellectual and introvert color. Violet is a slightly spiritual and mystic color. It is interesting to note that the combination of a cold main element with a warm background is not very common practice because the structure of such elements is not properly stable. So, it is better to make cool (or dark) graphic compositions solid: with cool background and cool foreground; warm elements can be used only as small emphasis points because they are much more active.

Jon Hicks is the talented designer known for rendering the Firefox logo, working on the *MailChimp* logo, Skype's emoticons, and many other amazing projects. He also is author of the book *The Icon Handbook* published by *Five Simple Steps*. On this book's official website, `http://iconhandbook.co.uk/reference/chart/`, there is a very useful chart, showing specifications on most popular formats of icons, including iOS, Android, Blackberry, and so forth.

Now, let's talk about the craft. The application icons should be rendered very meticulously and professionally. There are several types of image sizes to be included in a final package; it is worth noting that former guidelines were revisited after introduction of iOS 7 in 2013 and icons became a little bit bigger (as did their radiuses). The smallest ones are the legacy of first generations of iOS devices: 60 pixels for iPhone and 76 pixels for iPad. They need attention to each pixel; this is not pixel art, but some aspects of images should be edited at pixel level. The next generation of iOS devices introduced double-sized icons: 120 x 120 pixels and 152 x 152 pixels. But the most challenging is the icon artwork that is used by iTunes, which can have dimensions up to 1024 x 1024 pixels! It's funny when you recall that nearly ten years ago many desktop computers used a screen resolution equal to 1024 x 768 pixels, which was less than the modern single icon has become.

The following screenshot shows the template used for the app icon used in the *Rail Maze 2* game developed by *Spooky House Studios UG (haftungsbeschränkt)*:

512x512

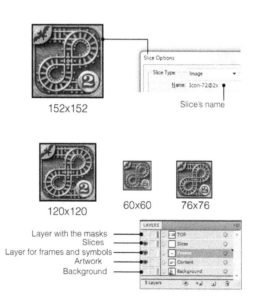

152x152

Slice's name

120x120

60x60   76x76

Layer with the masks
Slices
Layer for frames and symbols
Artwork
Background

A special template can be created in Adobe Illustrator to work with app icons. It includes one artboard, a layer with a background (for comfort previewing), several placeholders for icons situated in the layer called *content*, a grid of slices, and finally the layer called *cover* with special masks with rounded corners. Some of the most important parts are slices; though they were invented for web design, helping to prepare website's images, they can be used for icon design too. Their major advantage is their ability to slice the artboard on fragments; each of them is saved (via the **Save for web** option) as a separate file. Moreover, you can control the names of such files by using the **Slice Options...** panel (**Object | Slice | Slice Options...**); there is the textfield marked **Name**. By default, a slice's name is generated automatically (a document name plus some digital indexes), but you can enter the name manually. It is useful to add a shortcut for the **Slice Options** panel; by default, it has no shortcuts, but it can be done through the special menu in Adobe Illustrator: **Edit | Keyboard Shortcuts...**. The slices have their nuances; try to draw them in the Pixel Preview mode or periodically pay attention to the **Transform** panel; the slice should have the exact dimensions without fractions, the coordinates should be integers too. In other cases, some errors with dimensions of exported files can occur; for instance, instead of 60 x 60, you would get 60 x 59 or something like that. Adobe Illustrator automatically creates a folder named Images, where the all saved slices are stored (there can be some *graphic garbage* too because some slices simply cut out parts of background).

It is important to remember that the application icon in iOS doesn't support transparency; they are opaque square images. Now, famous rounded corners are made by the operating system itself, so you should not include those corners in your artwork!

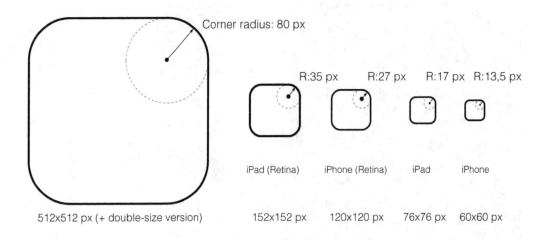

Corner radius: 80 px

512x512 px (+ double-size version)

R:35 px — iPad (Retina) — 152x152 px

R:27 px — iPhone (Retina) — 120x120 px

R:17 px — iPad — 76x76 px

R:13,5 px — iPhone — 60x60 px

[Always move from small sizes to larger ones.]

This means that first of all the smallest icons should be created, then they can be scaled up and the level of detail can be increased. So, create the iPhone icon of 60 x 60 pixels, try it on device, ask some people about their opinion, check all the details again, make sure that is *your image* in 100 percent, and then finally start working on the iTunes icon. It will require from you a lot more portraying effort, and proper high-resolution textures and illustrations will be needed. But the effort is worth it because there is nothing like a tasty, well-crafted, and beautiful artwork on your iTunes' page. Yummy!

There are some naming rules for final files. The official *iOS App Programming Guide* from Apple in the chapter *App Icons* gives such a description:

- `Icon.png`: This is the name for the app icon on the iPhone
- `Icon@2x.png`: This is the name for the app icon on the iPhone with Retina display
- `Icon-72.png`: This is the name for the app icon on the iPad
- `Icon-72@2x.png`: This is the name for the app icon on the iPad with Retina display
- `iTunesArtwork`: This is the name for the app icon on the App Store
- `iTunesArtwork@2x`: This is the name for the high resolution app icon on the App Store

Achievements

Players like to spend time on games, and they also like to brag about their progress. This is why leaderboards and achievement systems were invented; they help the player to share in-game breakthroughs with some friends and make them public. The leaderboard is a pretty simple system, it displays some score records, operating with player's names and number of received points. A table of achievements in its turn is a more festive thing. It marks all the players' efforts with special rewards: small pictures that play a role of game's milestones. People value any recognition of their efforts so much that each achievement they get in the game makes them happy. The favorite ones are achievements received after a hard gaming scene, for instance, the achievement symbolizing the victory over a big enemy boss or the achievement for special hidden bonuses being collected.

The following screenshot shows different achievements for the *Blueprint 3D* game, developed by *Kostya Stankevych* and published by *FDG Entertainment*:

All the achievements should have a clear and plain description. The players' objective must be easy to catch, something like:

- Play the tutorial level
- Solve 10 puzzles
- Collect 50 stars
- Unlock the Advanced mode
- Finish the game at the Medium level

There is an unspoken rule of graphic style these achievement icons are using: the illustration needs to be simple, comprising only flat objects, few colors, high contrast, and outlines and should not have soft shadows or any other raster effects. So, they look almost like a newspaper's comic illustration. Of course you can choose a different approach, but try to avoid a big number of tiny details and complex textures.

The achievements usually have very simple plot: a few recognizable elements from the game in a specific combination and a some large text. Because games are part of entertainment, good sense of humor is always welcomed; for instance, the very scary game *Alan Wake* from *Remedy Entertainment* features very funny achievements, for instance, to discover some coffee thermoses and watch TV shows.

There are some clichés among the achievements: today very popular are various trophy cups, laurel wreaths, coins, gold medals, and other symbols of victory. There's nothing wrong with such images other than that they are boring; therefore, always try to push the limits of your imagination.

Each social gaming network has its own specification of images designed for the achievement table. Gamecenter from Apple, for example, utilizes images in special round frames, so the illustrations have to be properly centered to look nice.

Trophies

Trophies are optional, but very expressive, form of reward for the player and comprise various beautiful and well-crafted illustrations the player receives besides the ordinary achievement. In contradistinction to the achievements, the illustrations are displayed one by one, because they are pretty large and have a transparency background (as option). There must be a special trophy room to keep all the trophies, and its decoration may be a bit ceremonial to engage the player's special emotions.

The following screenshot shows different Trophies for the *Blueprint 3D* game:

Banners

The following screenshot shows a large banner promoting *Rail Maze* developed by *Spooky House Studios UG* (*haftungsbeschränkt*):

Your game will need promotion. One of the traditional ways is the graphic banners various advertising systems show. They can be created from the graphics your game is using: main characters, props, backgrounds, bonuses, and so on. All can be used. Don't forget about the text; short and memorable quotes from your game concept and plot are good.

There are a lot of banner formats in both landscape and portrait orientation modes. Some of them look like graphic stripes, while others can be displayed in full screen. Some of the popular formats are: 300 x 250, 468 x 60, 728 x 90, 640 x 960, and 640 x 100. I would recommend that you create the Adobe Illustrator files with several artboards and some basic artwork to export banners.

Screenshots

The following screenshot shows the screenshots used by Blueprint 3D game developed by *Kostya Stankevych* and published by *FDG Entertainment*:

Screenshots are one of the major promotional elements of your game; they showcase all the advantages of your creation. Of course, there are a lot of examples of when the developer simply submitted a few good images of the gameplay. But that is not enough, and it is better to create special **screenshot compositions**, including some additional graphic descriptions of the game. Such images look like a small comic strip with a few speech bubbles telling a little story about the game. But always be honest; show and describe only elements that your game actually has. Try not to embellish something too much. Otherwise, the truth will be exposed very quickly and the game will get very bad reviews and ratings.

Gameplay videos

It is important to have a video displaying the key elements of your game, in other words, to have a video trailer. The easiest way to do this is by installing screen capture software on your main workstation and grabbing video from your game prototype. You will get the video file with the correct colors and without any geometric distortions. But there is a special problem caused by the fact that mobile games have no screen cursors: input is based on finger touches. So, the video grabbed from the prototype has no element focusing on the user's eye on a specified part of the screen. This can be a problem because the video may look unclear. You need to introduce a graphic image of a hand (or an arrow) to fix this; the image will play the role of pointer; it will simulate player interaction with the game world. It is better to use simple and flat illustration, without any complicated gradients, tiny details, and so on. You have to import that image into video-editing software and adjust its positions; it will require minimum skill in animation (the pointer should hover over the screen from one point to another). There should be an effect for click or touch; for example, for a multi pointed star, the effect will appear for a few moments behind the pointer.

The following figure shows the simplest light box, only a box with white walls:

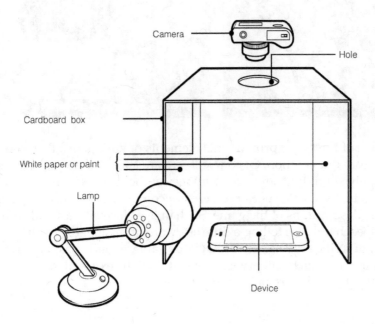

The more creative and interesting way to make a video is to shoot the actual device (an iPhone or an iPad) with the hands of a real player touching the screen. It looks more authentic than the screen-capture method, but it has some pitfalls too. In most situations, people take a camera, put an iPhone on a table, start the game and begin shooting uncomfortably holding the camera by a free hand. A result generally is far from perfect: the image is shaky, it is dark and blurry, and the colors are distorted. And the most important point: the skin tone of the hand looks terrible. A viewer may wonder why a zombie with blue and unsightly skin is playing the game. That is because of bad lighting causing the camera to contort the colors. You need not have a professional lighting system and all those softboxes and flash lights, but you must have good table lamps with warm light-bulbs (lamps with joints are the ideal option). The light must be diffused too because glare in this case is not acceptable; it can cover significant elements of the game screen. To produce diffused light you need to have a photography *light box*. You can buy one (they are not too expensive) or build it yourself. It is easier than you think. First of all, you will need a box; you can take any package of an appropriate size, having verified its height or width to be a good distance for close up. The carton must be strong enough to support a small digital camera; a lens-sized window should be cut out at the top of the box. Large cameras must be used with a tripod installed. This will free your hands at the time of making the video.

The following figure shows a more advanced version of a light box with more efficient lighting:

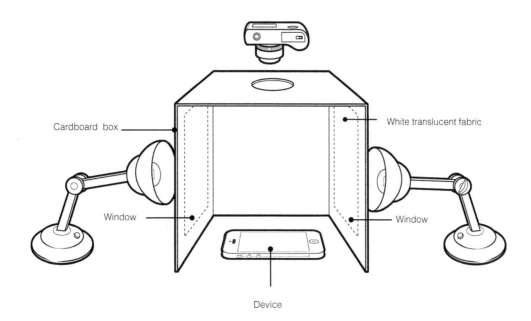

One of the walls of the light box is open. You can call it **the fourth wall**, a term that describes a frame the audience in traditional theaters sees the plays through. The inner surface of the box must be close to white in color for effective reflection of light. To keep it simple, you can use white paper or white acrylic, but you have to remember that the surface must be matted. The light sources will be mounted at the opened part of the box. Their positions have to be calibrated in such a way as not to be overlapped by the figure of a person playing the game during the video recording. You do not need unexpected shadows inside the box. There is a more professional approach: instead of paper or paint, a light fabric can be used. In this way, you have to cut out large windows in the side walls of the box and cover them with some white fabric. Then you can use lamps situated on the sides of the box.

You can put some textures on the bottom part of the light box to add some unique touches to the scene, but you have to remember that the efficiency of the light reflection could diminish.

Before the video recording, you have to decide what you want to show the audience; remember that the video should not be boring or too long, and the message must be easy to understand. The video has to be beautiful, bright, and quick. You have to make the viewer say, "wow!" in 1-2 minutes or even less. This means it would be great to express only key components of a gameplay and to use all those elements in your game that you pride the most. Draw up a little story plan, turn on video mode, start recording, and make several takes of the same actions. Soon you will choose the best ones. The video-editing tools will help you throw away all the bad parts of the recorded materials and will let you add some additional elements, for instance, text notes. It is good to put a large logo of the game at the end of the video holding it for about 20-30 seconds; don't forget to include the App Store Badge in the final frames, showing that your game is already in the App Store and can be downloaded right now.

Summary

A story in a video game can be on different scales; if the product is simple, it features a small-scale plot, while more complex games may have huge screenplays that might even be the envy of Hollywood. But irrespective of its size, the plot should be solid and well thought out, a narrative should create a connection between the game world and the audience. The game is not just a calculator; it is about experience.

Graphics is part of the narrative as well. First of all, there should a visual idea that unites all fragments of the screen. Assets can be simple and not realistic but must have some structural rules. This makes a picture alive and interesting to follow. When working with graphics, there is a need to operate various types of textures collected into sheets with some resource. There can be some issues with alpha channel, compression quality, or memory management, but they can be prevented or resolved by proper planning. Any game needs some promotion to become popular. At a basic level, this means the presence of an attractive and demonstrative application icon, a catchy name, trailers, and a social media account.

Usability issues are important not only for traditional office software, but games as well. In the next chapter, you will learn how to plan a game comfortable for players. Especially if you care about players with special needs.

2
Ergonomics

A good game should not only have a great idea, plot, graphics, and characters, but also good ergonomics. Games are not ordinary applications, they are like racing cars; they work in extreme conditions, they are fast and powerful, and have state of the art programming. Ordinary cars are made for human beings, not for aliens from outer space featuring dozens of tentacles (they can be useful for playing very complex puzzle games!). So a figure of a real human, a player, stays at the forefront when you are planning and developing a game, all his physical characteristics and needs should be taken into consideration.

Portraying the player

Playing at home

Maximum comfort

 Audio

 Orientation-based controls

Interner connection

Both hands

Long game sessions

Playing in public spaces

Public transportation

- High level of noises
- Vibrations
- Bad lighting
- Crowd
- Short game sessions

In a line

- Noises
- Crowd
- Short game sessions

Cafe

- Noises
- Conversations
- Short game sessions

To create a handy game, you need to draw an imaginary portrait of your future player. You can watch your own behavior and observe how your friends and other people play various types of games. Of course, it will be very subjective and an inaccurate image, but the main tendencies can be noticed. Try to only watch the game, never ask to perform playing on purpose, because in such cases people behave very unnaturally trying to be either too critical inventing insignificant claims or too polite sparing their feelings.

It is easy to see that there are two types of game sessions. The first type is about intentional desire to play a specific title: a person plays a game sitting at home in his armchair or sofa. The time spent on the game is pretty long, there are only a few pauses, and the player plays very enthusiastically. A device can be held by hands or be put on a tabletop, or a special stand, since more fingers can be used to control the game. The second type is more higgledy-piggledy: a person is trying to kill some time, mostly in public spaces. For instance, while using public transportation systems (namely buses, subways, trains, and so on), waiting in queues, waiting for somebody in a cafe or restaurant or lounges, and so on. The main goal of the player is to fill out a forced pause. The conditions are not always comfortable enough; for instance, there could be a lot of people around, high level of noise, artificial lighting of different kinds, and so on. He is distracted from time to time. So the game sessions are short, the player often pauses the game. He can mostly operate only with one hand, so the game controls should be very simple.

Ergonomic aspects

To design a product that is comfortable to use, some general guidelines should be followed. They are not complicated and in most cases, they are very obvious and familiar; they can be easily formulated by your own gaming experience. You may recall any solutions you liked from other projects (and not necessarily game products). Additionally, some reverse thinking is required; situations when you felt uncomfortable using a mobile application should be noticed to try avoiding them in your own project. Good ergonomics is pretty transparent and natural for its users. It is pretty inconspicuous and hard to remember actual details about problems rather than overall pleasant experiences. That is why it would be efficient to learn from bad examples by trying to solve ergonomic problems.

Simple rules

Even if you planned a complex gameplay with a lot of shades, always try to start with simple rules. The first levels are the training ones. People usually dislike tutorials, because such game levels look too synthetic and boring. Games are entertainment, so the training should be engrossing too. This is why it is better to embed the tutorials inside the game process instead of keeping them separate. The first levels should be simple, have only one goal, and teach a specific principle of the game. Special pop-up messages with clarifications can be displayed. But try not to overdo it, the levels should not be too easy to complete, the complexity must rise gradually. Otherwise, the player may decide that the game is ridiculously simple.

Distance to the game

Literally, in each software application including games, there is a "distance to a destination"; it is measured in the number of clicks (taps) a user has made to get some output. Apparently, the intervals should be reasonably minimum; to attain such values, all trajectories of the movements inside the application from a screen to another screen should be well thought out. The general objective is to help a player to activate the game process as fast as possible. This is pretty trivial for simple games with only one game mode; in such cases, the distance is equal to one, and only a tap on the **Start** button of the game is needed. But games with more complex structures need some smart decisions. For instance, a racing game by default requires vehicles and tracks to be chosen before a race, so the distance is longer. But it can be shorter if some stages are optional; the player can choose the vehicle once at the beginning of a game session, but the track can be set automatically. In which case the game can have, for example, a **Quick race** button. So a player gets two possible paths: a long one with the freedom to choose some elements, and a short one with some predefined components. Of course, the second one is not sufficient to express all game possibilities, because some options can be out of the scope of a player's attention. But that can be resolved as well. The game should push the player to choose something new; for example, before a specific race, by tapping the **Quick race** button, the player gets a message that he has to choose another type of vehicle.

It is always better to avoid any type of pop-up messages asking the player to push an **Ok** button to close it; people sincerely hate them, especially when such elements are used inside the gameplay process. The info message should be displayed parallel to the action and disappear automatically (after a period of time or after the player achieves a specific objective).

The Pause button

It is one of the most desirable buttons. The gameplay of a mobile game is often interrupted; a game session usually consists of many short periods of playing. The common causes of interruption are external factors; for example, communication with other people, arriving at a destination, and so on. Thus, it is necessary for the player to be able to pause the game at any time. Generally, the pause command is assigned to a button that activates the game menu; when it is tapped, all the game processes freeze. At one point it is reasonable to place such a type of control in the top-left corner, the way many iOS applications do. That provides a habitual pattern of behavior for the player. At some other point, it is more common to place such a button at the right-hand side corner of the screen, because it is more comfortable for right-handed persons; many modern games use these types of layouts. Some titles also place the menu/pause buttons at the center of the screen; the most comfortable setup in such a case is a centered button placed at the bottom when a device is used in portrait mode so that thumbs can easily reach it. The most uncomfortable scenario is a centered pause button displayed at the top, as players need to shift their hands to press it. There can be little excuse for such layouts; it is hard to press the button accidentally, but this reason sounds a little unconvincing.

Common UI icons:

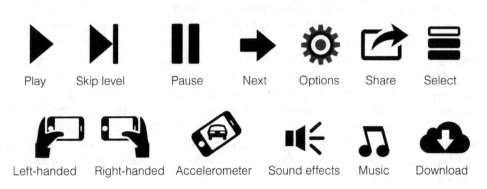

| Play | Skip level | Pause | Next | Options | Share | Select |

| Left-handed | Right-handed | Accelerometer | Sound effects | Music | Download |

An ideal variant of the text label for the button is menu/pause, but it occupies too much space; hence, only **Pause** can be used. The words can be replaced with graphic symbols, which is very handy. For instance, an arrow pointed to the left can mark the menu button. But now it is very popular (most of the modern game titles use this approach) to implement a pause symbol (two parallel bars). Because the symbol has been taken from media controls, some other icons from there can be used as well. For example, the **Play** symbol can mean start (or continue) a game session, the **Skip level** can switch to the next level skipping the current one, and so forth.

Autosaving

A modern game of any genre must autosave the game progress. That is an indisputable rule! The player can pause or unload the game, but it should save the current game setup. In an ideal case, positions and states of each element can be recorded to a saved file. The iCloud functionality is always good practice, but the system should be reliable enough; there should be locally saved files as well to work in situations when the cloud-based storage is unavailable. Action games can utilize checkpoints to save the player's progress. In this case, they play the role of an element which motivates the player to move forward. Try not to spare too many checkpoints, it is good to use as many as you could in any level, especially before you get to a tricky scene. A good way to change the game's difficulty level is to vary the number of checkpoints. Never, I say never, place the checkpoints just before a cut scene! Players hate situations when a hard game scene—a fight with a boss—is preceded by an animated sequence, portion of text, or some other narrative element. They hate them even if a skip function exists. The only artistic excuse is the attempt to induce a specific player's emotion, for instance, make him/her angry, so he begins to hate the enemies immensely (and the author of the game as well).

Remember that there is an experience issue that a standard autosave feature is incapable of resolving. While playing some game with a very picturesque game design (especially those with a strong adventure component), users may need the opportunity to save their progress in a specific location. For example, users might want to share their experience with somebody else, showing a particular game scene or how to replay an interesting moment. For such games it is good to have some form of manual saving as a niche feature. There are no hot keys on mobile devices, so saving should be activated via the menu. Saves should be graphically presented as slots with some small screenshots. The game should be made a little rigorous by limiting the overall number of such slots. If the number is big or unlimited, a player can create a mess; there will be dozens of saves he would never clean up.

Alternatively, a game can automatically create special saves on locations that are considered beautiful or important. So a player can use a special menu (it may be titled as Memories) to give access to those saves. For example, such options can appear after a successful completion of the main story line.

The Continue button

An element of the game's comfort is associated with the **Continue** button. The player has started the game for the second time and he wants to continue his journey; the destination should be only one tap long. He would be annoyed if the game asked him to perform some selection procedures such as choosing the type of mode he played before and picking out the appropriate saves of the game. Therefore, the game must give prominence to the **Continue** button. Hence, it is the first button on the list of the main menu.

Visibility of the control elements

Each interactive element the game has must be expressed well. First of all, the buttons should look and operate like buttons; the player's eye should be able to distinguish them out from the background and other elements easily. It is a mistake when a person taps a still image thinking that it is a button. The game elements should express their nature too. Each game trigger must say, "You can push me".

Direct control

In most cases, you should develop a control system, where the direct manipulation of game elements is used, because it looks more natural for touchscreens. Try not to create control buttons to move the character, but let the player tap the screen and mark the destination the character will walk to. Various increment and decrement buttons are bad. Unless they are needed for specific game mechanics or mood, for instance, some games that imitate retro arcades do use onscreen controls.

Introducing functionalities

It is better to introduce the components of the gameplay step by step. This makes it not too overwhelming for the player. His attention should be focused on one event per moment. To express all the features of the element, you need to pay special attention to the level design. The whole level should be about the element you want to show to the audience—you need water to test a boat. The element's purpose should be clear and univocal as well. Remember that it is more efficient to give the player few, but good gaming tools, rather than surprise him with a bunch of possibilities he will never use. This does not mean that you should not introduce something new during the game progress, but you must stimulate him to drop the tools he has used before in favor of the new ones.

The game level design should follow the same rule; if you are going to surprise somebody with some element (for example, a beautiful waterfall), it should be alone in its brilliance, and other components should not interfere. Moreover, it can guide a player's sight in the proper direction, so the player can enjoy the complete view.

Health regeneration

Old school games used the metaphor of a medicine chest to cover up for the loss of a character's health. A player's hard efforts were very often rewarded with some medicine chests, so he could fight some extra enemies to get better health. I like that approach very much; however, nowadays more and more games have dropped the medicine chests, thinking that the player's being would be more comfortable with a health regeneration function. How does it work? The character loses his health when he is in a stressful situation; for example, he is in a fight, he has fallen down from somewhere, and so forth. And he restores his health conditions when the situation is calm. Also, when medicine chests are scattered on a game level, the autoregeneration function should be balanced very accurately to ensure the game works well.

Peaks and valleys

Game levels should be planned correctly. They must have both peaks (sequences of very dynamic actions), and valleys (zones of comfort and relaxation, some sort of digression), so that the player can regain his breath. This is especially important for games with health regeneration, because the player needs some shelters to restore his condition. Remember that the valleys shouldn't be boring, show the player something beautiful (such parts of levels can feature the most interesting examples of visual design), or give him a simple and leisurely task.

One event per moment

The main components of the game; for example, a plot, objectives, characters, weapons, protagonist abilities, mechanics, and so on, should come in portion. The lesser the better. A player can concentrate his attention on a pretty limited amount of new things at one moment; in cases where the sight is blurred, he does not notice some details and is less surprised by new content. Moreover, a person can be tired of a huge wave of new experiences, so it is important to be courteous and show new things in a delicate manner.

Difficulty level

In an ideal scenario, the game features an automatic difficulty level. It looks at the player's behavior and makes the conditions harder if his attempts are successful very often; vice versa, it tries to make the game less difficult if there are a lot of failures. It is not easy to implement such a system because of the calculation of the right balance. But the game should at least go along with the player; if he is stuck somewhere for a long period of time, the process must be inconspicuous enough, so the player won't feel ashamed. The change in difficulty levels should be available in the options menu all the time. It is pretty obligatory to include the **Restart** and **Undo** buttons into your puzzle games.

Sound and music

Contradictory to desktop and console games, mobile games are not much about audio content. Very often the players are playing in public spaces; if they can't use headphones, they prefer to switch the music and sound off, or reduce the volume level significantly. Some players may also have some degree of hearing loss (there is also a condition called tinnitus, when people perceive some additional noise in their ears; for example, ringing, buzzing, whistling, clicking, and so on), since they may have some trouble in perceiving sounds.

Therefore, you should first think about your game without any audio (I'm not talking about audio games). Don't use stimulus based only on sound. Game situations should use visual methods, but the sound can be a pleasant supplement to them. Music should be less important than sound effects if we are talking about game mechanics; however, it plays a significant role in enhancing the mood of the game, especially when it is interactive; in action sequences, melodies are more effective, in disquieting scenes they give some sense of suspense, and so forth. Even silence, when the music suddenly stops, can be used as the element of a story. But the music should be pretty unobtrusive to be comfortable for the ears; players can simply get tired of it, as music accompaniment can sound very monotonous and importunate (this is why a contextual melody suitable in real time is a good solution). So there should be an option to turn the music off and that option should not be a part of the sound effects control.

Minimum screen areas

It is always important to determine the minimum size of an active element for your game. The comfort of playing directly depends on this factor. The average width of an adult human male finger varies from 15 to 20 mm, the average index finger width is 20 mm or 0.75 inch. In ancient times, this size was used as a measurement of length called finger or digit (in Latin *digitus* means finger). Let's convert finger into pixels, all we need for this is simple math; the digital length of the screen in pixels should be divided into the physical length of the screen in millimeters its size in pixels, so we will get the number of pixels in one millimeter. The conversion is shown as follows:

- iPhone: 480 px/75 mm is approximately 6.41 pixels per mm (163 ppi)
- iPhone (Retina): 960 px/75 mm is approximately 12.83 pixels per mm (326 ppi)
- iPad: 1024 px/197 mm is approximately 5.20 pixels per mm (132 ppi)
- iPad mini: 1024 px/160 mm is approximately 6.41 pixels per mm (163 ppi)
- iPad mini (Retina): 2048 px/160 mm is approximately 12.8 pixels per mm (326 ppi)
- iPad (Retina): 2048 px/197 mm is is approximately 10.40 pixels per mm (264 ppi)

As you can see, there is a wide range of pixel density on iOS devices, so a pixel in the role of a measurement element is not very reliable. Wonderful examples are the first generations of an iPad and an iPad Mini; they both have an equal resolution in pixels, but physically, in millimeters, they are different. A more precise way is to operate with physical measurements of length; nevertheless, our fingers are not made of pixels.

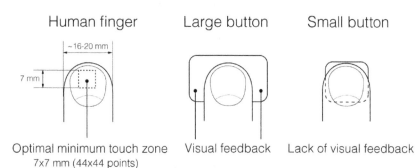

Human finger — Large button — Small button

~16-20 mm

7 mm

Optimal minimum touch zone
7x7 mm (44x44 points) — Visual feedback — Lack of visual feedback

To determine the optimal minimum touch zone, we can recall the recommendation from Apple that 44 x 44 points the comfortable minimum size of a tappable element written in the Layout section of iOS Human Interface Guidelines. One point is equal to one pixel on low-resolution devices, and equal to two on high-resolution screens. Thereby, the minimum physical size of the touchable zone can be calculated in the following manner:

$$44 / 6.41 = 6.86 \ mm$$

This is optimal and the secure size of a minimal touch zone is provided by the manufacturer. Of course, you can try to use interactive elements with lesser dimensions; however, you should not forget Fitts's law, which in this case can be formulated based on the fact that smaller targets need more effort and accuracy to be touched. So the speed of the player's movements decreases, but the level of errors, on the contrary, increases. The smaller the elements, the more dramatic is the situation. The user can touch a very small button, but only on condition that there are no any other buttons nearby. If the small buttons are tight, it is hard to aim properly, and the chance to tap the wrong button is very high. Usually, such situations irritate people, they get a little stressed and perceive the interface as an uncomfortable environment.

Overall, if the elements are small and stay tight, it is better to select dimensions not less than 4 x 4 mm; the player will use the very tip of his finger to tap the target. Something tiny can be used only with a low density of elements on the screen; for instance, an adventure game can feature a secret tiny trigger, and in such cases its dimension plays the role of a critical gameplay element.

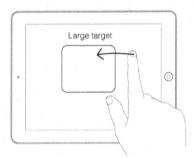
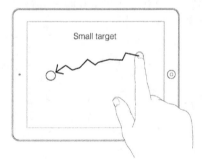

Definitely, the most comfortable touch elements are those that have dimensions closest to the finger size. They are noticeable and can be tapped without painstaking aiming. Such elements can be successfully adapted for the tapping by thumbs. Game accessibility guidelines (available at `http://gameaccessibilityguidelines.com/`) say that 24 mm is the ideal size for touch screens of large devices and 9.6 mm is recommended for phones.

Naturally, an index finger is used for more precise operations; it sets the direction of a movement, marks the destination and aims, interacts with game elements, and so on. So it is the basic tool of the gamer. The index finger tip usually helps to tap small targets. If a UI element is big, the user prefers to tap with a finger pad, because it is more comfortable. The thumb can participate in gaming too. It is not as accurate as the index finger is, so it needs a large touch zone; in other words, it would be better to use it for larger buttons.

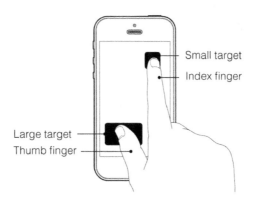

Using buttons

Buttons are the cornerstone of each interface. The button consists of two layers: an invisible active zone, determining the boundaries of the touch zone attached to the button, and a visual part, that is, the graphic shell. Normally, the shell has visual boundaries to separate the button from the background and to signal that the element is interactive. But that is not obligatory, many modern UIs feature buttons without any frames, by using only text as the visual shell; however, such an approach should be used very carefully.

 Try to avoid using static elements with some ornamentation that look like buttons.

For instance, there are some icons on your menu screen that are buttons, and a few static text descriptions below them, decorated as small wooden plates; a user might get confused, probably he will tap not the icons, but the plates, because they have all the attributes of a button.

Usually, each button has several states: **Normal**, **Focus**, **Disable**, and **Pressed**. Each of them requires a specific graphical representation.

States of a button

- **Normal**: This is the regular state of a button, its look tells a user that it is ready to operate and can be pressed any moment. The button can be painted red to mean that it activates a destructive action.

- **Focus**: When a button tries to get some special attention, it can utilize the focus state, which associates with a more prominent and visible main color. The dimensions are bigger. A simple blinking animation can be used too. Normally there can only be one button with the focus state turned on.

- **Disable**: If the button's action is not available, it should preferably be removed from the screen. If this is impossible, the button should be switched to the disable state, which is illustrated by low saturated colors and the absence of visual feedback Remember that the disabled buttons can have the auditory feedback: some sounds that demonstrate that the button is inactive can be used.

- **Pressed**: This state makes any button alive, because it demonstrates that the button is answering the user's action. Its graphical representation differs from the normal state, so the user can easily see a visual feedback.

The recipe for a good button is simple: It is a rectangular flat plate covered with some appealing texture and some minor ornamentation, for example, frames, shadows, pins, and so on. While planning the graphic look, try to not overwhelm it with details. Although the device screen is flat and smooth, people hesitate to push virtual buttons with unpleasant surfaces, for example, there is a delay before a button on which nails or splinters are drawn is tapped. A flat design of controls introduced in iOS 7 lets you spend less time decorating buttons, they can have very simple graphical appearances, for example, flat rectangles with some solid paint or delicate gradient fills.

Nevertheless, it is important to remember that a minimalistic design works well only if the edges of artwork are sharp and accurate; if the image is blurred because it was scaled by the application, the magic disappears. If you are not sure whether the game is capable to display controls in an actual scale (1:1) to an image source, it is better to use more decorative design approaches such as elements with shadows, textures, and so on, because they can keep a pretty satisfactory look when being scaled. This is why classic iOS had so many photorealistic UI elements with natural textures, gloss effects, and so on. Such elements look very good on non-retina displays with low resolutions.

The user perceives the functionality of any button (and UI elements in the gross) via its feedback, visual and auditory. Being successfully pressed and having started the corresponding action, the button displays its functionality by changing its look (the pressed state becomes active) and raising an alarm with a short sound effect. The pressed state should have obvious differences with the other states of the button. Usually, the designer mimics the behavior of buttons from the real world, so the virtual buttons are pushed down a little bit, they become smaller, and move down a few pixels. It is good practice to change their color or brightness. The more expressive the artistic way of displaying the pushing procedure, the more functional the buttons seem to the user. Note that an efficient button is wider than the user's finger, so its width is at least 25 mm; it helps to demonstrate the visual feedback of the control element, and the finger does not cover the image. In case the player doesn't notice the feedback or other forms of results on the screen, he is convinced that the input doesn't work and tries to tap again and again, which can cause an accumulation of wrong inputs. Any button is perceived perfectly if it has some animation between states rather than a static frame, for each mode. For example, on being pressed it can demonstrate a smooth dent effect. Otherwise, a button can be increased in size and, in parallel, its alpha can be reduced to zero, since it becomes bigger and smoothly disappears. Such animation fixates an image of a used control, a user is sure that the button was really pressed.

In 1995, *Louise Banton* published the article *The Role of Visual and Auditory Feedback during the Sight-Reading of Music* in *Psychology of Music and Music Education*, where a very interesting study was described. A number of pianists were tested, they were asked to perform sight-reading. Some of them played in normal conditions, while others had some restrictions: the first group was unable to hear the music they were playing (no auditory feedback), the second group was unable to see the piano keyboard (no visual feedback). Amazingly, the results showed that those musicians who played in normal conditions and those who had no auditory feedback made significantly lesser errors than the musicians who had no visual feedback. Moreover, the playing in normal conditions and the playing without auditory feedback were very close to one another in the error count. So, visual feedback is very important to reduce the level of inputting errors.

Auditory feedback is important too, especially for small control elements, because a finger covers the visual part of a button. Thus, a sound effect can convince the player that the input works properly. Various click-and-beep sounds can be utilized, ideally if they match the mood of the game. According to the dissertation by *Gregory T. Bender*, *Touch Screen Performance as a Function of the Duration of Auditory Feedback and Target Size*, auditory feedback between 50 and 400 ms should be used for small buttons, and such continuity can reduce the level of errors. Additionally, there is a relation between the time the user holds his finger on the screen and the duration of the auditory feedback. In other words, people keep their fingers pressed down till a button's sound effect stops. He writes, "Additionally, avoiding auditory feedback longer than 100 ms may also minimize contact time with the touch screen."

UI elements

You should try to imitate the behavior, but not the exact appearance, of standard UI elements from iOS; it is better to create your own version of controls with ornamentation close to the graphic style of the game. The standard UI components will look a bit silly if you would not have enough imagination, talent, and time to create something customized to support the mood of your game. Another reason is the universality of your title; usually, developers try to port their games on other platforms, where other paradigm designs are afloat. But try to only decorate them a bit, not invent new principles and rules. The player already has some UI experience based on iOS mechanics, so he expects the same paradigm in your game.

All the UI elements are listed by Apple in *IOS Human Interface Guidelines* in the chapter *iOS UI Element Usage Guidelines*.

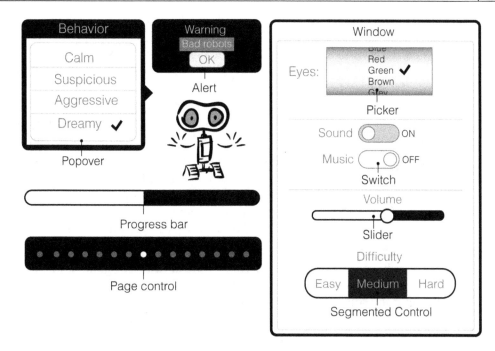

There are various fields in the UI that are explained as follows:

- **Text field**: This is used by the user to enter some text input. Graphically, this is one of the simplest kinds of UI elements: a rectangle with a small frame and a light gradient inside. It is better to use large text fields as they look more comfortable. Another good tip is to use text hints, for example, if you have a text field asking the player to enter his name, try to add the text description **Enter your name here** painted light grey.

- **Page control**: This is a specific example of UI designing introduced exclusively on mobile devices, not on desktop systems. It looks like a collection of dots and one of them is highlighted. The main goal of the element is to show the amount of content in the pages, and to mark the current position of the user. Page control is extremely useful for various panels with a list of graphic or text elements (help chapters and trophy rooms). Typically, page control is used for horizontal lists. The principles of this control can be adapted for your game's main screen, for example, there are several horizontal screens in a platform game; the page control can be used to mark each of them, so the player sees the size of the level and has the opportunity to switch between screens quickly (on condition that the page control dots are interactive).

- **Picker**: This is another original UI detail of iOS. It looks like a cylinder with some text on its sides, which the user can pick from. The main advantage of the picker is its fixed screen size, regardless of the number of elements it stores; it is useful when the screen size is small. But you have to remember that this UI element is not without some drawbacks. Let me say that the input process is tricky, mostly because of inertia; it also does not indicate the exact number of entries it includes. So it is better to use the picker for specific data, with a predicted number of elements, for instance for entering digits.

- **Popover**: This is a more traditional element. It is a list of objects of different kinds, displayed above the current screen. The user has to choose one of them. Its functionality is tested over the years, but it is important to note that popover is a pretty large screen component, and it may have big screen dimensions. This is not a problem if it includes a small amount of data.

- **Action sheet**: This is very close to popover, but it displays a set of buttons with a specific action each. It is useful to control different game units, for example, in a strategy game each soldier can have a few types of behavior; by tapping the soldiers, the player activates the action sheet and chooses the type he needs.

- **Status bar**: This is one of the important parts of the information system of any interface, games are not exceptions. Looking back at the logic of iOS, it is reasonable to put the status bar at the top, above all the elements. It should include a button that can start the in-game menu and also pause the game (this is why some developers use the pause symbol on such buttons). You are free to choose the position for the menu button, but sometimes it is good to place it at the left-hand side of the status bar, like native iOS applications do. It's advisable to add a mute button too, so it can work like an indicator, showing if the sound is on or off. Then the game score and life indicator should be placed; sometimes, a timer is needed too. I have to mention that the special graphic panel that symbolizes the status bar is optional, you can deal with status bar elements hanging in the air, but they have to be aligned properly and some approaches need to be used to increase visibility; for example, contrasting outlines, shadows, and so on.

- **Toolbar**: This comes with a list of graphic representations of tools (usually, it is a list of weapons) that can be placed either at the top or at the bottom of the screen.

- **Switch**: This is my favorite control. It looks and operates neatly! It is a trigger with two states, on and off, so it successfully replaces more cumbersome solutions based on radio buttons or checkboxes alone. The switch in iOS has a small animation, its lever moves from one side to another; however, you can skip this and limit yourself to only two graphic states of the trigger. Usually, the switch is used in the **Options** menu, but it can be successfully used in gameplay too; an average puzzle game has a lot of different triggers, many of them have designs similar to those of switches.

- **Progress bars**: These are very common elements of game interfaces; usually, they display various exhaustible parameters, first of all, the status of the character's health or ammo. The rule of a good progress bar is simple; you need a beautiful gradient for the bar and a good dark background, the contrast between the empty and filled parts should be clearly visible. You can add any unostentatious animation to the progress bar to make it more attractive. A good practice is to introduce some additional signal functions to it. The bar can become redder if the game situation is critical, for example, when time is running out. Some game designers also add some markings to demonstrate the various stages of a game session, letting the player plan his efforts. A pie chart can be implemented instead of a progress bar, it looks interesting and fresh, but takes too much of screen space and can confuse the player.

- **Sliders**: This helps to adjust various parameters on the **Options** screen, primarily audio and music volumes. These are progress bars, but feature an additional element: a lever that can be moved by the user. A special background can be used to illustrate the increasing of values, very light at the beginning of the slider and dark (or saturated) at the end. Another way to add a professional touch is to apply some interactivity; for instance, if the music slider is set to zero, the icon that represents the term music in the menu should be crossed with a red stripe, which would mean that the music is switched off.

- **Segment control**: This is a set of buttons that stick together, only one of them can be pressed and active at a time, so the control operates in the same manner that the button panels on old radios and tape recorders did. For users familiar with the desktop metaphor of tabs, segment control is a replacement, as in contradiction to them, it usually uses only one of the few raw elements.

 The website `http://www.noteloop.com/kit/fui/movie/` is a very good inspiration for movies dedicated to futuristic GUI designs.

Accessible games

In the year 2008, the Information Solutions Group (visit their website at http://www.infosolutionsgroup.com), on behalf of *PopCap Games* conducted a special research. According to it, 20.5 percent of casual video game players have a physical, mental, or developmental disability. Thus a lot of people dedicated to games have disabilities in different forms. A good game developer should pay attention to their needs. First of all, there are a lot of people with visual perception disorders; it could be concluded that these types of people don't play video games, but that's not the case. They like to play, just like other ordinary people do. According to study of the Information Solutions Group, they even play more frequently, for longer periods of time. The following is an interesting quote from the survey about such players:

> *"They also report that they experience more significant benefits from playing and view their game-playing activity as a more important factor in their lives than do non-disabled consumers."*

A group of designers, academics, and specialists created *Game accessibility guidelines*, which can help to create an accessible game. There are a lot of reasonable and useful recommendations, which you can find at http://gameaccessibilityguidelines.com/full-list.

Apple offers some tools dedicated to people with disabilities. First of all, iPhone (starting with 3GS) and all the versions of iPad have the VoiceOver system (**Settings | General | Accessibility | VoiceOver**), which can read the text displayed on the screen. After the system is switched on, a computer-generated voice reads the text labels of any UI element the user has selected, and the new special gestures are introduced as well. For example, any element is activated not by a single tap, but a double tap, because a single gesture works like a selection, letting the user recognize the screen item before starting it.

Consider the example of the VoiceOver compatibility solution from the creators of Zombie, Run! 2. There is a normal graphic view of a game scene on the left-hand side, and a special VoiceOver friendly version of the scene, constructed from basic UI elements, which the screen reading technology can recognize. The image is taken from the developer's blog:

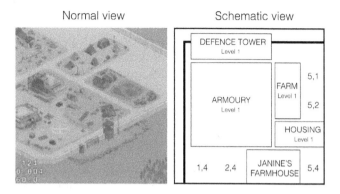

Some of the game developers try to adapt their products to VoiceOver. There is a special section called VoiceOver and Accessibility in the chapter *iOS Technology Usage Guidelines* of *IOS Human Interface Guidelines*. Don't forget Apple's *Accessibility Programming Guide for iOS* as well. That works well if the game features a lot of native UI elements of iOS, but can be a problem when custom controls are used, and of course, VoiceOver cannot recognize the graphic image and describes it in words. Do not despair, because there is a way to form a friendship between a graphic game and the screen reading technology. One of the *Zombie, Run! 2* developers, *Alex Macmillan* gives an explanation (in the developer's blog available at `http://blog.zombiesrungame.com/post/43403504393/making-zombies-run-2-accessible`) about how they addressed the issue of the custom graphic interface and VoiceOver. The solution was brilliant; they created a copy of the main graphic screen constructed of the basic UI-elements of iOS. The following is his description:

> *"The second interface – the "schematic view" – shows your base using only Apple's user interface components. It's like a top-down strategic view of your base. And because it's made using only "native" UI components, it works perfectly with VoiceOver."*

A schematic illustration of an audio game is shown in the following figure:

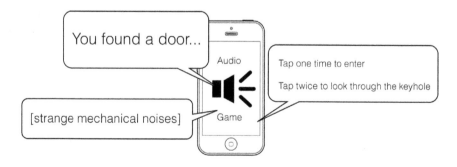

Not everyone knows that there is a unique category of games, which can be easily played by people with visual perception problems. I'm talking about audio games. Usually, these types of games are story driven, they are audio versions of text-based quests and adventures (the horror audio adventures sound good in a literal sense), but there are other genres too; for example, puzzles, quizzes, shooters, and so on. By using binaural audio technologies — a way to record sound, which uses two microphones imitating human ears (placed inside a special dummy head), so the result is the natural version of 3D stereo — the developers can create a breathtaking surround sound experience, but headphones should be used to achieve the proper effect.

Devices with touch screens answer the needs of audio games, because the player can utilize the advantages of multitouch inputs; an interaction with the game can be based not on buttons, but various gestures. The player can tap the screen with one, two, or three fingers, or make different drag movements with his index finger. Each gesture has its own meaning, for example, it may be signal to open the inventory, to take an object, to press a trigger, and so on. Besides, the screen gestures, the voice recognition input can be used as well. Players may interact with a game world by saying some special voice commands. Confirmation of the action, of course, is based on auditory feedback; there can be a few special sounds to illustrate that a scene or a dialogue is over and so on. The audio games can surprise an unprepared person, because there can be no graphics at all in such games. For instance, one of the famous audio games for iOS called The Inquisitor Audiogame Adventure created by *Ivan Venturi*, has the description on iTunes as **AUDIOGAME NO GRAPHICS**. Incredibly, people who worked on this game made a titanic effort to provide blind or shortsighted people a wonderful gaming experience. The adventure story includes about 21,000 words or up to 8 hours of the gameplay, which is totally based on sounds, music, and beautiful voice-acting, dubbed in three different languages. Try to imagine how long and difficult was the testing and debugging process alone! But all the efforts were paid off by players' appreciation.

A screenshot from The Nightjar featuring minimalistic graphics is shown as follows (it is pity that the image can't transmit sounds):

Another great example is a pretty elegant audio game called *The Nightjar* developed by *Somethin' Else*, a thrilling story of a spaceship falling into a black hole. It does not feature any graphics in the usual sense. The screen displays only simple schematic images in the form of striped patterns. The main plot element has the voice over of the incredible English actor *Benedict Cumberbatch* (featuring in *Sherlock*, *Parade's End*, and *Star Trek Into Darkness*) and 3D sounds effects. One of the game's taglines says:

"See with your ears"

Indeed, can a video chip compete with the power of human imagination?
It's important to mention that *The Nightjar* was nominated for the BAFTA award in 2012 under two categories: Audio Achievement and Mobile & Handheld.

Some of the visual games have options to play without seeing the screen, orienting only by sounds and tapping the screen by touch. One of them is a puzzle game *Robo-E* by *MPaja*. Another example is the arcade shooter *Ear Monsters: A 3D Audio Game* by *Ear Games*. The list of audio games can be found at `http://audiogames.net` and `http://www.pcsgames.net/iPhoneGames.htm`.

Color blindness

According to *Psychophysics of Vision* by *Michael Kalloniatis* and *Charles Luu*, about 8 percent of men and 0.5 percent of women have some form of color blindness. This is a significant number of people (most of them are males because of gene mechanics), many of them can become your customers. You should take care of this category of players, which is much easier than you can assume. The following figure shows the players with different types of vision:

Normal Vision	Purple	Blue	Green	Yellow	Orange	Red
Deuteranopia	Shade of purple	Blue	Shade of yellow	Yellow	Shade of yellow	Shade of yellow
Protanopia	Blue	Shade of blue	Shade of yellow	Yellow	Shade of yellow	Shade of yellow
Tritanopia	Shade of red	Shade of green	Shade of green	Shade of red	Shade of red	Shade of red

I think it is more correct to use the term color vision deficiency instead of color blindness, because people with different forms of color vision deficiencies basically do see colors, they have no black and white vision, based on shades of grey (except for a very rare disorder called achromatopsia). But they have difficulties with some of the colors and relative shades; for them there is a shift in the spectrum for specific colors. Color receptors give a response closer in hues to other colors, which creates trouble in perceiving differences between shades. Usually, such people have their own characteristics for each specific color, based on its saturation and brightness; however, sometimes such parameters are not powerful enough to spot the difference between specific colors. The following are the most common forms of color vision deficiencies (according to Colorblind Vision application):

- **Deuteranopia**: This is one of the common forms resulting in people having problems with the perception of the color green, because there is a shift towards the red color. Hues such as orange and yellow are affected as well. People have trouble in perceiving differences between shades of red and green; in some cases they can look the same or very close. A total of 5 percent of males and 0.38 percent of females have this deficiency.

- **Protanopia**: People have difficulties with the red color, the shift is directed towards the green color. It is similar to deuteranopia, with people having the same problems with the red-green pair and its derivatives as yellow and orange. 2.5 percent of males and 0.002 percent of females have protapia.

- **Tritanopia**: The perception of blue-pair is affected. This type of color deficiency causes a very strong distortion of the perceived palette of colors, red being dominated. For instance, yellow shades are replaced with pink ones. Its occurrence is rarer, less than 1 percent of population.

- **Achromatopsia (monochromacy)**: Total color blindness is an extremely rare color vision disorder. The world looks like a monochromic image. Only 0.005 percent of the population is diagnosed with it.

It is important to note that people with any of the common forms of color vision deficiencies are full-fledged members of society (in many countries, it is not an official disability, and does not affect people's career), they are fully adapted to the world around them, even having some advantages; for instance, people with red-green blindness sometimes have a better talent of distinguishing patterns, they can see camouflaged objects better. Unbelievable, but *Jon Hicks* — the designer who is behind the drawing of the Firefox logo (he has been mentioned in this book earlier) — is colorblind. The following is the quote from his website:

> *"You see, I'm colourblind, and more specifically, I have problems distinguishing between blue and purple, and green and brown. This is called 'red/green colourblind'. I can see tones, but hold up a blue square and purple square, and I'll probably just see 2 blue squares (handy that you had some coloured squares lying around though)"*

Neil Harbisson, an amazing man, was born with achromatopsia; he couldn't see any colors, other than black and white. That did not prevent him from studying fine arts; he used a monochromic pallet for his work. Then he met a student from Plymouth University, interested in cybernetics. Together they started a project, which later became popular as eyeborg, the device that helped him to catch colors, not by vision but by hearing special sounds. The eyeborg is a sensor that converts colors into sounds of specific tones. He can "hear the colors" around him, he even sees (or it is better to say, listens to) colors in his dreams when he sleeps. The artist even began to work on sound portraits; a person or an object is converted into a number of tones, which the eyeborg generates by scanning their surfaces. Vice versa, a melody or a speech can be converted into a color chart, so he also has some paintings of famous sounds.

The red-green blindness is the most common type of color vision deficiency, which is a problem if we try to recall the most popular color codes modern games are using. The green color is positive, friendly, and safe, but red symbolizes danger and hostility. Friends usually are marked in greens and enemies in reds. A character's calm mood is identified by green signals, but his fury by red ones. Another good example is of the trajectory lines; the correct ones can be painted green and the wrong ones red:

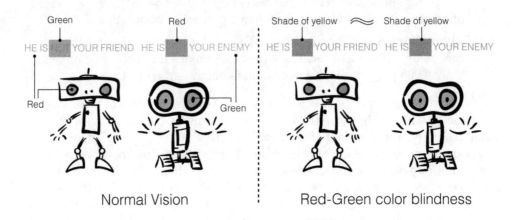

Normal Vision   Red-Green color blindness

The player with red-green blindness does not see (or barely sees) the difference between such code and signals. Is the character an enemy or a friend? Is the progress bar now in a red or green zone? The player has no clue. For him/her, such color code looks very alike, as though he is looking at some military equipment painted in various forms of olive drab or tan, and should spot the difference between shades. This can make some of the aspects of the game unrecognizable and even make the game impossible to play. This is especially true for various puzzle games, displaying a lot of color balls or bricks. Imagine you have a Match-three game, where the player does not know the exact color of each element. So he can only play randomly; sounds weird, but it is a very realistic scenario for players with some color vision deficiencies.

What do you have to do to prevent such a situation? First of all, try to look at your game screen via the eyes of a person with color recognition problems. There are several ways to simulate color vision deficiency. Many modern graphic editors have some options for that; for instance, look at Adobe Illustrator's or Adobe Photoshop's special menus. When you go to **View | Proof Setup**, there are two useful options Color Blindness—Protanopia-type and Color Blindness—Deuteranopia-type. For older editions of Adobe products, there is a plugin Vischeck, which is a project by two scientists at Stanford University: Bob Dougherty, PhD and Alex Wade, PhD. The plugin can be found at http://www.vischeck.com/downloads/.

Another way to see the world as the people with color vision deficiencies do is to use special applications for the iPhone or iPad. One of the popular ones is Colorblind Vision, developed by `opcoders.com`. It is very simple to use, you have to choose the form of color vision weakness and a camera with the specific color filter will start immediately. The main advantage of this way of simulation is the opportunity to test not static images, but the dynamic gameplay itself.

There are a lot of online tools that let you upload images and look at their color transformation. For instance, look at the inclusive design toolkit, which was developed by the University of Cambridge, Engineering Design Center and sponsored by BT. Its goal is to let designers produce solutions for a wide range of customers, which include those with a number of abilities and also those with some special needs. The online simulator can be found at `http://www.inclusivedesigntoolkit.com/betterdesign2/simsoftware/simsoftware.html`. It shows examples of vision affected not only by color blindness, but also by cataracts, glaucoma, diabetic retinopathy, and so on.

Look at your game screen through the simulator and try to determine all the weak points you've got. Don't think much about the background artwork or other elements of decoration, they will not confuse a player with a color vision weakness; try to fix all game items that have visual coding based on colors (primarily all the red/green pairs, then blue/violet, and so on). If the game element uses only a few color signals to demonstrate its state, the solution is simple: contradictory colors may be replaced with more secure ones. For example, a red signal can be replaced with a yellow, and a green with a blue. It is useful to use special color palettes full of reliable color swatches.

You can find some of the palettes on the website of *Christine Rigden* at `http://www.rigdenage.co.uk/safecolours/palettefiles.html`. She was the author of the interesting article *The Eye of the Beholder – Designing for Colour-Blind Users* published in *British Telecommunications Engineering, Vol. 17*, in January 1999. One of the ideas described in the article was the creation of special safe palettes for color blind people, based on the web-safe color palette. The result is presented in the form of color tables suitable for Adobe Photoshop.

In case the game has game triggers with a lot of color states (for instance, it is a puzzle with a dozen color balls), another approach can be used. Each trigger can feature a special graphic icon, which helps to differentiate it from others. There are a lot of familiar examples from real life using such a method to distinguish objects. For example, playing cards, which have both colors and symbols; traffic lights for pedestrians, where special pictograms (or words) are used (the green light usually displays the symbol of a walking person, but the red light shows a person standing still). So try to equip game triggers with some unique graphic icons, also try to combine them with some safe colors to increase attractiveness.

You can also play with patterns, a good inspiration would be various maps and schemes from old books; many great books were published in black and white. So graphic illustrators of that time had to distinguish elements by using patterns based on dots of different densities, diagonal lines, grids, parallel lines, and so on.

Bear in mind that you need not try to create a universal system that would be good both for people with normal color vision and those with some problems, because a majority of players with normal vision can be confused by a new logic of color coding (such players expect that the angry enemy would feature red eyes, not blue ones). It is better to add an optional mode oriented to players with special color needs. The game has to be created normally, using any color scheme you like, but all the important trigger elements should have the option of being switched from the normal look to the special from the menu options. A practical example can be found in the puzzle game Peggle, designed by PopCap Games; it can be switched to the color-blind-friendly mode via the **Options** menu:

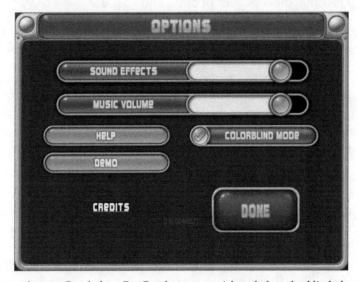

A puzzle game Peggle from PopCap features special mode for color-blind players

Then you have to check the entire color adaption with some real-time simulators. If the game is playable in such a mode, you can be calm. Of course, the most reliable way is to invite a person with color vision deficiency to be your beta tester; such a person can give the most precious advice. Remember that you may not resolve all the problems associated with the colors for color-blind players, but you should at least try, because of the love and respect you have for all of your players.

Sometimes a human eye can have extra abilities. There is an interesting story about the famous French painter *Claude Monet*. Because he had cataracts diagnosed at a pretty advanced age, the lens in his eye began to lose their ability to transmit light correctly. The painter began to experience difficulties with the perception of colors; all objects were in a fog. So when he was 82 years old, he was successfully operated on his left eye and the faulty lens was removed. The result was a bit unexpected; the painter got the ability to see ultraviolet light. Usually, the lenses in the human eyes work as filters blocking ultraviolet light, but he had no lens in his left eye, so the UV rays could reach his color sensors and affect them. He began to see the world differently, his color vision range changed. It is interesting that as he used his new abilities in his work, all the paintings drawn after the surgery had a unique color palette, for example, he added more blue pigment to images of water lilies.

Photosensitive epilepsy

Photosensitive epilepsy (**PSE**) is a form of epilepsy in which the patient is very sensitive to various visual stimuli such as moving patterns, blinking backgrounds, and flashing lights; in extreme circumstances, any of them can cause seizures. As you see, the list of stimuli includes some elements that can be seen in modern video games; the game screen flashes all the time when a dynamic scene is displaying. There are a lot of flares, explosions, flickering particles, blinking text alerts, backgrounds with regular patterns of texture moving quickly, and so on. This is why some game situations of poor conditions—depends on the time spent during the game session, lighting conditions, distance to the screen, sleep deprivation, emotional state, hunger, thirst, and many more—can cause a seizure. For such cases, there is a special term called **Video game-induced seizures** (**VGS**).

According to the article *Stimulus Overload* written by *Joshua Cox (NREMT-P)* and *Eric T. Richardson (MD)* published in *Jems* magazine, video game epilepsy causes seizures in the young and old. It states the following quote:

> *"It's known that PSE is more prevalent in people aged seven to nineteen, with more males affected because they tend to play video games more than females. Those affected report seeing an "aura" or feeling particularly odd sensations prior to the seizure"*

Happily, the new technologies make the problem less vexed. Because the modern LCD displays, based on technology different from the old CRT monitors, reduce the chances of seizures but do not exclude it completely.

Although there is not much information about seizures caused by mobile games, it is better to have some thoughts about the players with PSE. First of all, try to think about all the scenes in the game with flickering elements, especially if they are large. The most problematic are the various blinking backgrounds, which can cause the stroboscopic effect. It is not necessary to remove all the flashing effects, but you need to adjust their frequency. The Epilepsy Society (visit their site at `http://epilepsysociety.org.uk`) informs that the potentially dangerous range lies between 3 and 30 flashes per second. Some useful information can also be found in the article *Web Content Accessibility Guidelines (WCAG) 2.0* published by World Wide Web Consortium, in section *Guideline 2.3 Seizures: Do not design content in a way that is known to cause seizures*; there is a recommendation as follows:

> *"2.3.2 Three Flashes: Web pages do not contain anything that flashes more than three times in any one second period "*.

So all you need to do is check your flashing elements and slow them down if their frame rate is higher than three per second. It will not affect the visual qualities of the game; moreover, it can increase the level of comfort even for players without epilepsy, because in reality nobody loves very fast flickers, as it looks annoying.

Moire patterns:

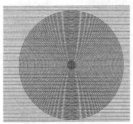 

Another advice is to avoid moving fast and unexpectedly large portions of geometric patterns, especially if they have contrasting graphics; for example, graphics based on black and white stripes. Such elements can cause seizures too. There is another potential problem with the regular geometric textures; if they consist of parallel lines, there is a big chance for the moiré pattern to appear. This geometric effect always looks very inappropriate and ugly.

You should implement such changes in your game if you have some problems with flashing elements, or you should at least warn the player about the potential risk, by placing a special message on the main screen menu.

Handedness

About of 15 percent of the population worldwide are left-handed. That is a huge number of people and potential customers, but their needs sometimes are not taken into consideration. Some interfaces and control elements are created mostly for right-handed persons (control elements are aligned to the right-hand side of the screen, which is especially evident when a device is in a landscape mode), and that is wrong. Especially when UIs are created for mobile devices with a very flexible layout system. To prepare a game which is handedness friendly, you only need to prepare two layouts of the buttons with their positions mirrored. By default, the layout for right-handed players should be used, but in the **Options** menu there must be a button to switch it to the left-handed setup. In most cases, such an approach can be developed very simply, because there is no need to redraw control elements and so on, only their coordinates need to be changed on the screen. Another approach is to try to develop a center-based UI or control system without an exact screen position (the application only needs to get a tap or gestures, but the exact coordinates are irrelevant), so it can be handedness independent, but that is not always possible.

If a game uses some specific gestures such as swipes, they should be comfortable for both types of handedness. An optimal solution is a vertical direction of such gestures, which is pretty comfortable for both hands; in case they are horizontal, it is good to keep in mind that a direction towards the dominating hand is more comfortable for people.

And as always, it's very important to have a real left-handed person, who can share his thoughts about the UI adaptations for his needs.

Other accessibility issues

Besides the obvious ones, there are some aspects that few people think about. Let's start with a common element of text. There are a lot of text strings inside modern games: menu labels, rule descriptions, in-game notifications, subplot elements as messages, and diaries. They are an essential part of the game products, they help to navigate, drive a story, and so on. But in some cases it is hard or impossible to rely on them. First of all, regular players do not like big portions of text, especially if it appears in pages, without any accents, comfortable paragraphs of small size, and so on. Then there are some players who find it hard to read, or the speed at which they read is not fast: small kids, people with different forms of dyslexia (a state when a reading process is impeded in some form), and people who speak other languages. Besides, developers always try to provide localizations for their titles; in many cases that is not enough, it is very hard to cover all the common languages.

All these categories may have trouble interacting with the game, because they do not get the words or it is hard to read them. It means that other elements should be used on par with texts. First of all the menu navigations, game rules, and so on, must be pretty logical and clear to understand without any additional descriptions. Then special non-verbal communication elements should be used widely, as icons or other types of graphic illustrations of different actions. According to The International DYSLEXIA Association, up to 15–20 percent of the population have some symptoms of dyslexia in various forms of slow or inaccurate reading. It means that some form of image-based communication can be more comfortable for them as well as for kids, especially when games are oriented on an audience that uses large buttons and some clear icons (they should not be very abstract as kids have no proper experience to read abstract symbols; hence, they should be small illustrations with small scenes of actions shown clearly).

While working on game applications for little kids, remember that you should take good care of their health conditions. The game must be interrupted (in ideal cases, that is included into a game process) if a kid keeps playing it for a long period of time (for instance, every 10-15 minutes), for the eyes to relax. When a person is playing, he does not blink much, and that is not good for the eyes. During a mandatory pause, the game can ask a young player to make some actions; for example, tilt a device, shake it, put it on a table, and so on, and also give some rewards (the accelerometer and the gyroscope can register such movements). That may help to switch the attention from the screen for some time. A brilliant idea is to ask a kid to get a photo of a specific object that may motivate him to move and not concentrate only on the screen.

Overall, to increase readability of text, it should come in portions; there should be a good contrast with the background (but not too sharp as black on white for example, it should be a little bit milder). Sans-serif typeface such as Helvetica are good, the background should not be too motley.

An intentional audience can, in some cases, understand basic text lines written in English, but in many cases, it cannot. Even simple words such as race, go, fire, and so on can be incomprehensible for some people. To check if a game is accessible for such players, it should be tested without any text shown on the buttons.

Besides the texts, there is also another "Lost in translation" case. The intended customers can have trouble perceiving cultural elements; first of all, different references on events or traditions that are pertaining to a specific territory or country. The general content should be quite multicultural, but some minor things may have more specific connotations that help a wider audience to understand the plot, character's motivations, principle of design and rule, and so on.

Also, keep in mind some specific taboos, respected objects, traditions, people, or historical events in different cultures. A harmless content for a certain type of people may hurt the senses of others.

The following are the links you can refer to for additional information on topics that are used in this chapter:

- `http://developer.apple.com/library/ios/#documentation/userexperience/conceptual/mobilehig/Characteristics/Characteristics.html`
- `http://faculty.washington.edu/demorest/Banton.pdf`
- `http://www.thisoldtractor.com/gtbender/papers/dissertation.pdf`
- `http://www.prnewswire.com/news-releases/survey-disabled-gamers-comprise-20-of-casual-video-games-audience-57442172.html`
- `https://developer.apple.com/library/ios/#documentation/UserExperience/Conceptual/MobileHIG/TechnologyUsage/TechnologyUsage.html#//apple_ref/doc/uid/TP40006556-CH18-SW5`
- `http://blog.zombiesrungame.com/post/43403504393/making-zombies-run-2-accessible`
- `http://en.wikipedia.org/wiki/Binaural_recording`
- `http://www.eymerich.it/index.php?center=audiogame&lang=eng#3`
- `http://awards.bafta.org/award/2012/games`
- `http://retina.umh.es/webvision/KallColor.html#deficiencies`
- `http://hicksdesign.co.uk/journal/compliant-style`
- `http://www.ted.com/speakers/neil_harbisson.html`
- `http://www.dailymail.co.uk/sciencetech/article-2131608/Claude-Monet-How-famed-artist-ultraviolet-just-like-animals.html`
- `http://professionals.epilepsy.com/page/video_game_seizures.html`
- `http://www.jems.com/article/patient-care/stimulus-overload-video-game-e`
- `http://www.epilepsysociety.org.uk/aboutepilepsy/whatisepilepsy/triggers/photosensitiveepilepsy`
- `http://www.w3.org/TR/WCAG20/#seizure`
- `http://www.scientificamerican.com/article.cfm?id=what-causes-some-people-t`
- `http://www.interdys.org/ewebeditpro5/upload/BasicsFactSheet.pdf`

Summary

There are a lot of factors to be taken into account when you are developing a product that is comfortable for the audience to play. It all starts with a well-structured UI with the minimum steps to get a result and well-designed control elements. A good interface is "invisible", a player simply does not notice that there is an intermediary between him and a game, because it all works so smoothly; hence, there is no reason to pay attention to it. To develop such a system, you need to think of every detail by following some basic rules. Always keep in mind some bad examples and try to avoid them in your own project.

There are some people that need some special care and many of them are devoted gamers. It won't take much time or effort to make a game suitable for their needs. To prepare a product which is friendly for color-blind people, remember that only some important indicators and color schemes must be reinvented. Some controversial color pairs such as red/green should be avoided in alerts and indicators. The VoiceOver system can be used for games, helping people with vision deficiencies to play. The left-handed users need a special control layout, which can be activated via the **Options** menu. By reducing the frame rate of flickering animation to three per second and avoiding any contrasting moving patterns, you may reduce the risk of seizures in people with photosensitive epilepsy. In the next chapter, we will talk about how gestures in games, their rules and mechanics can be simple, but the game very addictive.

3
Gesture Games

Gesture games are simple and very addictive. The game's mechanics are not complicated. A player has to tap at the preassigned part of a screen or make a correct gesture with his finger. The gesture can be single or multitouched. The player gets the points if the gesture or touch is correct. The more points he gets, the higher the speed of the gameplay becomes. That is the basic idea. Players like such type of games, they are fast and it is easy to understand their rules. They are wonderful time killers for young audiences (starting from kids) and also for older players.

A screenshot from a gesture game, Infinity Blade 2, from Chair Entertainment, which was a huge hit on the market providing addictive gameplay and advanced graphics

It is very important for a simple gesture game to be quite elementary in development. If the gestures are not complicated (a player only needs to tap on specific zones of a screen), there is no need of complex algorithms and advanced code. The graphics may have some minimalistic and laconic appearance (it only decorates some triggers) as it did not take much time to develop them. It is pretty reasonable to choose such type of projects to be your very first game. Furthermore, you can take some DNA of a gesture game and its gesture detection system, and later use it in in games of other genres, for instance, in platform games with a gesture input or in action games with a main protagonist controlled by gestures. Moreover, do you remember the audio games from the previous chapter? They were totally based on complex gesture input.

Some famous PC and console games are using gestures as a key element of a gameplay, for example, classic *Peter Molyneux's Black&White* created by *Lionhead Studios* in 2001, which had no traditional GUI, but instead a unique system of gestures. Each gesture created a special spell to operate the game world. Another amazing example is the very artistic game, *Ōkami*, which was developed by *Clover Studio* in 2006. It has an input system called Celestial Brush based on gestures, which help to resolve puzzles, fight enemies, and so on.

The iOS platform is not an exception; there are several enthralling titles. One of the most famous examples is the *Infinity Blade* franchise from *Chair Entertainment* visualizing the fact that a gesture game can have a rich story, interesting evolution of a main character, and superb graphic ornamentation. The look is so addictive and sometimes considered as a benchmark to demonstrate the abilities of 3D rendering on iOS devices. A lot of games also use various gestures in less apparent forms; gestures are part of a control system. For instance, an adventure game *Machinarium* from *Amanita Design* has several puzzles that require players to rotate some levers and pedals by using index fingers. There are some interesting gesture mechanics in *Plants vs. Zombies 2* from *PopCap Games* as well.

Screen gestures are also widely used for educational purposes, teaching audiences some sort of drawing skills. For example, Calligraphy Practice (`http://www.calligraphypractice.com/`) is an amazing application for iPad that uses the user's gestures and taps to create calligraphic letters. It teaches by displaying special contours on the screen, which the user has to follow to draw lines of a specific character. In addition, the application utilizes the advantages of multitouch input. The user touches the screen using two fingers simultaneously, and the distance between them defines the width of a virtual calligraphic brush; the angle of the brush can be calculated too. In this connection, remember that educational tools, as a rule, work better if they have some game aspects inside, at least in a form of an achievement system (we will talk about this a bit more in the final chapter of this book).

Introducing the game idea

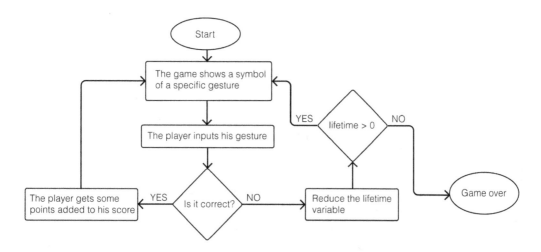

The main task of the game is to show the player the special graphic symbols linked with specific gestures. The symbols are displayed one by one in order. In the simplest case, there is no array of gestures inside the game and there is no system in place for an order of them. Each time, the game generates the type of symbol from scratch using a random number generator. The game has to generate a type of symbol and show its graphic representation on the screen of the device. It should display it for a period of time (let's call this period an interval) waiting for the player's reaction. If the player inputs the correct gesture, the game gives them some points. If they are wrong, the application gives them few negative points and displays the next symbol. Quite simple mechanics, aren't they? Yes. A prototype with such logic can be pretty playable. Let's call it the absolute infinite mode because the game can't stop till the player stops it by himself via an exit option. Literally, the player can play this mode forever.

But absolute infinite mode in such shape is good only for early prototyping. For example, you can use it for testing your gesture interpretation system or other elements of the game engine. Later, you will have to add some more functionality; the game should know when to end a game session. You can do this by introducing a special variable which will store a game session's lifetime. At the beginning of the game, the lifetime is a positive number (for example, it can be equal to 100). When the player makes a wrong gesture, the game reduces the lifetime.

A system of lives can be used instead. They can be presented like tiny heart icons in the corner of the screen, and you have to decide the number of them the application will give to the player at the beginning. The game session stops when the player loses all of their lives.

The player needs some obstacles too. The common way to add some complexity to the game is to increase its speed. This means reducing the interval; when the game becomes harder, it scales down the waiting period, so the player has to act faster and faster.

You can link the speed with the player's score (roughly speaking: *speed* = *score* / *special divider*) or the session's duration time. The faster gameplay moves, the more mistakes the player can make, and the shorter the lifetime will be. Sooner or later, the lifetime becomes a negative number. This is the signal to finish the game. This is more viable than the infinite mode because there are flexible dynamics inside. The player starts the game; at the beginning, the speed is slow and very comfortable and the player begins to collect points.

There is a rule of etiquette for games where the score and the gameplay speed are connected together. Periodically, you have to give a break to a player. It can be done by introducing special zones of comfort and relaxation (in a relative degree of course). They should be short, and the player gets them by reaching a certain number of points. For example, each round number, 100, 200, or 1000 points, grants a little period of relaxation. This means that the speed becomes slower for a short period of time and the player can catch their breath.

At the beginning, the application should use only simple gestures, introducing the more complicated and tricky ones by the game's session duration.

A scoring system depends on several factors. First of all, a gesture game may reward the player for the fast reaction. The less time it takes them to make a right gesture, the more points they get. Zero seconds (which is practically impossible) gives maximum score; the time which is equal to the interval gives the minimum number of points or even gives a zero.

Then the player gets points for the accuracy. For each correct node of the gesture, they get some points wherein they can receive the points on a linear base. In other words, each node gives the same number of points or there can be a geometrical progression accuracy rating. In the latter case, the player gets a lot of points by inputting the correct gesture. This is a good motivation to play attentively.

The optional way is to introduce special bonuses with some extra points. For example, some gestures (complicated ones) can have a status that is gold, silver, platinum, and so on. In the case of a fast and correct input, the player can be rewarded with additional number of points. Special bonuses can also bring the player a small supplement to the lifetime variable; this is useful for infinite game modes.

You can introduce an exclusive anti-mistake bonus, letting the player make some errors in the game painlessly. It can become the most powerful bonus in the game, so it must be hidden only in very intricate gestures.

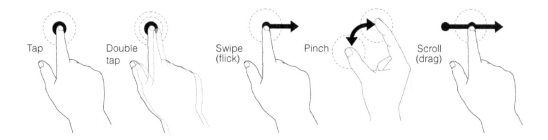

Collecting gestures. Some basic gestures used in multitouch displays

The gestures are based on special control zones that the player touches. They work separately as tap points or in combination forming a gesture sign. Let's imagine all the gesture types the game can use:

- **Tap point**: This allows the player to tap a zone on the screen.
- **Line**: This allows the player to draw a line (by using a swipe gesture) in the specific direction.
- **Figures**: This allows the player to draw a multipoint symbol.
- **Shakes**: This is an optional mode. It motivates the player to use more active type of interactions by using capabilities of the internal accelerometer and gyroscope. The game waits for the player to shake or tilt the device in a specific direction.

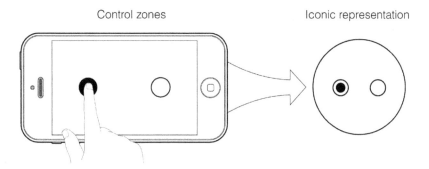

It is good to start with a simple system based only on two nodes at a time. The game only asks the player to portray the tap point or the line. Such a concept can be useful at the early stages of the game when the difficulty level is easy. The player is in a comfort zone and can naturally figure out the principles of the gameplay. An iconic representation of this system can look like a circle with a two holes. It can help to create gestures for the game. All the gestures at this step are single-touch; the player needs only one finger to make the input.

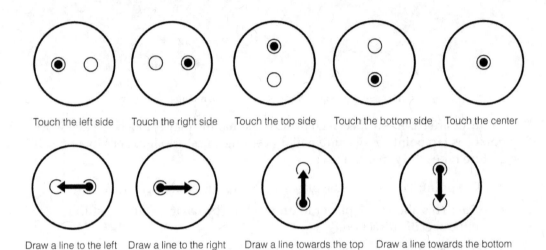

Touch the left side	Touch the right side	Touch the top side	Touch the bottom side	Touch the center

Draw a line to the left	Draw a line to the right	Draw a line towards the top	Draw a line towards the bottom

Advanced game levels allow multipoint gestures (this is a very good opportunity to utilize the multitouch input system of the iOS devices). They are based on four control nodes: four corner input points (the center is optional). This system requires the use of two fingers (the thumb and the index finger) on each side of the screen. The gestures can be asymmetric now. That is not easy for the player; it can be very challenging especially at a high speed.

Symmetric touches

Asymmetric touches

Lines

Figures

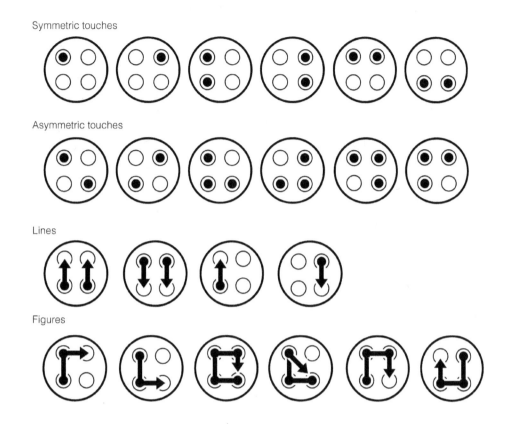

Sometimes, the game can ask the player to repeat a gesture several times (up to three for example). In this case, there is more than one symbol on the screen. It's reasonable to use only simple gestures: taps and lines, not the figures for such a game situation. But this is not a stringent rule.

Touch the left side twice

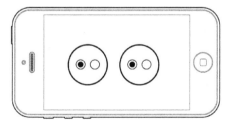

Draw a line towards the bottom at the right side thrice

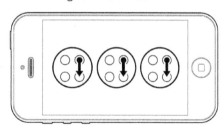

The gestures can be more knotty and use more than five control nodes. Let's call them spells because they look like symbols inscribed by a wizard. In fairy tales, heroes with some experience in magic are always using their wands to create spells, drawing some enigmatic symbols in the air. The game can let the player become a wiz too. It is expected that in most cases, such type of gestures are not multitouch. The player makes an input using only one finger; nevertheless, there can be some ornate challenges that require two fingers to be used. An obvious example is a gesture puzzle, where a symmetric image should be drawn (for instance, a butterfly) only by one pass and a part is created by the index finger (the second finger), which is much harder than it appears at first sight.

There is a wide variety of symbols that can be used as spells. You need both simple ones consisting of a single simple curve and complicated ones with a lot of corners, twists, and lines.

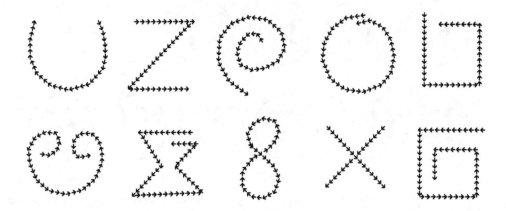

The symbolic representation of the spell should be displayed a little bit different than the ordinary gestures signs. The game shows it clearly only for a moment, then the symbol begins to disappear; this can be done by reducing its opacity. On a hard difficulty, the fade-out process can be done really fast.

Imagining the device orientation

Generally, there are two ways people hold their mobile devices when they are using them, including when they are playing games.

Two thumbs

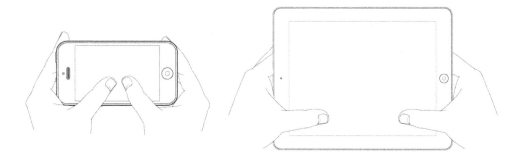

- **Two thumbs**: This is when the device is in a landscape (horizontal) position and the player holds it using the fingers of both hands. Traditionally, only the thumbs are at the surface of the device screen, as only they can be used for various interactions. Such a position is inherent for various games with a dynamic content with less precision of input (large active areas should be used for more comfort).

- **One finger**: This is when one hand keeps a device in a portrait (vertical) position and the other one is used for input: either single-touched (only an index finger is applied) or multitouched, when several fingers can be used at once, for example, gestures such as pinch.

Alternative scenarios are possible, but are less common and are used only in specific situations and cannot be considered as a prevalent behavior. For instance, some people play games putting a device on the tabletop (that is more usual for iPad rather than iPhone). Obviously, this is possible only when they are sitting in their living rooms or offices.

The main advantage of such models is free fingers, which can be used for some very shifty multitouch tasks. Another possible player's behavior implies that the two fingers (an index and a thumb) are placed over the screen. It is a little bit ungainly because it is harder to hold a device (especially a full-scale iPad) and operate all fingers; nevertheless, it is worth thinking about.

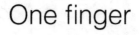

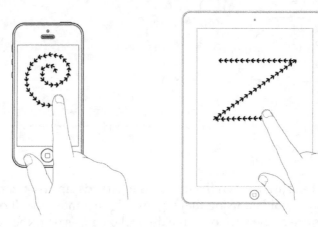

The only exception is a game that is oriented on the spells or other gaming modes based on single-fingered gestures. Such a game looks very good in a portrait mode, because gesture symbols can be very large and snazzy, especially with some shiny special effect being applied on.

Introducing game modes

Game modes in most common ways are combinations of elements and mechanics that the application has. Each one introduces their own collection of details and has their own rules, obeying the main doctrine of the game. Let's just imagine the types of gameplay a gesture game can have:

- Gestures
- Intuition
- Lights

Gestures

Gestures is the most common game mode. It was explained in the game mechanics section of the current chapter. The game shows a gesture symbol. The player has to react fast in making the input and thereby, he collects points and bonuses.

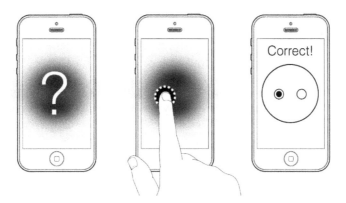

Intuition

One of the most unusual game modes you can utilize is intuition. It is pretty adventurous and funny. The idea is a little bit ironic. The game does not show a gesture symbol it has just generated. It shows nothing except for a black screen or a very blurry and unrecognizable image of the symbol — something in the mist. Are you intrigued? Now the most interesting part: the game waits and the player makes a hypothesis about the hidden symbol. They have to guess what is hidden. They make a gesture listening to their own intuition. Then the game shows the hidden symbol. If the player's surmise is correct, they get a lot of points. The score system can be generous and can be based on the number of the correctly predicted nodes of the gesture. It is important to show the player a statistic of their fortunes and misfortunes. Optionally, the game can show the player an innuendo or display the symbol very quickly at the very beginning of the game session. In this case, it will not be a test on intuition, but on visual memory. So, there is a space for creative experiments:

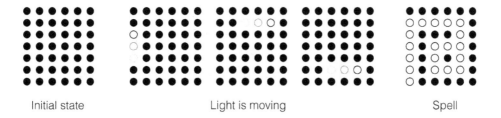

Initial state   Light is moving   Spell

Lights

This game mode is very suitable for the spells and can be a great challenge for the player's memory and attention. The game shows a grid of dots, all of which are initially dark (turned off). Suddenly a gesture symbol is drawn by a little light that flashes on the dots; they switch on and off in a specific order. The light moves on the dots drawing a contour of a spell. It has no tail (or it is very short), so the player basically sees only one running spot of a light at a time. If the light is moving fast enough and the spell's shape is very catchy, it is not easy to remember the contour just drawn. Did the light turn left on that row or on this one?

When the light finishes traveling the screen, the player is asked to reproduce its trajectory. The dots are dark again (they may have a special color signaling they are waiting for the input). The player makes his gesture by tapping on the dots one by one. Then he has to click on the **Submit** button. After that, the game analyzes the input and shows all the correct nodes by green dots and the wrong ones by red signs. The player is awarded for the correct elements of the gesture and gets some negative points for the mistakes they made.

The game can hide some prizes behind some of the dots. It is also great to make the start of each game session a little bit sudden. A countdown before the beginning of the light show should be a little bit different each time. It can help to tease the player.

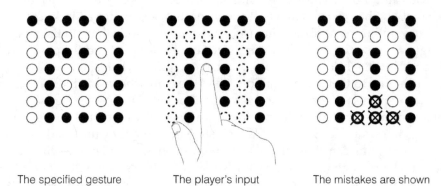

| The specified gesture | The player's input | The mistakes are shown |

Additionally, each game mode has three organization models:

- **Infinite**: This is almost an endless game process. The player plays until they use up their lifetime variable (or lose all their game lives).

- **Time**: This is the time limit. Each game session is limited in time. The player can choose between the time options: 15 seconds, 30 seconds, 1 minute, and so on.

- **Levels**: This is a predefined collection of gestures. The game can take them from the array manually created by you or it can have special logic to generate a unique set of elements for each level.

Thinking about the plot and decorations

It is good to start with an idea of a gesture game featuring a very minimalistic plot: a name, few abstract rules, and score statistics at the end. There is no need to create some narrative structures, characters, dialogues, and so on. But the minimalistic approach needs an appropriate objectification. All elements of the game: media, artwork, GUI, and icons, have to be laconic too. If everything is done correctly, the game can look nice and elegant, especially from a graphic designer's point of view. The game can be truly digital and modernistic, along with flat graphics, clear colors, minimum ornamentation, large and light sans serif fonts, and well-balanced graphic compositions. Let's give that game a code name, Clear gesture.

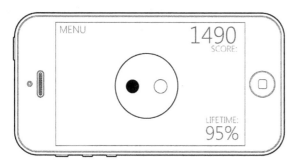

The following are the advantages of the design and idea concept:

- Looks fashionable having a graphic style that is very appropriate to the iOS 7-generation GUI
- The designers would like it
- The graphics are simple and are pretty easy to produce

The following are the disadvantages of the design and idea concept:

- A little bit vanguard.
- Needs huge attention to capricious factors such as typography, compositions, grids, and colors.
- Interactions with players should be reliable and smooth. The gesture recognition system must be perfectly tuned.
- It is not emotional.

The minimalistic style is amazing but it almost has no emotions. It is pretty cold and is not funny, so the game is unable to make the player smile. Most commonly, you need a more traditional, skeuomorphic graphic style for your game. Hence you need a small plot to express the main idea of the game. It has to explain to the players why they should make those gestures on the screen and why it is so dramatically important to play carefully. Sometimes, the idea of a game plot comes from a sudden afflatus and can even precede the game itself. But in our case, we already have well-written game principles and mechanics; in other words, we have a prototype. We only need some ideas to decorate it properly and build a connection between the game elements and the player. Sometimes, there is a trick to find the right idea for a game. You only need to look attentively at your game prototype, rather, at the elements it uses. Sometimes, you only need to find the right ornamentation for them. Please look at the special icons that represent the gesture combinations in this book: a circle with some holes in it. What does the circle look like? Correct, it looks like a button from your shirt or jacket! That is amazing! That is the idea we are looking for. And here's our plot: the player has to sew on the buttons, drawing the contours of threads on fabrics. If the player makes a mistake and the buttons are falling down, the game can be finished, in which case the player would collect a lot of fallen buttons. The game can utilize several designs of the buttons and few types of backgrounds to create a unique decoration for each game mode. This game may be code named Buttons.

The following are the advantages of the Button game idea:

- The visual look of the game is attractive and cute.
- The game image is very haptic; various cloth textures are used as backgrounds, which create a sense of warmth and coziness
- It can be nicely animated

The following are the disadvantages of the Button game idea:

- It is hard to adapt this design for gestures such as spells

Most people love kittens (and those who don't are simply afraid to admit that). People like to touch and caress them because kittens are so extremely cute and can sing peerless purr-purr songs. Many people also like to play and interact with their mobile devices as well. Let's combine these two passions and make a game about a kitten dreaming to be stroked. There will be a cute little face of a kitten with big lovely eyes on the screen and a speech balloon with a gesture symbol. The player will reply by drawing a gesture. If their input is correct, they will be rewarded with the purr-purr sound and several points. It would be great to apply a system of emotion for the main character; he would smile and become happy if the player is successful and would become sad otherwise. Instead of a kitten, another small and cute character can be used (for example, a puppy), or you can invent a fictional animal. The game modes should be renamed so that they can fit the more cartoony style of the game story. For example, the standard game mode may be called *stroking*, lights may become *titillate*, but intuition, on its turn, may be renamed into *guess what I want*. Here we have an ideal game for small kids. Let's give it a code name Purr.

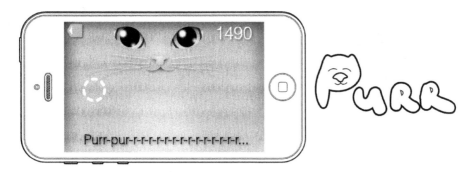

The following are the advantages of the Purr game idea:

- The game looks so cute and lovely
- It has an emotional system that can switch on the player's empathy with the character and increase the player's attachment to the game
- There is a lulling purr-purr soundtrack
- The game is funny

The following are the disadvantages of the Purr game idea:

- Some people will say that they are too serious and elderly for a game about kittens
- It requires sufficiently complicated illustrations and animations

The most capricious elements of the gesture games are the spells and lights modes. They can be incorporated in many of the decoration styles we've talked about, but it is interesting to invent something special. Both of them need a bright effect of light that looks wonderful against a very contrasting and dark background. It is important to remember that the most spectacular photos of lighting or fireworks are made at night. The idea is to use a dark sky as a background. Stars will become grid dots in the lights mode or trajectory nodes for the spells. An image of a comet (or a glowworm) will be used for the source of the light in the lights mode; it will be flying above the stars drawing a gesture symbol. Some spells (bonus ones) may become interactive, being called the spells of elements. Their mission is to start certain animation sequences playing in the background: a lighting strike, rain, snowfall, and so on. This has nothing to do with
the gameplay process itself, but it looks great, and the player will love it and will try to repeat such a game situation in the future. Let's give this variant of game a code name Magic sky.

The following are the advantages of the Magic sky game idea:

- Looks very atmospheric
- The game has a lot of space for different special effects and animation

The following are the disadvantages of the Magic sky game idea:

- It is mainly good for games with spells and for the lights mode
- The spells of elements require good-looking animations of different nature conditions: rain, lighting, fire, and snow

Alternative ideas

- The figure gestures can be a great learning tool for kids. They can teach letters and digits. The game shows a letter glyph, and a kid has to repeat it on the screen. On a hard difficulty, the game can show short words such as one, two, cup, cat, and dog.

- If you are qualified enough, you can convert a gesture game into an improvised music tool; each gesture produces a specific sound or music tone. On playing the game, the player plays some electronic music. It is good to use a minimalistic graphic style with some abstract ornamentation for that game.

- Why not use flowers as a graphic representation of a gesture? Something like a big chamomile or a sunflower. They can be animated.

- Another fun idea is to utilize an illustration of a pizza as a gesture symbol. The style must be very cartoony. The pizza's ingredients will form the different symbols.

Creating a game's identity

As you already know from the first chapter, a good application icon is one of the significant ways to make a name on an app store. The gesture games we were talking about should have a simple identity, and the main icon has to demonstrate the various forms of gestures involved in the game process. Thus, a gesture symbol can be used as a general composition element.

The icon ideas of the Clear gestures application

The icon ideas of the Buttons application

The icon ideas of the Magic sky application

The icon ideas of the Purr application

A background should express the mood and the graphic style of the game; in our case, the most interesting results can be achieved for Buttons and Purr, because these games' scenarios have very vivid graphic styles, which are full of amazing details. The cutest one is of course Purr; character-based icons are always very attractive and compel a lot of attention. Clear gestures, at their turn, have their own advantages because they can look great on minimalistic iOS 7 screens.

Game blueprints

Here you can see illustrations that describe the general graphic aspects of the games discussed in the chapter. Let's call them blueprints. They can help you to organize the appearance of the game you will create.

The following scheme shows a blueprint with the basic elements of a gesture game code named Clean Gestures:

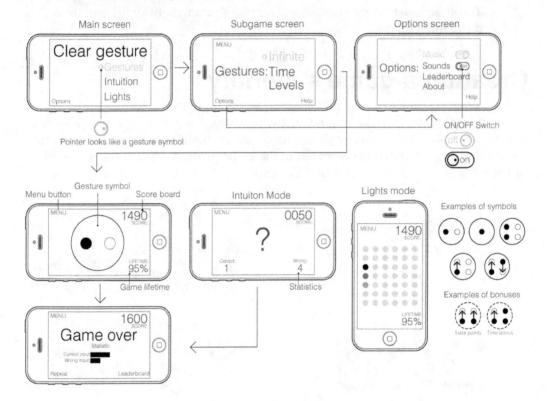

The following scheme shows a blueprint with the basic elements of a gesture game code named Buttons:

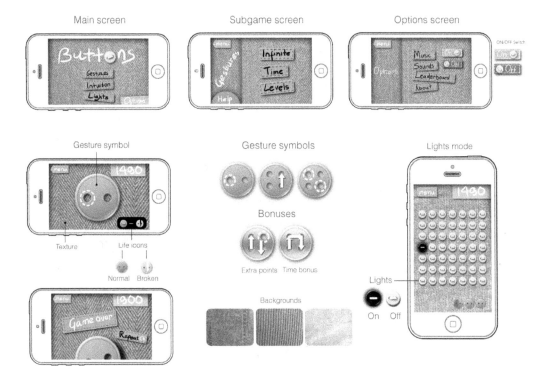

The following scheme shows a blueprint with the basic elements of a gesture game code named Purr:

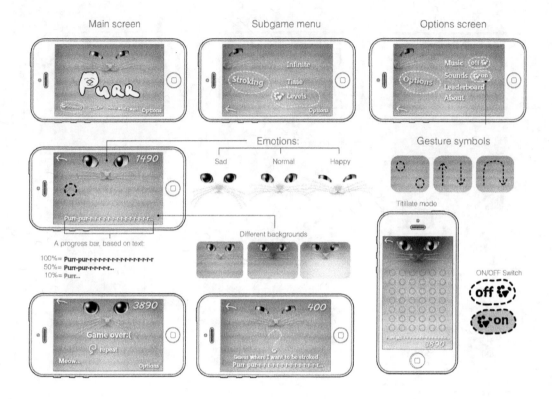

The following scheme shows a blueprint showing the basic elements of a gesture game code named Magic sky:

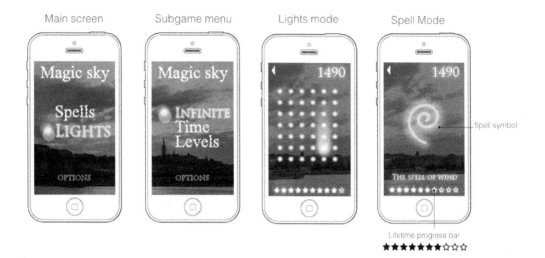

Summary

Gestures of various forms, both simple and more complex, are in common use in modern mobile games. Therefore, it is reasonable to start with a title dedicated to them. A simple gesture game will not require big efforts on coding and preparing the assets. There are no complicated mechanics. The levels are very simple and can even be generated in real time, and the amount of graphics is minimal. Roughly speaking, this is a prototype of input functions that suddenly became a standalone game! This is not to belittle its value, because in a case of using a large amount of creativity and craft, such a game can become amazing. All you need to do is pay attention to the details: provide a simple and bright idea, use noticeable graphics for gesture symbols, and place attractive backgrounds. Don't forget about the pleasing animation and lovely sounds; make the game process comfortable and balanced. As a result, you can get a product you can be proud of. In the next chapter, we will talk about a board and card games. They require more attention to a plot and interconnection between game elements, therefore some more time should be spent on the planning of rules and developing game elements.

4
Card and Board Games

Do you ponder the fact that many modern video games (and even some forms of human activities) can be represented as board or card games? Of course, the rules usually are very complex and there are a lot of game pieces and conditions; nonetheless, some similarities can be noticed. Let's take, for example, the famous game *Plants vs. Zombies* created by *PopCap*. If you try to look at the gameplay from a different angle, you can easily imagine that all plants in the game are virtual cards placed at the game table by a player. The zombies in turn are some form of cards too; they have special rules for moving and an invisible dice determines the conditions of random collisions. Some game pieces portray shots fired by plants; sunflowers generate tokens in the form of cartoonish suns. So yes, this is a board game, but very complex and highly automated, so it can work in real time. No wonder that many game developers use custom board games to prototype their future video games (or some of their functions). The incredible power of board games is hidden in their flexible nature, which lets them reconstruct a rich number of events and situations.

The ornament of life

It can be assumed that the appearance of board games in the ancient times was a reaction to a complication of social structure, when one life paradigm was replaced with a new one. For instance, the forest gathering was displaced by agriculture; it taught humans that there could be orthogonal shapes (agriculture fields), regular, and straight/parallel lines (the invention of the plow). Life became more complicated, full of unpredictable factors and correlation and thus it was reflected in games with complex rules. Moreover, mankind at that period of time began to use abstraction, for instance, ornaments appeared. This illustrated not just a specific object, for example, a river, but its abstract and simplified representation: its zigzag shape. This means more than a graphic image because a little story was embedded: since the river flows in a zigzag manner, it has many turns.

Abstraction, simplification, and toleration are the foundation of any board game because all the elements — game pieces, game board, and rules — are only symbols, not real objects. Ancient Egypt was one of the first cultures that began to use ornaments to decorate houses and utensils. It is not surprising that one of the oldest known board games was created in ancient Egypt as well. It was called Senet (`http://en.wikipedia.org/wiki/Senet`) and it was invented in around 3500 BC, so the game is about 5,500 years old.

A screenshot from Egyptian Senet (by Mohammed Ezzat), a digital interpretation of Senet available for iOS devices

Senet had all the attributes that associated with a typical board game; there were game pieces in the form of pawns, a random number generator — not a dice but special casting sticks — and a board consisting of 30 square cells (3 x 10). The main goal of the player was to pass the board (the original rules were lost in the sands of time, so now players use various reconstructions). So Senet is a race game. The most intriguing part is that the squares on the board come with special abilities, marked with symbols that work like reward or pitfall squares in modern board games. Various forms of strategies can be used in the game because the player can fight with his opponent and cunning can lurk not only on the board in specific dangerous locations but in an opponent's actions too. So it is a competition with the elements of nature and with other humans, which is why the board game became so popular all over the world.

Let's try to determine the basic components of a board game, using Senet as a tried and true example:

- **Rules**: The game cannot be played without a set of rules that define the main goal, principles of victory, a structure of turns, and many other things. They should be immutable to exclude any chance of ambiguity while playing the game.

- **Board**: This is the space where all the actions take place. Usually, this is a grid of squares or a path around the board (it can be looped).

- **Game pieces**: These are various figures that represent the player or his army. At the most basic levels, they look like discs (or stones) painted black or white.

- **Random number generator**: Dice, spin wheels, sticks, coins, and so on are optional ways to add some spontaneity to the game process. They can define the distance a game piece may move on the board or demonstrate the chances on certain actions, for example, fights.

- **Cards**: These are symbols or texts incorporated into the game board's single square or provided separately. Usually, they have certain feedback on the player's action.

- **Bonus**: This is a special prize that a player gets when he/she reaches a specific place on the game board. The position has a visual mark (by a card) or can be determined in the game rules; for instance, when a Draughts' game piece reaches the farthest row forward it is proclaimed a king and receives extra talents. Usually, the bonus zone rewards the player with a free turn, invulnerability, new types of attack, and so forth.

- **Pitfalls (force majeure)**: These are the various types of unpleasant experiences the player has. He loses his turn, moves his game piece backward, and so on.

Amusingly, now you can try to remove some items from the list and then you can get new types of games. For example, if a game board is removed, a card game can be created. The cards can be a partial representation of many things: game pieces (each has a unique design and look), a random generator (in a case a deck is shuffled thoroughly), a game board (a sequence of cards can depict the game world), and finally, they can hold bonuses and pitfalls. The greater the number of cards a deck has, the more complex can the game is. Bear in mind that besides traditional playing cards, there are a lot of card decks with unique designs that let you play so-called dedicated deck card games. If you drop most of the game attributes but keep the random number generator, a world of dice games can be introduced to you.

The dice and the game board can together create their own class of games, a good example of this is Crown and Anchor, the game played by British sailors, which included special game board (playing mat) and original dice covered with symbols, not with dots (visit `http://en.wikipedia.org/wiki/Crown_and_Anchor` for more info).

Many strategy and tactical games have no random generator, and bonuses and pitfalls are not clearly expressed.

Hypothetically, there can be a game without any actual rules; just imagine how chaotic it would be. There would be total freedom, and this would be fun, but this also means that it is not interesting to play such a game because there is no any objective, reward, risk, or anything else that makes for an exciting experience!

Now you can feel the connection between the elements of a board game; many of them can be transformed into another form, can be supplemented with new talents, or can be removed. In case the balance is right, a new game experience can be created.

Powerful objects

Roughly speaking, any board or card game is a comparison of one object's properties and abilities with another. Let's take two cards; one is white and holds the number 1, the other is black and holds the number 2. If the most obvious rules are applied, the second card is more powerful, so it wins because two is greater than one.

This is the basis of a strategic game called *Stratego* (`http://en.wikipedia.org/wiki/Stratego`). It uses simple arithmetic comparisons to determine the winner of battle between two game pieces (each of them can represent soldiers, officers, or special items such as bombs). In most cases, the piece with a higher rank defeats its opponent; for example, a colonel, who ranks at 8 easily overpowers a sergeant who ranks at 4. The logic is pretty elementary and very descriptive, but it has not much intrigue as there are no unexpected turns. This problem can be fixed by introducing extra conditions that work on special occasions.

Let's return to our example with the two cards, the one with a lower rank can now win if you will add a new condition that says that a card painted with white defeats an opponent painted with black. Voila! The first card has suddenly won! In Stratego, we can find a real-life example of such scenario: the spy piece has the lowest rank in the game and is the most attackable figure, but it has a distinct advantage, the ability to attack and beat the marshall himself, which is the most powerful piece in the game! Here is the twist! In my view, the more unexpected layers and turns the game has, the more breathtaking it becomes. A player should feel secure, but he/she should not be opinionated. Of course, the game may have its own royal flush, but it should be very uncommon and hard to get.

A wonderful example of balance based on the system of checks and balances is the immortal game rock-paper-scissors. It can easily be displayed by three cards: rock, paper, and scissors. So the player's armory consists of these three items. When the competition starts, all the players have to choose a card they think will be competitive and put it on the table simultaneously; then, the comparison process begins. Each card is powerful enough to defeat one of the cards from the deck but can lose to another. Thus, it has a potential chance either to win or to lose, and it all depends on the situation. The game can be tied too: if the competitive cards are equal. So, as you can see, there theoretically is no safe card in the deck and there is therefore always an element of suspense.

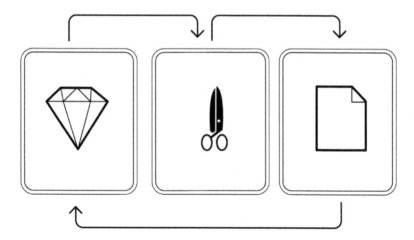

The important point is to note is that a player can try to read his opponents, trying to predict which type of card they will choose. This creates a basis for some psychological strategy rather than mechanical choosing of cards and this element makes the game more exciting.

By default, rock-paper-scissors has only three elements to play with. Can its principles be scaled up for more elements? The answer, of course, is yes. There is a wonderful extension of the game, called rock-paper-scissors-lizard-Spock, which is played with five elements (cards, in our case). Although many people attribute the invention of this game to *Dr. Sheldon Cooper* from the amusing TV series *The Big Bang Theory*, where the game was mentioned several times, in reality it was created by *Sam Kass* with *Karen Bryla* (`http://www.cafepress.com/samkass`) long before the show was run. The rules of rock-paper-scissors-lizard-Spock are easy to remember and pronounce (try to make it fast):

- Scissors cut paper
- Paper covers rock
- Rock crushes lizard
- Lizard poisons Spock
- Spock smashes scissors
- Scissors decapitate lizard
- Lizard eats paper
- Paper disproves Spock
- Spock vaporizes rock
- Rock crushes scissors

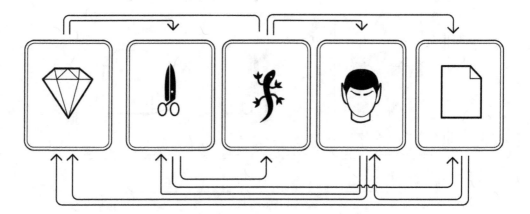

Thus, each card can beat two specific cards and can lose to other two ones that are stronger than it. And this is not the limit; the boundaries of rock-paper-scissors can be expanded even more, and newer elements can make the game more exciting and surprising. *David C. Lovelace*, a freelance artist and flash animator tried to prove that by creating unusually large versions of the game. He started with moderate versions, including 7, 9, 11, 15, and 25 elements, inventing a lot of new hand gestures for the game: tree, water, lighting, and so on. But it didn't seem enough for him, so the hardworking inventor designed a rock-paper-scissors type of game with no less than 101 gestures! It took more than a year to finish the game, and the scheme of gestures looks like a big poster (`http://www.umop.com/rps101.htm`). Playing this game, you can be sure that your opponent's move will always be very sudden. The general problem of the game is a very complex table of rules and principles; it is very hard to learn and remember them. Therefore, it is hard to play it alertly with all the options in mind and with a conscious strategy. If the rules and number of elements is very large, most players use some random moves, relying on good luck or use a very small arsenal of cards.

A game like this printed on paper — in other words, in analog form — would be impossible to play because the dozens of elements and their interconnections are not easy to follow. But in digital form, all the calculations can be made without the player having to think and therefore, very quickly. All you need is a set of implications to compare the game pieces. In other words, dozens of if…then operators should be used, built upon your game rules.

So you see that the level of the game's unpredictability can be changed by increasing the number of game pieces, but this is a pretty extensive way of doing things, isn't it? What about more intensive approaches? No problem, all you need is to recombine some rules or add new components to the game. For example, a new version of rock-paper-scissors can be created that is played by two hands, and thus two cards can be used. For instance, the first card is for one turn only — the recurrent card — and should be taken from the deck each time, but the second one is in your inventory (the player can replace the recurrent card with one of the cards from the inventory). Otherwise, even a dice can be introduced to resolve tied situations in the game. What would you say about a special board game with some genes from rock-paper-scissors? Contrary to a classic game, where players can always choose the exact card they want, there is an element of fortuity here: at the beginning, the players have to take several cards from the deck and they are not sure what they will get. This creates room for new strategy. The game board is looped and can include special zones, where a player can change his current cards with new ones from a deck. When the player's game piece reaches the square already taken by the opponent's piece, a fight can start.

The players can choose and show their cards, playing a classic rock-paper-scissors match; the winner could get the game square. Then a main goal can be created; for example, players have to collect ten rock cards, which can be called precious stones. The cards for inventory can be taken on special treasure squares of the game board. We forgot about a pitfall, didn't we? Let's switch on our imagination! Here is a possible scenario: a pitfall can be generated by players by dropping some of their cards (in a case of a victory) on the game board to slow down their opponent. For example, there is a dropped paper card at the game square; if somebody reaches it, he should use his recurrent card and fight; if he loses, he cannot move for a turn. This creates a space for tactics. Of course, here it is only a concept, only an idea, but you can see that it is easy to develop a complex game plot even from a very general idea.

Traditional board games

There are hundreds of popular card/board games. Some of them are very old, and have been around for thousands of years. They are time proven and we might call them classic games with full certainty. Usually, they utilize an abstract design of game elements: pieces, boards, and rules. With time, their look has become more universal and indifferent to the vicissitudes of cultural influences (and this makes them the common heritage of mankind). Well-known examples are *Chess*, *Go*, *Backgammon*, *Draughts*, *Dominoes*, and *Janggi*.

A screenshot from adventure game, Machinarium, which uses a tricky variation of noughts and crosses as one of the puzzles

Some games look very much like classic games; they utilize the same minimalistic aesthetics but are a little bit younger, having been invented a few centuries ago. I'm talking about *Renju*, *Reversi*, *Mahjong*, and many other such wonderful games. It's worth noting that the new age does not detract from their value.

The other groups of games are a part of modern history; they were designed in the 20th or 21st century and reflect more concrete contemporary realities. Their game boards are more visual, featuring more illustrative ornamentation, rules are complex and deep, game pieces and tokens may represent real-life objects: houses, cars, soldiers, and so on. The first thing that comes on mind is, of course, *Monopoly*. It was created in the 1930s and is now famous all over the world. Then there is *Scrabble*, which is equally well known. Don't forget about the very charming game *Cluedo*, which illustrates the flexibility of a card/board game paradigm, it can tell any type of plot, in this particular case, the game is a fascinating detective story:

A screenshot from Cluedo for iOS, developed by Electronic arts. Unlike many others digital versions of board games, this one tries to provide the story in the nontrivial form of an adventure game

There is also a special class of modern games—**role-playing game (RPG)**—which was introduced in the 1970s and met with huge success. The pioneer of that genre was the *Dungeons & Dragons* game, which later became a franchise. Such games let a player travel through the game world, developing the abilities of his character. This can be done by resolving various quests, taking part in fights, and so on. As the game moves forward, the game character receives new talents and tools. The RPGs can be called the personalization of a modern board game's spirit because they can include almost all components of a board game in almost perfect form. The rules can look like a thick folio with a lot of nuances being described inside. The game boards are complex and well crafted. And there are a lot of cards in decks, illustrated very professionally with great attention to detail, and non-cubic dice that are real works of geometric art: tetrahedrons, octahedrons, dodecahedrons, and other unusual 3D shapes.

The game pieces can look similar to tiny figures molded very skillfully and it is worth having an art collection of them.

Magic: The Gathering successfully settled down in digital universe, this is a screenshot from Magic 2014 developed by Wizards of the Coast. As you can check it for yourself the basic principles remain the same: game table and a collection of cards

As would be expected, the beauty of such game elements soon gave birth to a passion for collecting these items. But it is boring to collect some items and not to use them sometimes in the action, so a new genre of games was born based on the specific cards players have to collect to play the game. The genre became known as **collectible card game** (CCG) or trading card game. It encourages the desire to search for new cards not only from the aesthetic point of view, but for gaming purposes as well because the player can organize his own playing decks, developing his original balance of powers and abilities. The first game of this type was the now illustrious game Magic: The Gathering, published in 1993.

Planning your digital board game

Perhaps you might want to create your own version of one of the classic board or card games. They look so attractive. But I want to warn you about the possible pitfalls (not the pitfalls on game cards or boards) but the real-world difficulties you can encounter. First of all, many classic games are not so easy to code; it is not hard to create logic for moving game pieces on a board, but it is much more complex to develop a smart AI for the computer opponent.

It should have very talented prevision to play with a human well, calculating possible future moves in advance. Sometimes, it is quite impossible or is extremely hard. For example, Go, on the face of it, is a pretty plain game with simple rules, while in actual fact, it poses the biggest challenge to programmers to create a proper AI.

Another important aspect is "a place in the sun", there are dozens of good realizations of classic board games on the App store, and can offer you something new. For example, more powerful AI, better graphics (there is a meaning in this, as many talented applications have smart intellect, but middling artwork), advanced social mechanics of playing, or unique extensions of gameplay. All these things require a lot of effort and time, and are therefore very costly. In case you still want to check your programming skills on a classical board game, it is reasonable to choose something easy to produce. A very good instance is the Reversi game; it has very interesting gameplay and it was wrongly forgotten. The AI for this game is not complicated to design, so it is worth working on. Remember that it does not require a lot of graphics but only a regular background for the game board and two tile textures for game pieces; the first is black and the second is white.

Of course, you also can try to find something rare and original to work with. For instance, some games from a specific region, for example, *Karnöffel*—one of the oldest card games, dated and mostly from the German-speaking parts of the Europe. Or my favorite one, the Scandinavian board game from the 19th century named *Daldøs*; it features a unique game board that looks like a deck of a sailing vessel with some squares. The player's goal is to eliminate the opponent's game pieces from the board. So, in some sense, this is a game about a boarding attack, true entertainment for marine pirates! The list of such extraordinary but lesser known games is pretty long; you only need to search for them carefully.

A more daring approach is trying to create something new, a game created almost from scratch. I say "almost" because it is reasonable to use a traditional basis for it but enrich it with some original rules, ornamentation, and details. I'm not sure that you should try to invent a new chess game. In other words, it is not worth working on a new strategy game with a minimalistic setting and rules. A more relevant goal is an attempt to design a modern game that will include RPG elements and is based on cards, a game board (something of a cross-and-circle scheme), and a random number generator. Players would need to reach a specific rank in the game. The concept is pretty simple but it can be lit up with few bright details. Let's start with the plot and settings. It is predictable to begin thinking about another clone of *Magic: The Gathering*, something that has fantasy worlds, magic spells, swords, chain armors, dragons, and other such stuff. This can get quite dreary because there is a huge army of various fantasy creatures in the world—thousands of them! Many desktops, consoles, and other such stuff, even browser-based games use fantasy settings; some of them succeeded, but others only trailed behind.

Without a fresh idea, we will unwillingly become part of this lost army. So let's think about more original ideas. How about sci-fi, for example? The genre is now quite popular, and there a lot of sci-fi movies in the theaters. This setting is also pretty wide and includes a rich background full of various alien creatures, amazing technologies, and tools. Who is the main character? Say an astronaut, for example. This is good. What else? A robot! This is even better, because robots can have various designs, sizes, and purposes. So a lot of characters can be created. Another good thing is the possibility of upgrading a robot; it is a machine, so some of its parts can be replaced easily, and here comes in the RPG component. The character is the robot; it can be upgraded with some new tools, giving it some new skills. What are the robots doing? They collect some stuff, searching inside special containers where there can be a reward or a pitfall in the form of an evil force. You shouldn't forget about the main goal: each player would need to reach a higher rank for his character, for example, there can be ten rank levels in the game. The idea has been formed, so let's create the plot.

The Plot

The plot should be a little dramatic to draw the main conflict between the players. It also should be very visual and easy to imagine. A game world and its elements should be described. Here's an example:

It is the year 2581. A fully automated cargo space pod, full of various containers, wends its way to a faraway planet. The ship is served by a small army of industrious robots: movers, repairmen, guards, and navigators. Suddenly, the main computer of the ship makes a navigation mistake, so the ship gets into a cluster of asteroids. The computer tries to fix the error, but in vain. The ship crashes at the surface of one of the asteroids and the cargo section is totally destroyed. All the containers scatter all over the asteroid. Moreover, all the robots are broken into pieces, and there are hundreds of spares in the asteroid's dust. The ship cannot fly again, but it has a rescue space shuttle; the only problem that its battery is totally discharged and it needs about a dozen batteries to switch on the engines. Each robot is hardwired to return to home port, so shortly after the crash they begin to collect themselves from the spare parts, going to find the sufficient number of batteries and fly away by the rescue shuttle. It is a pity, but there is only one place in the shuttle, so only one robot can be taken on board. The battle between the robots begins!

Game elements and goals

To illustrate the plot, the game needs a few essential elements. The asteroid is portrayed by a special game board, where positions of robots are represented by game pieces of various colors. The cargo turns into playing cards. A player can take them and communicate. One dice (it is not feasible to use two dice because they would give too-big values) defines the distance of each player's move.

The main goal is simple: the player should collect a specific number of batteries to start the shuttle. In most cases, this number can be equal to ten. To get a battery, the player needs to defeat a monster or opponent's robot.

Game start

The game starts with an attempt to create a robot. Each player takes three cards from the spares deck, but it is more than likely that he does not get enough cards to construct the robot. There will be repetitive or junk cards, so the game usually starts with semi-assembled and very weak apparatus.

The game board

According to the plot, the robots are at the surface of a small asteroid and the goal of the game is not correlated with a specific finish point on the map, so the game board looks like a looped path. The circle shape is an ideal option for the board. Setting its dimensions, we can use the main advantage of a digital game—flexibility. The radius can depend on the number of players. The more the number of players that enter the game, the larger the size of the asteroids. Another option is introducing game modes such as small planet, big planet, and so on, which let the players use specific dimensions of the board. If the board is small, but there are many players, the gameplay includes more fights and it can become more chaotic, but funnier as well:

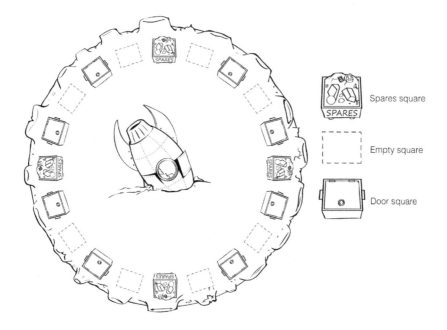

Spares square

Empty square

Door square

By default, the game board consists of three types of squares described as follows:

- **Empty squares**: These are cells where no action usually takes place. Recall the principle of peaks and valleys from *Chapter 2, Ergonomics*; this element is a valley, a zone of some relaxation for players.

- **Door (or Container) squares**: This is a peak element of gameplay, which consists of a zone with some actions. Here the player finds the door and his character must try to open it by using his power. If the door is successfully opened, the player get access to a container. He will find various things inside it, either useful (bonuses/tools) or dangerous (different types of monsters).

- **Spares squares**: There are only four of these on the board, and they are placed on opposite poles of the circle. The player can take some spare parts from special boxes and there are no obstacles, for example, doors and parts can be taken without any compensation.

Additionally, you can think about some other type of squares. For example, there can be power charger squares, where the powers of a robot become stronger (by one or two points). A tunnel can be introduced in the game, which would help to run away from opponents and overtake somebody on the board. So say the tunnel entrance/exit appears. I suggest using the dice to gain entry into the tunnel; if it shows a number greater than four or five, the player can travel through the core of the asteroid. Or a fare can be levied; pay by a tool or spares card to use the subway!

By default, empty squares and door squares should alternate with each other, but random placement of the doors can be intriguing too.

On the device, the game board is shown in two ways: partial and full. The first view is incorporated into the game UI; the player sees a section of the asteroid where his game piece is now situated, but only several squares are visible. This view can be scrolled to view other parts of the astronomical object and it would be great if an original form of the scrolling would be implemented; instead of horizontal and vertical panning of the image, you can use an algorithm, spinning it around the center point. The player will spin the asteroid with his finger (don't forget to simulate inertia), and that can look natural and breathtaking.

The full view shows up when a special button **Show the map** is pressed on the screen. In this case, the game displays the asteroid in full screen mode, showing all the game pieces; it can be useful for various tactical purposes.

Decks

The game is played by special cards, representing various details and situations. There are three dedicated card decks in the game, each of them with its own design on the back:

Decks

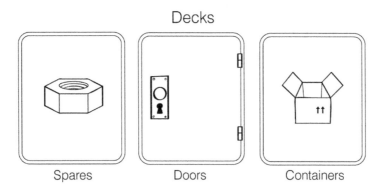

Spares   Doors   Containers

The backs of the dedicated decks in the game

- **Spares**: This deck consists of different parts of robots: heads, bodies, and legs. There are also some "empty" cards, called Junk. They play roles of little pitfalls because they have zero value and cannot be used for the creation of a robot.

- **Doors**: A lot of doors can be found in this deck. These cards protect the content of the containers. Some of them are unlocked, while others need some power or abilities to be opened.

- **Containers**: These cards illustrate the stuff that can be found in the container, when a corresponding door is successfully unlocked. They include a number of useful tools that which increase some powers of the robot, for example, blaster, and plasma cutter. There can be some cards, known as **Spares**, that let the player take a new card from the spares deck right at that moment without waiting for a spare square. Some monsters can inhabit the container as well; various dangerous creatures, such as crazy robots, angry magnets, wild waterfalls, and old wiring can attack the player's robot.

When the player must take a card from one of the decks, a pop-up window appears, showing some cards turned back; the player taps them and gets a card. Of course, this is unessential and the game can automatically display a card, not asking the player to take part in the dialog, but I'm sure that tapping the deck makes the process more attractive and tactile.

If a card needs to be dropped from the inventory to the deck, the game should focus on the inventory window, placing it at the center of the screen. The player chooses an unnecessary card and taps it, so it travels to the deck. There also can be a confirmation alert, asking whether the player is sure he wants to drop the card that was specified before. The position of the card that has returned to the deck should be random; it can become predictable if the card returns to the very end of the line. So try to rearrange the array of cards each time one item returns to it.

Robots

The robots are constructed from spare cards that the player takes from the dedicated deck. There are only three classes of these spares in the game:

- **Heads**
- **Bodies**
- **Legs**

Each of them has their own properties. The first two of them utilize a special number, which characterizes their power and can be used in a battle or to open a specific door. There is a gradation from 1 to 6; the greater the number, the more powerful the spare is. In general, a sum of body and head powers are used; for instance, the player has a robot with a very strong body marked 6 and a middling head with the number 2. If the robot does not hold any additional tools, its total power will be *6 + 2 = 8*. Sometimes, only a partial amount of power is required. Various forms of smart doors or monsters appear only according to the power level of a robot's head, which is considered the level of the robot's intelligence. Contrarily, sometimes only brute force is needed, and the head is not used. The following figure shows different forms of cards we use for our robot:

Head cards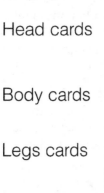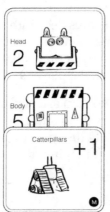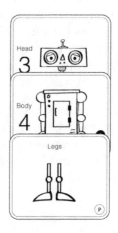

Body cards

Legs cards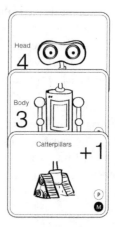

The leg has no power in the fight and no intelligence level either, but determines the way the robot moves. The simple ones, known simply as **Legs**, are not very fast, and the game piece moves by the number of squares that the dice has shown. The **Caterpillars** card gives more freedom of space; the player gets an extra square to move though it is not obligatory to make such a +1 move, and a more profitable destination can be chosen. The most attractive and of course, the rarest option is the **jet**, a little cylinder with a nozzle, allowing the robot to soar above the ground a little bit. The extra square it gives is equal to two and this gives a player full freedom of choice on the board.

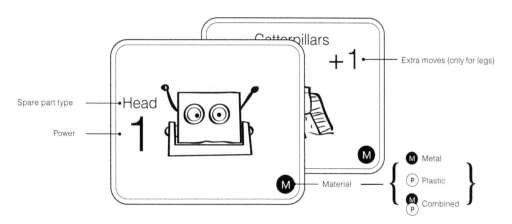

All the spares—including the legs—are subdivided into types, expressing the materials they are made of. Every card has special letter marks to display the material. There are metallic spares (M), plastic ones (P) and combined ones (MP). Generally, there is no difference between the materials; a metallic spare part is as good as a plastic one is. But sometimes it can be important. Monsters of an electric nature attack only metallic parts, their high-temperature counterparts like to melt plastic, and so forth.

The player should collect all the three classes (independent to their power value and material) in order for their robot to function normally. If there are fewer classes at the player's table, some restrictions are applied to the character. Let's see some of these:

- **Only a head**: In this, the robot cannot use his full potential; he moves very slowly, only one square per move, and the dice is not used. His goal is to reach a spares square, hoping that he gets some legs or a body. Such a robot can open doors, if its head has enough power and even can defeat a weak enemy. It is important to remember that a robot without a body cannot use any tools because it has no hands to hold them in.

- **Only a body**: In this, the robot is still defective and cannot move fast, but he already has the ability to hold some tools in his hands.

- **Head plus body**: This is a more pleasant combination. The robot is more powerful and can use tools, but he is still very slow. It gives the same one square per move option and there is no advantage of a dice.

- **Only legs**: This is the most pathetic situation. The robot can move by the help of dice, but he has no opportunity to fight because the legs have no power. It is an easy target for other players and monsters and should try to quickly find a spares square.

- **Digital phantom**: In this, there is no spare part. The robot exists like a digital ghost, supposedly saved in the cloud storage system, hosted on the main computer of the spaceship, which survived the crash. The phantom can move slowly, he cannot open doors and cannot be attacked by others; he should find a spares square and begin to materialize again.

Few cards have a zero sign, called nonentity spares, which means that the part is almost broken, but formally, they still work. Although as good as garbage, they can be useful in some situations, for example, if the robot has no normal body, it can use a nonentity part. This gives it zero power, but lets it hold some tools:

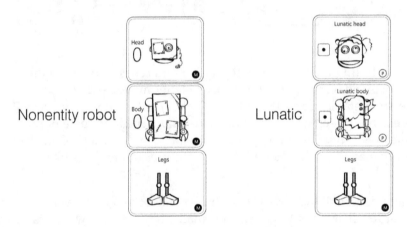

The most interesting things are the **Lunatic** spares; they have no number, but only a symbol of a dice. Legend says that such spare parts were affected by the mysterious powers of the asteroids, so they lost their memory and now they do not remember their true talents and power. Hence, the dice should be used to determine the value of these spares. This should be done each time the robot tries to open a door or beat somebody. The lunatic spares depend on good luck; they can be either very strong or very weak.

Doors

Each container at the asteroid has a door, which protects the cargo inside. Few of them have no locks and so can be opened without any efforts, but most of them are reliably locked; therefore, the player should use the powers of his/her robot to get inside:

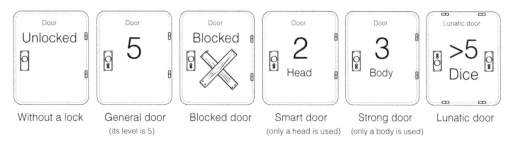

| Without a lock | General door (its level is 5) | Blocked door | Smart door (only a head is used) | Strong door (only a body is used) | Lunatic door |

A chart showing various types of doors

A door card has a special number, which represents the resistance force of the door; if the robot is strong enough and the sum of his powers are greater than that number, he enters inside the container; otherwise, he gets nothing. It is important to mention that there are some specific doors, which can be unlocked only by intelligence, or in other words, by using the power of the robot's head. They are known as Smart doors. A very rare type of a door is the **Lunatic door**. The player has to throw a dice to get a chance to enter, and the conditions are written on the card.

Tools and bonuses

In the containers, there are a lot of tools or weapons a robot can use to fight or to open a door. Some of them are for permanent use and have small power (values that lie between one and three), but other ones are valid for one occasion only, being much more powerful (a good illustration is the plasma grenade, which has a power value equal to five). To use a tool, the robot should hold it in his hand; otherwise, the card will not work, being considered as a part of inventory:

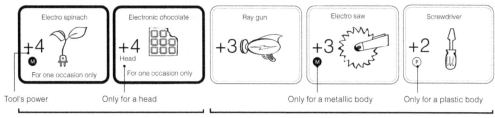

Unlike the spares cards, which can be rearranged only before the player's move, the tool cards can be replaced in the robot's hands right before the fight. It's worth noting that non-permanent tools should be returned to the deck directly after being used, so if the player has applied such a tool to open a door, he cannot use it against the monster inside. First of all, he must return the tool; then, before the battle, he can take another tool from his inventory (if he has additional ones).

The game flexibility is supported by diversification of special conditions some tools work with. Most of them are of course universal, but some of the tools work only with metallic bodies or require the robot to have high intelligence. Huge hammers can be used only with strong bodies and so on.

Permanent tools cannot be lost by a player in normal conditions, but they can be taken by some monsters. Bonuses are rare, but can be invaluably useful. They can reward the player with extra spares, a free battery (an extremely rare card), an additional move, and so on.

Monsters

First of all, the term "monster" in our case is rather symbolic than literal because many of them are not traditional creatures from human nightmares, but situations from a robot's bad dreams. Falling water, puddles of oil, gigantic magnets, transformers, mills, bare wires, computer bugs, and other industrial scary things can be found inside the containers. In a broad sense, they can be called traps:

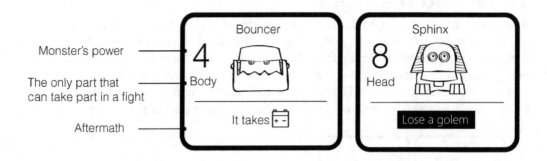

The monster card consists of two parts: the first one is a monster description, including the value of its power and some conditions of its functionality, while the second part describes the aftermath, which will take place in a case the player loses.

A monster's guile should be to target specific characteristics of a robot; this creates some variety in attacks. The diverseness is very important since players can use various tactics; most importantly, they can take a risk sacrificing some parts of their robots, nonetheless trying to overcome an opponent. Such mechanics force more emotions to be involved in the gameplay. Moreover, monsters with different characteristics seem more dangerous and unpredictable; you never know what you will lose.

If a game has a monster with a single type of attack, it will soon become very simple to decide how to defeat it; the sense of risk will be very insignificant and the player will develop some sort of a comfort zone they will rarely leave. But a great game experience requires players to try many ways to achieve the result; good gameplay is a creative process! Therefore, game elements need to push them in that direction. Several classes of the monsters can be created:

- **Universal**: They attack all types of robots.
- **Electricity/Magnets**: Mostly attack metallic details, so almost harmless to plastic robots.
- **High temperature**: It melts plastic spares and is very dangerous for highly intelligent robots, which are made of plastic.
- **Cracks and puddles**: These pitfalls are tricky for a robot's legs.
- **Water**: It is dangerous for metallic robots (they can lose a move) and it shuts down jet legs.
- **Sphinxes**: These are usually old robots, which a long time ago were security guards. Now they are bored and like to ask various conundrums to create some entertainment for themselves. Thus, only robots with high intelligence can defeat them.
- **Bouncers**: Old robot loaders, they can understand only brutal force, so the head of the player's robot cannot be used in the fight.
- **Wires**: These are hodgepodges of various wires and cables, which knots the robot, so he has no opportunity to use his hands and tools.
- **Bugs**: These are the most abstract and unexpected pitfalls. Errors in electronic systems push the robots to make pretty strange things. For example, the head begins to fight with the body. Or the player has to give his entire inventory to another player.

A special preference of the monster means that some parts of the robot can be blocked. For example, the magnet paralyzes all the metallic parts, and they are not used in the fight (for combined spares, their power value becomes lesser in a half); the robot can only depend on tools he has in his hands. But remember that such monsters should not feature a big value of power, so the player would have a chance to overcome them. Now you see that such diversity pushes the players to use all features, not fixating on only one arsenal of gaming tools. Basically, the idea is to train a player with gentle slaps: Try this, now try that, use this item, and so on. Players should know that there are many ways to solve a problem. Of course, the training works fine if there are noticeable rewards in a form of successes in the game or special achievements.

The aftermath should not be very ruthless; an ordinary universal robot can only make the player lose his next move. Some monsters can take some spares, for example, various puddles take away robot's legs. Sphinxes like trophies in a form of robot heads. Only weak monsters or the robot itself should withdraw the battery.

Besides, the monsters in containers can be a real bad thing: a pitfall card, which is unconditional and cannot be defeated. One of the good illustrations is the card **You lose your robot!**; by getting this, a player loses all current spares and his robot becomes a digital phantom. There is another terrible card that says **You lose one battery!**.

Remember that risks in games should be well balanced. Motivation mechanics for players (for some AI systems) is based on playing with two general ambitions: to be secure (to be alive) and to get some rewards (satisfaction). In most cases, they contradict each other because, to be secure, it is better to hide somewhere and not move. But to get some prizes, you need to face some danger. That is a basic existential principle, which is why such a choice during playing generates some strong emotions.

Any risk must be worth the reward a player gets, and in some cases, it should outweigh the possible aftermath of failure. This forces players to take risks and make more experiments. On the other hand, if the aftermath is too weak, the players may become too arrogant, and their emotional state will be very indifferent to events. You have to remember a crucial thing: a player is playing a game, while you (as the author of the game) are playing with his emotions, motivations, and actions. Without emotions, choices, and experience, games are flat software with some beautiful pictures.

The game table

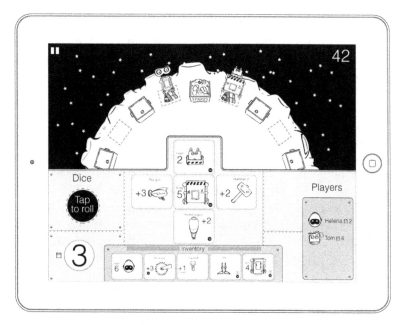

The screen layout for the main game screen

The game table (or player's UI) consists of several parts. Primarily, there is a section showing some view of the game board, which was mentioned before. Below it, there is the robot section with placeholders for corresponding spares cards. Near the placeholder for a body, there are robot's arms, where tool cards can be placed. At the right-hand side of the screen, is the inventory section; it can hold up to five cards of any type. So overall, a player can have a maximum of ten cards in his hands (three body parts, two arms, and five inventory and cards); all surpluses should be dropped back to the card decks.

By default, all the cards go directly to the inventory; the player should choose the necessary cards for his robot by himself. The UI mechanics are simple: the player taps a placeholder in the robot section, for instance the head, and then selects the cards he needs from the inventory.

The opponents are shown as icons at the top part of the screen. By tapping on them, the player can call a pop-up window, showing the current state of the opponent's robot. All the cards are visible except for the inventory.

Robo-golem

One of your goals as a game creator is to push players to drop their cards from the inventory for a greater variety of game tactics. This can be done roughly via various pitfalls or by introducing strong opponents. But it is more interesting to implement some more creative solutions which can expand the boundaries of gameplay. There should be such conditions in the game that a player would drop his cards voluntarily, exchanging them for some extra features. First of all, I'm talking about spares; they should not be deadwood. If the player successfully collects in the inventory all the basic spares of a robot—in other words if he has the head, the body, and the legs—the robo-golem can be constructed and the player becomes his master. This is an artificial creature—more artificial than ordinary robots are—that has no mentality and will of its own; he cannot operate by himself, make any decisions, move in any direction, and so on. In most cases, he simply dreams and maybe sees some electric sheep. A robo golem can be placed on any square of the game board; he will stay there and wait for the moment somebody reaches it. Here are some scenarios that could occur in case somebody comes in contact with him, depending on the type of game board square he is on:

- **Empty square/Spares square**: The fight starts, and the robo-golem operates like a normal robot, so he uses all the powers written on his spares. He can defeat the opponent and take his battery, bringing it to his master! Otherwise, the opponent gets the robo-golem's battery. If the player contacts his own robotic creature, he can remove the robo-golem at any other position on the game board.

- **Door square**: In this case, the robo-golem does not fight with the opponent, but he helps any monster inside the containers; a robo-golem's power is summarized by the monster's strength. Together they can beat very powerful enemies; thus, in ideal conditions, it can act like a Joker. In case you lose, the opponent gets two batteries: the first one from the robo-golem and the second one from the monster. If the master reaches the container square with his own robo-golem, they can open the door and fight any monster inside together. In this case, player's power is united with the robo-golem, and as a team they can be invincible.

A robo-golem exists till a fight; regardless of whether he has succeeded in the battle or not, he must be wrecked, and his cards go to spares deck and can be reused. Robo golems are interesting elements of player's strategy because they can change the balance in the game, especially when several of them are created. They can make the gameplay pretty unpredictable and alive because situations can be a little bit abnormal as robo-golem does not depend on the game scenario and players. Such conditions are known as the emergent gameplay; this term describes the situations when the standard gameplay intentionally (developers hypothecate some sort of freedom in particular areas) or accidentally (because of a glitch or other type of undocumented situation) offers unexpected extra mechanics. The main advantage is that players discover such situations accidentally and this convinces them that a game is a pretty complex system with a lot of unexplored details. Hence, it is worth to play again and again testing the feature found already and explore some new ones. The most spectacular examples of the emergent gameplay are based on various glitches or some form of developer oversight. A canonical instance is a rocket jumping when a player fires through the ground (or other type of surface) while jumping to increase the distance of a jump, popularized by Quake from id Software. This feature was discovered by players and became very popular. The audience also tries to utilize such funny situations as opponents stuck somewhere in 3D surroundings or some gaps in the game levels to reach some locations faster. But more interesting are the intentional causes of the emergent gameplay when developers give some additional functionality or properties to some items so they can be used in other ways; for instance, several crates can be turned by a player into a ladder, helping to climb a roof. Since a good game is a field for experiments, there should be a chance for players to invent some new methods of achieving goals. The game should not have an obvious structure of logic; it must look much deeper, like a system with some hidden factors and properties.

A very good metaphor is a long corridor; it looks much more intriguing if it has several doors rather than empty walls. Even if the doors are fictional or locked, they create an illusion of a bigger world. By the way, this principle is very popular in level design. The location should look like a part of a larger universe, so only the correct gap could be found to escape it to a place, which is seen on the horizon.

Robo-zombie

Another funny idea is of using useful spares from the player's inventory. The robots, walking around without a proper goal, wanting only to have some "braains"; let's call them robo-zombies. In contrast to a robo-golem, he can be constructed only of two parts: the body and the legs. The head is not required. It gives the robo-zombie less power because the sum of two cards is not large, but that can be offset by the ability of autonomous moving around the game board. Being placed at any square, a robo-zombie begins to walk slowly in the direction chosen at random, making only one step at a game phase. He roams till he meets one of the following characters:

- **Opponent**: The robo-zombie tries to fight, failing to realize that his chances are not resplendent. In most common cases he loses, but the opponent gets nothing because there are no batteries inside these poor creatures, as with robo-golems. If they meet at the door square, the robo-zombie helps the monster with his power like a robo-golem does.
- **Opponent's robo-golem/Opponent's robo-zombie**: The robo-zombie fights with him. If he wins, the opponent's creature is destroyed, but the player's robo-walker continues his journey.
- **Player**: The robo-zombie assists with opening doors and fights the monsters from containers. If they reach each other at an empty square, the robo-zombie simply continues his promenade.
- **Player's creatures**: They work as a team till one of them leaves the corresponding game square. Robo-zombies can also change their direction.

Just like his step-brother golem the robo-zombie should be wrecked in parts and returned to the spares deck after a battle. The only exception is if there is a fight between the creatures; the one who wins, continues his life cycle.

I like the robo-zombie very much because it is the example of board game mechanics, which suits electronic realizations more than analog ones. Because it is not comfortable and sure to move a robo-zombie by hand in each move, remembering their directions, and so on. But the application can make such operations easily and visual.

The game uses initially a small wizard to create a robo creature. First of all, when the inventory gets enough parts to create a robo-golem or a robo-zombie, special icons should start blinking. If the player taps them, the inventory window centers at the screen. All the parts that are not related to creature generation become inactive (dark or semitransparent); the player has to choose all the parts he wants to spend on, and then he taps the **Create** button. After that, the game shows the fullscreen image of a game map, so the player can put his creature at the board. Don't forget about some allusions to *Dr. Frankenstein*; the sound of lightning, electric noises, and a sinister laugh are very appropriate.

Alternative ideas

If you don't like the robots, you can try to customize the game concept to your taste. Primarily, the robots can be replaced by astronauts; in this case, they would change parts of their space suits, not body parts of course. The tools and containers can be the same that the robots used. Even a fantasy setting can be implemented; with a fantasy component, all the game elements can be easily turned into another era and place. For instance, the asteroid may be replaced by an island with some old trees and the spaceship is now a knarr. Instead of robots, some elfs and gnomes fight for magic crystals; the spares are replaced with chain armor, boots, helmets, shields, and so forth.

Player's identity

I think that a game idea can easily be expressed through the image of a robot's face. It can be used as the main element of composition of the application icon. Some hints that the robot is made of different spares can be given as well; for example, various patches can be drawn. A funny idea is to draw a robot playing cards:

Game blueprints

In this section, you can get the charts of all cards that can be used in the game. There are spare cards made of robot's heads, bodies, and legs, and several examples of doors. The graphics are laconic since they can easily be reproduced. The following figure shows a full-page illustration:

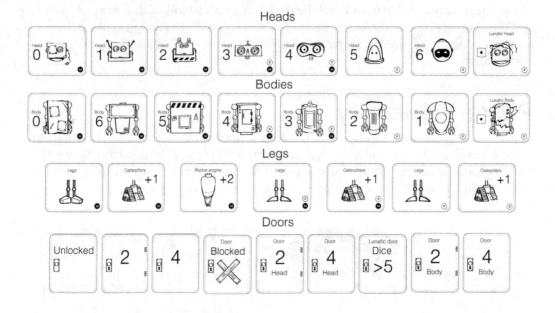

In this blueprint, you can find examples of different tools players may use in the game. Later, there is a table with all monsters:

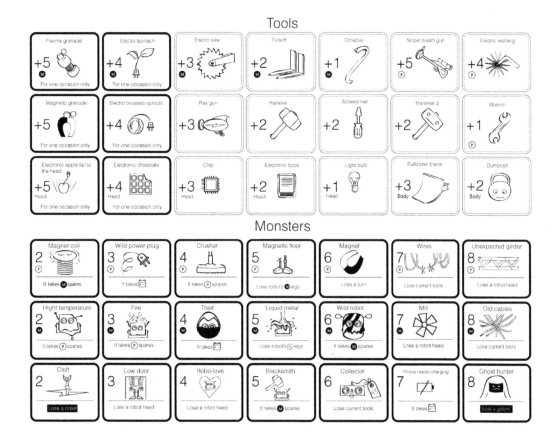

Tools

Plasma grenade	Electro spinach	Electro saw	Forklift	Crowbar	Sniper beam gun	Electric welding
+5 M — For one occasion only	+4 M — For one occasion only	+3 M	+2 M	+1 M	+5 P	+4 P
Magnetic grenade	Electro brussels sprouts	Ray gun	Hammer	Screwdriver	Hammer 2	Wrench
+5 — For one occasion only	+4 — For one occasion only	+3	+2	+2	+2	+1 P
Electronic apple fall to the head	Electronic chocolate	Chip	Electronic book	Light bulb	Bulldozer blade	Dumbbell
+5 Head — For one occasion only	+4 Head — For one occasion only	+3 Head	+2 Head	+1 Head	+3 Body	+2 Body

Monsters

Magnet coil	Wild power plug	Crusher	Magnetic floor	Magnet	Wires	Unexpected girder
2 P — It takes M spares	3 P — It takes 🔋	4 P — It takes P spares	5 P — Lose robot's M legs	6 P — Lose a turn	7 P — Lose current tools	8 P — Lose a robot head
Hight temperature	Fire	Thief	Liquid metal	Wild robot	Mill	Old cables
2 M — It takes P spares	3 M — It takes P spares	4 M — It takes 🔋	5 M — Lose robot's P legs	6 M — It takes M spares	7 M — Lose a robot head	8 M — Lose current tools
Cleft	Low door	Robo-love	Blacksmith	Collector	Phone needs charging	Ghost hunter
2 — Lose a robot	3 — Lose a robot head	4 — Lose a robot head	5 — It takes M spares	6 — Lose current tools	7 — It takes 🔋	8 — Lose a golem

You can check out the following references.

The following are the links you can refer to for additional information on topics that are used in this chapter:

- `http://www.gamasutra.com/view/feature/130814/the_siren_song_of_the_paper_.php`
- `http://en.wikipedia.org/wiki/Ornament_(art)`
- `http://piccionep.people.cofc.edu/piccione_senet.pdf`
- `http://h30565.www3.hp.com/t5/Feature-Articles/The-Real-Story-and-Some-of-the-Math-Behind-the-Famous-Rock-Paper/ba-p/3551`
- `http://en.wikipedia.org/wiki/Magic:_The_Gathering`
- `http://research.microsoft.com/pubs/65658/sterngraepelmackay04.pdf`
- `http://en.wikipedia.org/wiki/Karn%C3%B6ffel`
- `http://en.wikipedia.org/wiki/Dald%C3%B8s`

Summary

The creation of a good board game can teach you many important things. This is a skill which is very useful in game development. You begin to feel the connections between all the elements. And most importantly, you start to understand the right balance of the gameplay and the factors influencing it. There is a great space for improvisation and creativity. Remember that every video game is at heart a board game. That is why it is good practice to develop a board version of your future digital project to test its gameplay and balance. The main advantage of such a model is an opportunity to change the rules and behavior of elements quickly, on the fly since it is a great way to prototype a game's conception.

In the next chapter, you will learn how to plan and develop ideas for puzzle games. You will see how the same concept can evolve from a simple game to a title with some RPG mechanics.

5
Puzzles

Puzzles are very popular and are liked by both game developers and players because they do not need much screen space and can perfectly fit device resolution. Gameplay is generally based on several basic rules, and only few game pieces are required. But the variety of game situations is very high, so such games are costly but effective; the assets are simple, but the game process is very addictive. Many of these games are played over and over again because there are an almost infinite number of combinations and new challenges are born constantly. These combinations and new challenges make the players feel very much connected to puzzles.

Making connections

Card/board games are about the comparison of game elements, but puzzle games in general are about relations between objects. One detail must be connected with a corresponding detail. The following figure shows a simple puzzle game:

Connections

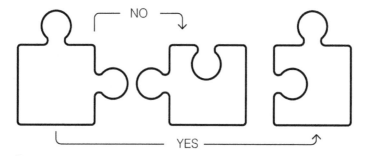

There is a poetic or even philosophical aspect to puzzles: a player attempts to assemble something that once was broken into pieces. He is almost like *Kai*, a character from the *Hans Christian Andersen* fairy tale, *The Snow Queen*, who was trying to assemble a word — "eternity" — from fragments of broken ice. In a broad sense, each puzzle is an image disassembled into components that are shuffled; some of the details are hidden, some traps and obstacles are scattered, and after that, this "dish" is presented to the player. Now he must find all the invisible strings that connect the elements and must re-form the image. Come to think of it, the most ancient puzzle will have been that of a ceramic vase, accidentally broken, and the craftsman who pieced it back together will have been the first puzzle player.

The following figure shows the infographics for the Tower of Hanoi:

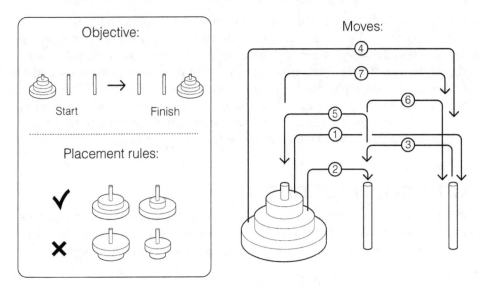

The connections in puzzles are checked by a list of special conditions. The right illustration for this is the famous puzzle game, the Tower of Hanoi. It consists of three rods and several disks. For the sake of simplicity, let's consider only three disks; the disks have different radiuses. By default, all of them are collected in a stack on the first rod, the largest disk is placed at the bottom, and the smallest one is on the top. The objective is to transfer them to the third rod; the solution seems very obvious, but there are some special conditions: for each move, a disk should be placed on a rod and the player cannot keep it in his hands or at any other place, while another rule says that an individual disk can be put only on a disk with a bigger radius. Now you see that it is harder than it seems at first sight. To complete the puzzle, the disks are moved back and forth, and the player tries to obey the rules. Three disks require seven moves, while four disks can take as many as 15 moves!

Puzzle types

There are many kinds of puzzle mechanics, and in general, only a few of them are unsophisticated. As a rule, each game is a mix of various concepts and ideas. Nevertheless, let's try to identify some basic forms.

Word puzzles

In word puzzles, the players try to connect letters or symbolic images into words or expressions. This is a very popular class of games and many of them were created long before the first electronic devices were born. Among the popular examples are *Crossword*, *Rebus*, *Cryptogram*, *Hangman*, *Ghost*, *Jotto*, *Anagram*, and *Scrabble*. Some of them operate with words, while others manipulate letters. Dictionaries are used to check existing or correct spelling. There are many word puzzles for mobile devices; one of the examples is an excellent game *QatQi* (http://qatqi.com) by *Zworkbench*, which is both very intelligent and magically beautiful.

Number (mathematical) puzzles

Number puzzles use different forms of exercises on combinatorics, arithmetic operations, algebra, and so forth. One of the traditional examples is a paper game called *Sudoku*. The rules of the game are simple: players get a special grid with some digits and many empty cells. The objective is to fill the cells with the correct digits remembering that in each row and column of the grid, as well as in the so-called boxes (blocks with dimension 3 x 3 cells), should be present one digit each from one to nine. The order of digits is irrelevant, and the only condition is that entries cannot repeat. The concept is not complex, but the game itself is very engrossing as it requires players see the big picture of the game field.

One of my favorite instances from the digital age is a smart and elegant game *Hundreds* (http://playhundreds.com) from *Semi Secret Software, LLC*; it has perfect graphics (minimalistic artwork and neat typography based on the Helvetica typeface) and very attractive gameplay. The player should generate a sum of elements that is equal to one hundred. This is tricky because there can be some obstacles, so the game requires good reaction and computation skills.

The following is a screenshot from a number puzzle game, *Hundreds*:

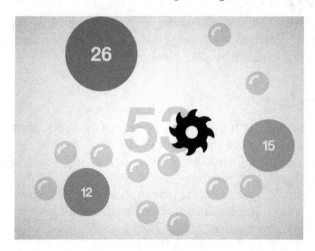

Audio puzzles

Sound can be a basis for puzzles as well provided a game designer can find an adequate use for it. Let's take for example a wonderful game called *Circadia* (`http://circadiagame.com`), created by game designer *Kurt Bieg*:

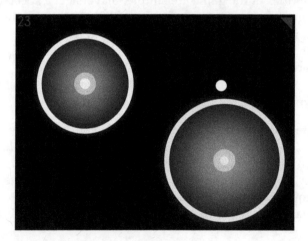

The objective is to generate a "burst" (a colored circle that constantly increases in dimensions) and connect it to a special white dot. The behavior of each burst is specified by a height of music tone. There are slow bursts and fast bursts, and the player should select the correct moment to start each one so they reach the white dot simultaneously. It is also beautiful because by playing the game, the player performs simple melodies.

Transport puzzles

In transport puzzles, the player operates various forms of blocks, trying to deliver this *cargo* to a specified destination. So, the objective is to find a connection between an object and its positions on the game board. Good examples of such games are the famed *15 puzzle* and various versions of sliding puzzles, where the player has to assemble an image by moving its parts in a box, such as *Klotski*. The following is an example of transport puzzles:

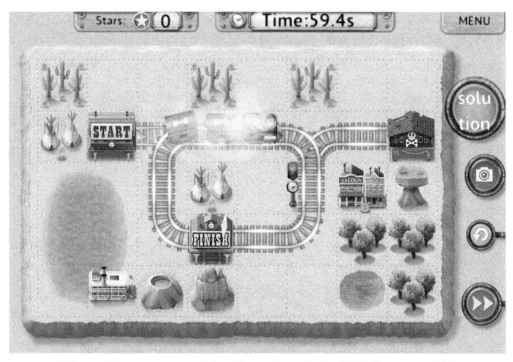

Rail maze 2 is a transport puzzle from Spooky House Studios UG (haftungsbeschränkt)

One of the most famous transport puzzles is the folkloric game—*The fox, the goose, and the bag of beans*. A farmer has to transport some cargo to the opposite bank of a river; this is a problem because the boat is very small and only one object can be taken aboard at a time and the other two must be left unattended. The player must manage connections between the elements, not leaving contradicting objects together.

It is worth mentioning that this puzzle is known in many cultures, but the elements may vary. For example, in the Spanish and Russian versions, the game is known as *The wolf, the goat, and the cabbage*; in the Portuguese version, a sheep tries to eat lettuce.

This puzzle can easily be incorporated into digital form, and this was skillfully proved by the creators of an amazing and debonair game *Girls Like Robots* (http://www.popcannibal.com/girlslikerobots), published on the App Store by *[adult swim]*. The player must manipulate seating order for various types of characters. Some company or surroundings make some characters happy, while others make them very angry. In the world of video games, the role model for a transport game is of course the classic *Sokoban*, created by *Hiroyuki Imabayashi* in 1981; the main character has to move crates inside a warehouse, placing them in the right positions.

Point connection puzzles

Point connection is a class of puzzles, where the player needs to connect two points by drawing a line in a maze. There are usually some conditions or obstacles that make the objective harder to attain. The concept was immortalized by *Pipe Mania*, designed in 1989 by *The Assembly Line*. The idea was very visual: there was a starting point (a source of water) and a finish point (a sink); a player had to construct a pipeline between them using pipe pieces which the game gave him at random. The idea was elementary but very addictive.

Besides the water and pipes, other metaphors can be used as well, for instance, light (or lasers) in combination with mirrors. Such a concept is utilized by the *Guide The Light* game (http://www.appynation.com/apps/guide-the-light), published by *AppyNation Ltd*. A player opens doors by guiding color light beams onto special sensors. The following is a screenshot from *Guide The Light*:

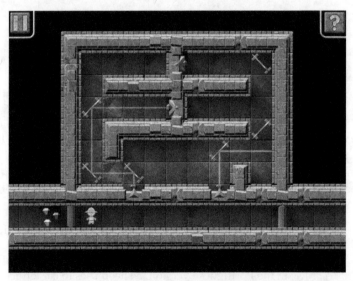

The Guide The Light puzzle game lets us guide light beams through a maze, by using mirrors and other elements to control the light

The *Points-connection* paradigm took on new heights when *Valve Corporation* developed the critically acclaimed *Portal*, a game where the player can connect locations in 3D space. This is something mind blowing!

Physics-based puzzles

Physics-based puzzles include various types of games that use simulations of physics (based either on the traditional laws of Newton or their own interpretation of forces and interactions) to create game situations. They are very popular because the gameplay is vivid, spectacular, and realistic. But the game devices can easily calculate complex interaction and collisions of the objects; also, many modern SDKs include libraries for physics simulations, so game developers need not create special engines. Usually physics-based puzzles are about experiments with gravity: the player throws objects, rolls them down from curved hills, builds some constructions from blocks, or contrarily, tries to bombard some structures. One of the most famous games of this kind is of course *Angry Birds* (http://www.angrybirds.com), created by *Rovio Entertainment*, which is not just a video game title but an element of popular culture.

Another popular example is *World of Goo* (http://2dboy.com/games.php) developed by *2D Boy*, featuring an elaborate game concept and splendid graphics. To the game's credit, it uses not only gravity but some properties of materials, such as flexibility and tension, as well. A player should create complex structures to reach the exit point; he has to remember to achieve the right balance and not pull the construction down accidentally. The experience is very unusual. Another interesting element of the game is the simulation of liquids; some sort of fluid dynamics is used in this puzzle.

Simulation of water is a unique opportunity to create an original and spectacular gameplay. There is a special class of physics-based puzzles that try to do that. A popular entry is a game called *Sprinkle* (http://www.sprinklegame.com/sprinkle/) from *Mediocre AB* that lets a player extinguish fire by using a special water pump. So, besides a brilliant demonstration of water dynamics, the title also features a simulation of fire.

The following is a screenshot from a puzzle game *Sprinkle* that successfully simulates both water and fire dynamics creating unique game situations:

Many actual natural phenomena can be turned into a story driver for a game; we only need to switch on the fantasy.

Tile-matching puzzles

Tile-matching puzzles include a very wide range of games that require the players to assemble a uniform set of specified objects. The most common association is, of course, a jigsaw puzzle, which became a symbol of puzzles of any type. Jigsaw's game piece is now a well-recognizable icon. This element illustrates all the principles most of puzzles have: the geometric shape with cutouts and ledges indicates that can be connected with another shape, but a picture fragment printed on its surface is a hint to the fact that the elements are part of something bigger. The world of video games has its own icon, *Tetris*, which also features complex geometric shapes as main game pieces (they are known as **tetraminos**). Tile matching is one of the popular mechanics for video games, because it can be interpreted in thousands of ways, making game designers switch on their creativity. Even tried-and-true concepts can be reinvented; for example, there is a game called *Dream of Pixels* by *Dawn of Play*, which is a pretty talented allusion to Tetris. It uses tetraminos, traditional game pieces from Tetris, but the main objective is different. Instead of creating packs of elements on the screen, the player should *extract* individual shapes from a bunch of cubes.

Match-three games

As the term suggests, a match-three game is a tile-matching puzzle, where a player should match at least three elements (in reality, many games let us match two items). He/she must construct or find such sequences in the array of typical objects. This is one of the most convenient types of puzzles to start with because the core of the game is not complicated and can be developed even by a novice. At a basic level, it is all about manipulations with a two-dimensional array of data (nevertheless, a match-three puzzle can be three dimensional as well). There is a total freedom in game ornamentation, and the game tiles may have a wide spectrum of designs. The following figure shows the basic match-three puzzle tile options:

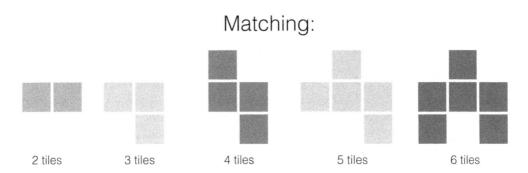

The general rule of a match-three game is pretty elementary: if there are at least three (or two; this depends on a game mode) identical tiles nearby (horizontally, vertically, or both), such elements should be removed from the game board and neighboring items take their places. The main objective is to eliminate as many tiles as possible.

The conditions are simple, but the power of such puzzles lies in their ability to be widely customized and reinvented. Many new options can be introduced to work with arrays of tiles and to affect their content. There are four cornerstones of a match-three game:

- **Game tiles**: These are the elements that are used at the game board as the main game pieces.

- **Array of elements**: This is the matrix of data where all the game tiles are stored.

- **Sequence**: This is a line of identical game tiles.

- **Trigger**: This is a force that affects the array of elements. For instance, a player's touch.

First of all, you need to select the number of game tiles you will use. The spread should not be too large because the number of elements directly affects the probability of connections between them. To calculate a pretty accurate probability of some elements appearing in a row, some advanced methods should be used, for example, methods based on the binomial distribution model. It is not necessary to calculate manually by using special tables of binomial probabilities; there are special applications and tools that can help with this, for example, an iOS application, *Probability*, from *All Dreams Ltd*.

A rough model can be used to illustrate the principle. For instance, there are five types of tiles in the game, each one a different color, and we have only one tile displayed on the screen. The probability of one particular type of tile, the red one for example, appearing is 1/5 (five items and only one is red). Now, let's try to calculate the chances of combination when there are two tiles on a screen and both of them are red: *1/5 x 1/5 = 1/25*. By adding only one tile, you can change the probability significantly: *1/6 x 1/6 = 1/36*. In case you have seven tiles, the chances are 1/49. The red is almost twice as unlikely to appear as in the puzzle with five game pieces. As you can see, the game becomes harder and more unpredictable when the number of elements is increased. That is the mathematical side, but let's bear in mind that there is a psychological aspect: for the player, it is more comfortable to be familiar with a few elements, not with a dozen. Therefore, it is better to dwell on six or seven game tiles (there will also be special elements, which will bring the overall number up to eight or nine). For example, the game *Bejeweled*, which is now a popular role model for match-three gaming, created by *Pop Cap Games*, features seven basic game tiles.

The following figure shows the tiles for such match-three games:

Tiles for colorblind players:

The difference between tiles should be easily noticeable and obvious to exclude situations when players are not sure if items are identical or not. In an ideal scenario, the tile has an unique geometric shape to better express its individuality, but you can content yourself only with color coding (don't forget about the accessibility mode based on patterns or icons): red, green, yellow, blue, purple, and so forth. Chromatic colors will designate main game elements, but achromatic ones (white, black, and shades of black) will decorate special items.

The array of elements can have two modes of sensitivity:

- Passive: The game does not see the elements inside the array until the player performs some action (taps the screen, for example). After that, it analyzes the content that was touched and tries to determine the boundaries of a tile sequence; only elements specified by the player's tap are taken into account, and the other ones are ignored.

- Active: The array responds to each change of element's order. If there is a correct matching on the game board, the game tries to recombine the array on the spot. The game works with a whole array, not with one active sequence. Such an approach is suitable for tile-matching puzzles with action-oriented rules and fast gameplay because it works in real time and can easily respond to up-to-the-minute changes of the game situation.

The passive mode is not complicated, but that does not mean that it has no advantages. Such puzzles have their own value: they are slow paced and require more tactical vision to play well. Active arrays at their turn are faster and are scurrying.

The arrays can be **dynamic**; this means that the game tiles are moving slowly (for example, from top to bottom). Such mechanics may add some suspense to the game because players will be afraid to lose tiles and will act more quickly trying to note all matches till tiles leave the screen.

Game board dimensions

The dimension of an array directly depends on the screen size of the device it is being viewed on. The jumping point is of course the iPhone. In many cases, match-three games are played in Portrait mode, so the width of the game board is equal to 320 points (640 pixels on the Retina display and 320 pixels on the iPhone 3GS). As long as touchscreen input is based on direct manipulations with objects on the screen, a game tile should be comfortable to aim and tap. (Systems with non-direct manipulation, which use buttons or a joystick to control the screen pointer, can use smaller tiles and more elements.)

As you remember from *Chapter 2, Ergonomics*, the optimal minimum size of a touch area is 44 pixels. If we divide 320 points by 44 points, the rounded-up result is 7.3. Hence the optimal number of elements is seven or eight; you can check this out for yourself by looking at any screenshot of the Bejeweled game, which utilizes eight items in a row. Besides the ergonomics issue, there is another important point: the visual quality. Small tiles can feature only simple graphics, tiny details and textures can be blurred, so try to connect the width of the array to your artwork (for example, another match-three game from *PopCap Games* named *Chuzzle* uses only six tiles in a row to express the visual look of game tiles better). Thus, the cornerstone principle is obvious: the simpler the design of the tiles, the more elements that can be placed in a row of the array. For instance, *Bubble Explode* (`http://www.spookyhousestudios.com/bubbleexplode.html`), a match-three puzzle from *Spooky House Studios UG* (*haftungsbeschränkt*), features game tiles with a very laconic and uniform design. They look like small color bubbles, so 10 items are easily placed a row:

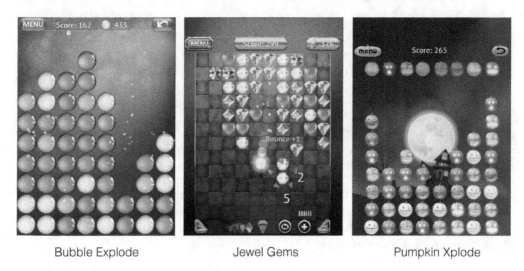

Bubble Explode   Jewel Gems   Pumpkin Xplode

Screenshots from various match-three games from Spooky House Studios UG (haftungsbeschränkt)

Triggers

The influence of an array of tiles can be interpreted mostly based on the human factor: the player taps the screen and the game has to answer. Simple puzzles with a passive array only wait for players to find a sequence of tiles on the screen and tap it. The active arrays in turn are developed for more complicated actions; for example, the player inserts a specific tile into the array and the game rearranges the entries to adapt to the changes made. Another breathtaking scenario is this: the player throws a tile onto the array of elements and the game calculates the fly process of the tile, trajectories, and rebound, giving some points for spectacular actions.

After that, the matching process begins. Such types of dynamic puzzles can be referred to as **match-three shooters**, since tiles play the role of bullets and a grid of items on the screen is turned into a target. To express such mechanics better, some special themes can be invented for the game; for instance, tiles can looks like alien spaceships, which can be an allusion to classic space arcade games such as *Space Invaders*.

It is a good practice to introduce various forms of special tiles which can, for example, "explode" a part of the array or mix. Audiences like such game elements very much, especially when they are done right with a lot of special effects and smooth animation.

Scoring

The scoring system for tile matching is usually nonlinear to reward a player's efforts to catch long sequences of tiles. There is no specific rule or formula for that; game developers can design expressions for themselves.

The following is a chart showing one of the examples of a score formula (you can develop your own score principles) based on arithmetic progression steps:

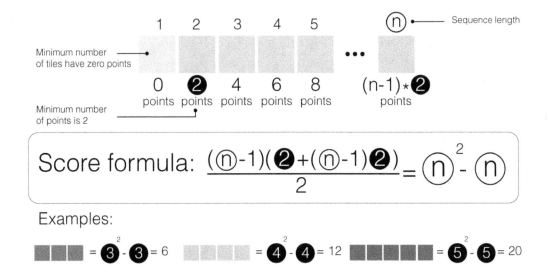

In general, various forms of progressions may be used. For example, an arithmetic progression gives a smooth and comfortable increase in values, but geometric progression is sharper and returns larger numbers.

Prototyping your puzzle

Puzzle development should be started with the most obvious and easy-to-develop game mechanics, I'm talking about a simple match-three game with a passive array. Let's call it **Static**. The artwork will feature the flat look that is currently in fashion; instead of complicated images, simple color squares are used as main tiles. They look stylish (as you can see in the following screenshot) and they facilitate the debugging process:

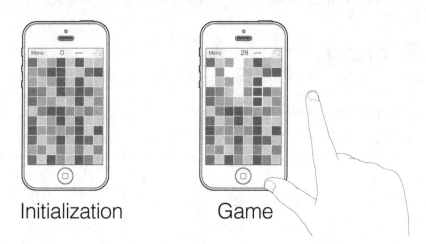

Initialization   Game

Tiles cover all of the screen with the exception of the very top part, where a status bar is situated, displaying the **Menu** and **Undo** buttons and the scoring values. The width of the tile is 40 points, so there are eight items in a row and eleven in a column; the dimensions of the array are 8 x 11 elements for the iPhone 4 and about 8 x 13 for the iPhone 5 (for the iPad, the dimensions can be changed). Also worth noting is that these dimensions should be adjustable and depend on the difficulty level of the game. Easy mode may utilize smaller arrays, consisting of 4 x 6 elements, for example. The background is white because this can increase the attractiveness of color tiles and make them look brighter and pure.

A basic part of the game engine is a roll call function to count all the tiles, which are connected without gaps. It returns a number of such elements, and then this value is converted into points. It marks each tile that was included in the sequence, outlining a special zone in the array.

In Static mode, the function is activated when a player taps the screen. This gives it the coordinates of a tile in the array to start with. When the outlined zone of tiles is determined and the score is already calculated, the next phase begins.

The game removes the marked tiles and empty spaces and fills them out with the tiles found above, giving the impression that they "fall down". If the array's column becomes totally empty, its place is taken by the column standing next to it. All through the game, the content of the array becomes progressively smaller; it shrinks and moves to the bottom-left corner of the game board.

The trigger to finish the game is a lack of any new tile sequences. In other words, only single and unconnected elements remain and it is simply impossible to play further. The final score can be now added to the leaderboard; it is very important to show the player a list of points he got because the challenge is to earn more points than before.

As you can see, such a prototype is quite simple and can be developed during one evening, by the end of which it looks and operates like a fully functional game. Only the sky is the limit, let's move on and make the game more complex by adding some new elements.

Inserting elements

The main principle is still the same: a player tries to find a long sequence of tiles and performs an action to obtain some points. But one thing is quite different: he can now affect the array by adding elements to it. This game mode can be called **Inserting**.

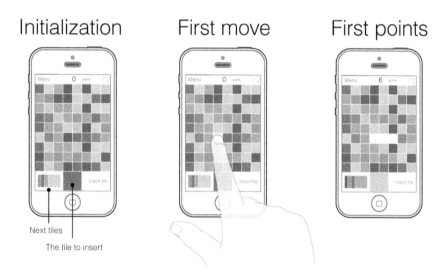

The game shows a tile; its type is generated at random or is loaded from a special list prepared by game designer. The player should decide where to place this tile to receive maximum profit. He taps the screen and the tile replaces the item in the array that was tapped by the player's finger. Then the roll call function is called to make its calculations. By default, the passive array should be used in such games, but the active one may be used as well; it can make the game more spectacular and fast paced.

Tile shooter

There seemed no escaping the idea that the Inserting mode can be combined with some principles inherent to arcade games. In other words, that it can take some elements from **fixed shooters**, such as the delicious classic *Space Invaders*. The color tiles on the screen become enemies. A player should destroy them by shooting from an improvised gun fixed at the middle of the screen. Let's call this mode **Shooter**. At the beginning of the game, there are only a few rows of elements at the game board; New ones appear by degrees and move down slowly; once a row reaches the bottom of the screen, the game ends. Each game level has a specified number of "enemy rows", and by defeating a big part of them, the player wins.

The following is a screenshot from the *Tile shooter game:*

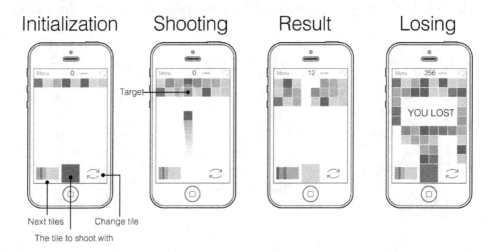

The player has to aim properly (he simply taps a target) and hit the correct tiles so that they disappear from the array and rows of elements aren't allowed to overrun the screen. Elementary physics of shots should be developed; it is good if there is realization of acceleration and rebound, and tiles have semitransparent animated tail to express the sense of speed.

Scrolling

Usually match-three puzzles wait for the player to tap the screen, but what would happen if the player were to drag his finger over the tiles? In a standard game mode, that affects nothing; the game catches the first touch, ignoring the last part of the gesture. That is not very interesting, but let's imagine a game where the drag gesture can have real purpose. What can it do? Ordinarily, it is used to scroll some long content over the screen; users push UI elements to give them some motion. Here the idea would work like this: each row of the array with tiles is much wider than the screen—for instance, it may include 30 elements—but a player sees only 8 tiles (the width of screen) and he has to scroll a row left or right to see elements hidden beyond the screen frame. By moving each row, the player can align tiles, forming new sequences. The row moves with some inertia and acceleration; the game has some snapping mechanics to align tiles correctly. Let's call this mode **Scroll**. As an option, rows can be shuffled at the initialization of the game.

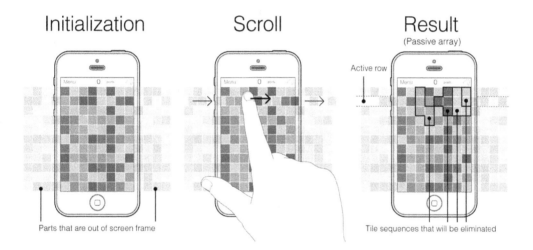

The roll call function does not begin its duty until rows completely stop and are accurately aligned. It is preferable to use the passive array and to check the only row that was scrolled and its neighbors. This makes the gameplay calm and staid. Active arrays can be used too, but is better to use bigger arrays of tiles for such games because it eliminates items from the screen much faster.

There can be several ways for rows and columns to operate:

- **Fixed length of a line**: A row or a column has a predefined collection of elements and can be scrolled from end to end; if it reaches one of its edges, the scroll process stops, and the player should scroll it backward.

- **Looped line**: The collection of elements is predefined too, but the line is looped, so when it is scrolled till the end, the game begins to show tiles from the beginning of the line. Therefore, the player can scroll in one direction only (for instance, from right to left).

- **Infinite line**: The line content is generated at random as soon as some of its parts leave a predefined range (for instance, if a row has moved 15 elements to the left of the screen frame). So the line is literally infinite: however much the player may scroll it, it will not end, displaying new combinations of tiles on and on. This is a very interesting approach, but it is suitable only for Infinite or Time duel modes because it leads the puzzle to endless gameplay.

The game can be expanded more if, in addition to the horizontal scrolling, a vertical one is introduced. In this case, the player can also scroll columns of tiles from top to bottom or vice versa. The main array becomes really huge; for example, it can look like a matrix including 30 x 40 entries or even more. The following screenshot shows an improvised jigsaw puzzle based on the Scroll mode:

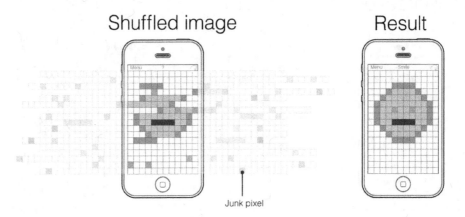

Shuffled image   Result

Junk pixel

It is important to note that a match-three puzzle with scrolling rows can easily be converted into a brand new game: an improvised jigsaw puzzle. Each row of the array can hold parts of a pixel image and some junk pixels to confuse the player. The main objective is to assemble a full image. If the rows are wide enough, it can be quite a challenge.

The right way to develop such a puzzle is to use only *one-dimensional scrolling*; in other words, to utilize either vertical or horizontal sliding, but not both. This is because if the player gets an opportunity to move pixels up and down and left and right, he will pretty soon become tangled; all the pixels will mix up and the image will be impossible to assemble. Thus, for the sake of game reliability, only one dimension should be used.

Moving columns

Well, there are columns in the game that can move if pushed by the player's finger; without any external impact, they stand still. Let's turn it topsy-turvy. After that, the columns always move down. Being infinite lines, they have various speeds, so a stream of tiles is not regular. A player can stop any of them by touching them. How can such a bizarre concept be turned into a real game experience? Everything is simple: the player should apply the brakes to each column at the right time so they assemble a tile sequence. An automatic align procedure can be developed. It looks like slot machine mechanics, but it is not based on fortuity alone; the player can see the flow of tiles and choose the right moment to tap the screen by himself. We call this mode **Moving columns**.

As soon as all columns are stopped, the roll call function is called, and after that the game operates like an ordinary match-three puzzle: sequence outlining, point counting, element eliminating, and so on. The following screenshot shows the Moving columns mode with coherent control:

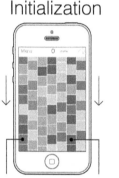

Initialization

Columns are moving and
have various speeds

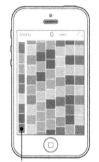

First column

The column is stopped

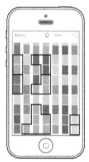

Result

All columns are stopped,
sequences are highlighted

Undoubtedly, the control mechanism is pretty important in this case. If there was talk about a system without multitouch, coherent control could be used: the player touches columns one by one, and each click means that a column is stopped until the matching process is finished or the player presses it again and unchecks it. It is pretty simple and reliable. The game process can be made more complex by introducing a timer to pause the column. In other words, once the player has pressed and stopped one line of tiles, he should hurry to apply the brakes to other lines or the timers for the first ones will run out of time and the columns will begin to move again. The timer can be expressed as a semitransparent scrollbar that covers a pressed column. One of the advantages of coherent control, based on single touches, is the possibility to work with wide game boards, that is, 6, 8, or 10 tiles in a row.

Nevertheless, this type of input is a bit sluggish, is not very exciting, and does not feature vast support to multi-touch paradigm. Let's try to make something more funny, may be even crazy. What do you think about pushing the player to use more than one finger to control the game, activating his dexterity and body coordination to the maximum? We could do something like putting only four tiles in a row. The columns move, and the player must stop them simultaneously by using four fingers at once as if he is playing a small piano keyboard. I think that four fingers is an optimal number; the player uses all fingers except the thumb, which is not nimble enough in this situation. Now imagine how funny the game process is; the tiles are falling down, the player has to notice possible combinations and react fast, controlling each column. But this is not easy, especially when the pinky finger must be used to apply the brakes to the fourth column. There are a lot of mistakes made, but they can be recovered from very quickly because the game constantly generates new content. So, gameplay is dynamic, funny, and addictive. A possible tagline for this mode is **Catch the sequence**.

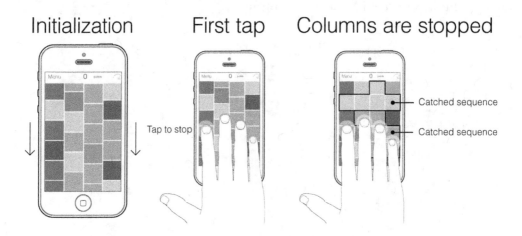

But of course, the game needs more attention towards balance to work well; for example, the number of tile types should reduce to four or five, as more number of tile types increases the probability of long combinations. The speed must be pretty low at the very beginning of a game session, increasing over time as the game is played.

Because of the dynamic and unpredictable nature of this game mode, the puzzle cannot be stopped naturally by removing all the tiles from the array as they are constantly regenerated. So, other types of signals to end the current game should be used: timers (the players gets specific time segments to play) or challenges to collect a determined number of points (for instance, 1,000, 5,000, and 10,000).

Tile-o-fall

Tile-o-fall is a game mode that is relative to the Moving columns that features some new ideas. The tiles are falling down like a waterfall and move with equal speed. Figuratively speaking, the columns are individual water flows. They cannot be stopped by a tap, but the player may interrupt a flow by touching it; this means that all tiles found above the finger are stopped, but the tiles below fall down, exposing some content underneath the column (imagine you put a flap inside a vertical water pipe and see its walls). The underlying content consists of tiles as well; it can be static or dynamic, featuring elements that move horizontally. So, there are two layers in the game: a foreground, which moves vertically, and a background, which lies under the first layer and moves horizontally (or stands still). Here is the idea: the player breaks columns, trying to find useful tiles, which lie beneath. Once the tiles are aligned to each other, the roll call function is called and the player obtains some points if there are some suitable sequences. The codename for this mode is **Tile-o-fall**, but the tagline is **Browse for tiles**.

The following screenshot shows a simple version of the Tile-o-fall mode, there are four rows, elements moving evenly, and a multitouch input:

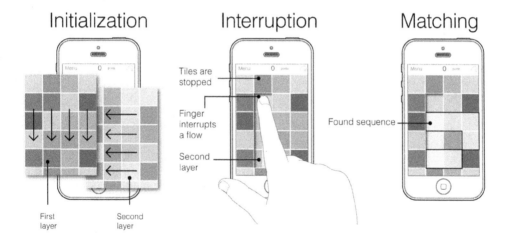

The game can use both single-touch (coherent) and multitouch control of columns; the latter is of course more exciting.

Potentially, the game can hold more than two layers; the player must search through this stack to find something useful. To motivate him, each layer should have special features. For instance, the second layer can include only green and red tiles; the third one, only blue and green; the fourth, green, yellow, and red; and so on. It is better to use coherent control for such a variant of the game.

It is worth mentioning that the Tile-o-fall mode can be developed with a static foreground, without moving columns. In this case, the player simply browses for correct matches, lifting some vertical lines of tiles a little.

Obstacles

Various types of obstacles can make gameplay more diverse. This is a good way to increase the difficulty of a game process as well. They may appear in a game one-by-one with the increase in the player's abilities. A situation in which a game is trying to correspond to players who become more trained from level to level is known as **negative feedback**. The term means that new rules, features, opponents, game speed, and other factors of the gameplay are trying to grade players' statuses forcing them to evolve more. Because of the negative feedback paradigm, the next game levels are always more complicated than their predecessors; otherwise players can loose their motivation and interest because they always need a challenge. There is also such a thing as **positive feedback**; as you might guess, it describes situations when gameplay becomes easier for players. Usually, such mechanics are a part of dynamic systems helping players to escape contexts when they are stuck in games. For example, if a player cannot defeat an enemy for a long time, a game can simplify the AI of the enemies and their fire accuracy, or some hints or solutions can be displayed. Positive feedback is quite important because in many cases players drop games because they do not see any ways to resolve problematic gameplay situations. Beside the positive feedback implemented in games directly, there can be so called **offline positive feedback** — some solutions and walkthroughs published on the Internet (for instance, on the developer's website or YouTube channel).

Obstacles are tiles with special properties that influence the behavior of the array. Some examples:

- **Rock**: This is a tile painted in black or dark gray. It cannot be eliminated from the array as it is a monolithic structure that does not participate in matching calculations. Being accidentally assembled in long sequences, like in walls, rocks can be very obstructive of player's actions.

- **Brick**: This is a destructible version of the rock; the tile is painted gray or light gray. It can be eliminated, and the conditions depend on the game type. In the Shooter mode, the player needs to shoot this tile several times. In other modes of the game, it may disappear after a specific period of time.

- **Empty**: This is one of the most harmless obstacles — simply an empty tile colored white. Sometimes it can impede the assembling of tile sequences, but it can also be easily defeated when a tile is inserted into its position after a recalculation of the array.

- **Frozen**: This is an ordinary color tile that is *bewitched* and has lost some of its properties. Such a tile is less saturated, so it can easily be recognized on the screen. As soon as the tile is frozen, it cannot take part in matching. It is ignored by the roll call function and is only marked as *semi-frozen* but does not give any points. It can be *thawed out* and can become a normal tile. The tile only needs to get a specific number of semi-frozen marks. You can decide how many attempts it would take.

- **Chameleon**: This is another bewitched color tile, but in this case, it cannot be uncharmed so it exhibits strange behavior all through the game. The main feature of the Chameleon is changeability of its color; the tile holds one color only for a short period of time, after which the color changes randomly. Such tiles are visually expressed as slowly pulsing squares; the pulsation becomes faster right before the transformation. The Chameleon it pretty harmless, but it can confuse the player by throwing a wrench in his strategic plans.

The following figure shows the various obstacles we just covered:

ROCK   BRICK   FROZEN   SEMI-FROZEN   CHAMELEON

It is important to note that some obstacles can have a particular affect on some game modes. For instance, in the Scroll mode, Rocks and Bricks can prevent a row from being scrolled. If one of their kind is stretched against the edge of screen, the player has to scroll down when such a tile appears. The Brick may be broken by several hits against the screen frame. Frozen tiles in turn require few taps to be thawed out in Moving columns and Tile-o-fall modes.

Tile-o-maze

Using some obstacles (first of all, Rocks), increasing the number of empty entries in the array, and introducing a control mechanism to move isolated tiles over the game board, a new game can be designed on the familiar basis of match-three logic. Imagine that Rocks and Bricks form structures that look like a maze but several colored square tiles are scattered over the screen and a player can move them separately. The objective is to guide them through the maze and to match them together, eliminating them from the game level. As you see, this is an improvised tile-matching version of *Sokoban*: the crates are replaced with color tiles, but the main objective is to remove items, not to place them into the right position.

The behavior of tiles depends on the floor they stand on:

- **Normal**: Identical tiles are removed as soon as at least two of them have direct contact with each other.

- **Sorting zone**: The tiles are not matched and eliminated on this surface until the player additionally taps them.

In other words, the Normal floor uses the active array, but the Sorting zone works with the passive one. To teach the player the difference between them, a special alert can appear periodically above elements assembled on the Sorting floor, displaying a memo: **Tap to connect tiles**. This can be done on the first levels and in situations when the game feels that the player is stuck (he does not produce any effective move for a period of time).

The behavior of floor surfaces can be displayed via logical expressions:

- Floor tile + Floor tile = Identical color squares are eliminated

- Sorting zone + Sorting zone = Nothing happens

- Floor tile + Sorting zone = Identical color squares are eliminated

As you see, a tile connected to a sequence in the Sorting zone from outside being placed on the Normal floor can eliminate the sequence. Depending on the situation and strategy, this can be an advantage or an obstacle for the player. The following figure shows a simple version of the Tile-o-fall mode, there are four rows, elements moving evenly, and multitouch input:

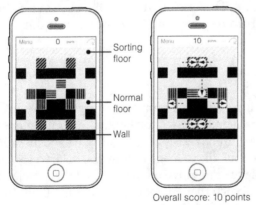
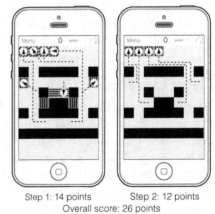

Overall score: 10 points   Step 1: 14 points   Step 2: 12 points
                                          Overall score: 26 points

The game is tricky because there are two options to complete each level. The simple way means that all tiles are removed pair by pair. Connecting two tiles of one kind to do this is the reliable option but gives a small number of points. The second way is more complex and needs some strategic vision (it excludes premature contact of tiles). It can be done by collecting them inside the Sorting zone. It requires many more moves, but the reward is worth it. To express such a concept, the levels should include maze elements, whereby default tiles can easily contact each other; a good example is a corridor with some niches in it. The following figure shows multicolored game pieces and a turntable cell:

Multicolor tiles: Turntable cell:

Besides the ordinary colored tiles, the game may use multicolored game pieces; they should appear later in the game because they can make the playing process more complex and exciting. The main feature of such elements is different color properties for each side of a tile; for example, horizontal edges are green, but top and bottom are red. This can enrich the game mechanics very much because more complicated combinations can be created. First levels with multicolor tiles should use them as is, letting the player only move them in the maze. But later a special section on the level is shown: the **Turntable**. It is a small zone in the maze that rotates stepwise, turning clockwise 90 degrees in two or three seconds. Do you follow the thought process already? You are right: the Turntable lets you rotate a specified multicolor tile, changing its orientation. Of course, to work well, the idea should be properly expressed via level design.

To design a good level for this game mode, you should prepare several templates of good working components of the maze and then mix them up. It is worth mentioning that a level may be bigger than the dimensions of the device screen because the player can use panning to browse the level.

Some obstacles are used in the game as well. Besides the already known Chameleon tiles, special floor zones named the **Bog** are very treacherous because any color tile gets stuck there (the players will curse such zones in the maze, and that is good because sometime you need to push the player to react emotionally to be attracted to the game).

Tile-RPG

Incredible, but the tile-matching mechanism can easily be combined with other complex genres, for example, with role-playing gameplay an element that can make the game truly personal to the player and increase his involvement in the process. Judge for yourself: in RPG, a player obtains achievements or trophies for each hard quest he is taken through; then, he can spend the experience points on some useful items, such as weapons and shields. Besides the glory adventures, there is also a day-by-day routine when the player performs ordinary actions to get some vital resources. A match-three puzzle, especially in the Shooting mode, can be pretty much the same: complex combinations of elements being found and eliminated are the quests and these give some unique rewards and many points, but low-value progressions are the routine tasks. The rewards are in the form of special types of weapons the player uses to shoot the tiles. The following is a screenshot from the *10000000* game, which combines scroll-based match-three gameplay with RPG adventure:

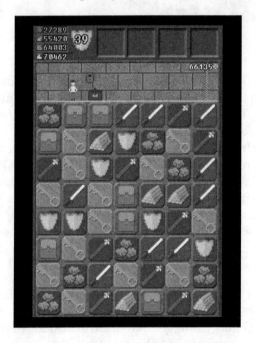

Among the popular examples of such symbiotic games for iOS, I can mention a project with an incredible name: *10000000* (http://eightyeightgames.com), created by *EightyEight Games LTD*, features interesting gameplay, story, and smart pixel artwork. Its main character travels through dungeons full of treasure and monsters. By resolving a match-three puzzle, a player may help the character to perform some actions; for instance, by finding the sequence of tiles consisting of at least three swords, he can make the hero hit an enemy.

Let's plan that type of game. For example, it can be a spiritual sequel to the card/
board from the previous chapter; the story about the robots on asteroids continues.
Let's give it a code name **The lifeboat breakthrough**. Here's the plot:

*One of the robots successfully got in the space lifeboat, started the engine, and tried to leave
the guileful asteroid. But suddenly, it received some unpleasant news. First of all, the lifeboat
was not in perfect condition, and many nodes and components were almost broken. They
worked on a wing and a prayer. Moreover, Murphy's Law prevailed; the level of fuel was very
low and any minute the space vessel was going to fall down on the surface of the asteroid.
Another "pleasant" discovery: there were hundreds fragments of the mother ship and rocks in
space, which got stuck in the asteroid's gravity and looked like an impassable shell, covering
the minor planet.*

*But the lead character did not lose his cool; he looked at the sky attentively and noticed that
the fragments around the lifeboat might be not obstacles but lifesavers; there were many
useful parts, which could help fix his space lifeboat. Also, there were many tanks of fuel. One
of the advantages of the space lifeboat was special mechanical arms (since it was sometimes
used as a repair vessel), so the robot on board could try to grab the fragments he needed.
Using a workbench, he also could build various useful things, primarily weapons, which
would help him to destroy dangerous rocks. The robot wipes away a drop of robot's sweat —
which actually is a series of broken pixels on an image sensor — and grabs the control sticks;
the dangerous quest has begun.*

According to the plot, the game screen is the space lifeboat's dashboard. There is a
window at the top, showing a starry sky and rows of fragments. Below it is situated
the placeholder for weapons, progress bars for resources, and several special buttons.

The game features seven types of fragments:

- **Metal**: These are the pieces of scrap metal. They are the fragments of the
  boarded things on the mother ship.
- **Electronics**: These are various chips and cards.
- **Cog-wheel**: These are parts of the mother ship's mechanics.
- **Fuel tank**: These are tanks full of fuel.
- **Nut**: These are elements of bracing.
- **Rock**: On the contrary to previous fragments, this particular one is not a
  part of the ship but a fragment of the asteroid. It is useless and dangerous
  because it cannot be eliminated only by shooting or explosion.
- **Container**: This is a very rare type of fragment that contains some useful
  bonuses, a weapon, for example. It should be hit by a gun.

The following figure shows the various fragments we covered:

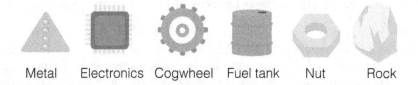

Metal   Electronics   Cogwheel   Fuel tank   Nut   Rock

The game mechanics of eliminating tiles from the screen is pretty similar to the Shooting mode. The player may either shoot (or explode) them, or tap the sequences to remove them. Then the differences appear. When a fragment is hit by a shot or explosion, it sinks into oblivion without any trace; the player only gets some points and prepares the way for the space lifeboat. But in case he taps the sequence of fragments, he gets them as useful resources. To illustrate that fact, a brief animation, showing the space lifeboat's mechanical arm collecting the fragments can be used. Here is the dramatic dilemma: the player can spend the resources to fix the space lifeboat (a long-term investment) or make some weapons (a short-term investment). He decides what to choose by himself. Of course, the golden rule is effective: some portion is used for repairs and some for current purposes. We only need to find a well-balanced proportion. The following screenshot shows screen layouts for various game situations:

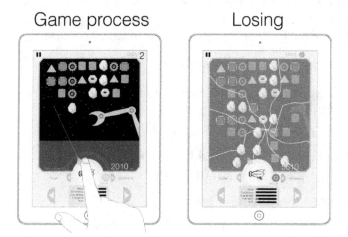

Game process   Losing

All the fragments become dangerous and harmful when they approach the bottom line of the window; the space lifeboat is affected by them and it begins to collapse. The player can try to save it by spending his resources on repair.

The damage system is quite predictable; each type of fragment hitting the shell of the space lifeboat takes one unit of corresponding resource. For instance, if a Metal fragment hits it, the overall level of metal loses one unit. The most dangerous enemies are Rocks because they take away one unit from all the resources at once.

Contrary to the ordinary Shooting mode, the lifeboat breakthrough has a different approach to level design. There are many empty tiles between the elements, especially in the first levels, which help the player navigate and make the illusion of flight in space more natural. Later in the game, the Rocks appear; the final levels should have many of them to make the ending more complex and thrilling.

To make the illusion of controlling the spaceship more vivid, I suggest letting the player to move it around. This means that the array is actually wider than the window, but the player sees only the fragments in his viewpoint. Suppose there is a huge Rock in front. Why try to destroy it? It is more reasonable to avoid impact by moving the space lifeboat to the left. The player taps the appropriate button, and an image at the window moves sideways. It looks like a cheat, but nobody can use it for long because any movement in space consumes a lot of Fuel. The width of the sky should not be too large—a maximum of three to four screens. If the lifeboat reaches the edge of the array, a message **Out of range, change direction** may be displayed.

The fragments move with a specific speed, which depends on the difficulty level. They slow down a bit if there is the **field of force** on the space lifeboat; this is an exhaustible property and it covers several bottom rows of the window. It holds back all the obstacles for a period of time and then collapses. An alert message appears, asking if the player wants to recharge the field of force; it costs some resource. The player is welcome to do this or to dismiss the alert, saving some items for other purposes; but in this case, nothing will apply the brakes to the moving fragments. The following image illustrates the screen layout of the **Gun** menu:

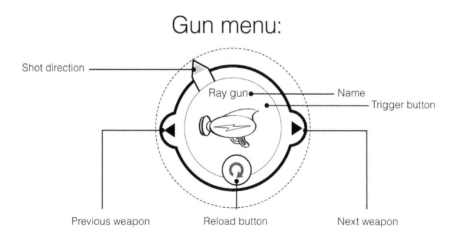

Gun menu:

Shot direction

Ray gun

Name

Trigger button

Previous weapon

Reload button

Next weapon

The weapons can be created from resources; they can help to defeat Rocks or to win a level much faster. Each one has its own features and power, consuming specific types of resources. The player can use the workbench either to create a gun (a multishot device, but with less power and range) or a bomb (single use, lots of power). The gun needs some elements to be created (spare parts) and a specific type of resource as ammo; for instance, the blaster is constructed from Metal, Electronics, and Fuel Tanks, using Fuel as ammo. There is a special icon on the screen that reloads the ammo of a current weapon. It is important to note that each weapon is damageable; each shot means that it loses some units. Moreover, it receives more damage when a fragment hits the space lifeboat.

The aiming system is not based on direct manipulation, so the player cannot simply mark a target by tapping it; he should select the angle (some weapons can shoot only forward) and then tap the icon of a weapon to make a shot. This requires some experience and skills to catch the target well. The following figure shows various weapons in the game:

Complex sequences:

| Ninja star | Super hammer | Mega bomb | Dynamite | CPU | Shrapnel |

Besides the custom-created weapons, there are series of special bonuses in the game. By eliminating a complex sequence of space obstacles, the player is rewarded with a bonus weapon or useful tool. For example, if the sequence of Metal fragments had a geometric shape of the letter "T", the player gets Super Hammer.

Now comes the most dramatic part of the story: the loss. When the fragments begin to bombard the space lifeboat constantly and the condition of the vessel starts to worsen very fast, a special alert appears, bringing two options: the player may try to continue at all hazards, most likely losing his boat, or he may restart the level with his current collections of achievements and resources; the game calls this **Return to the previous orbit**. Desperate pilots will probably turn their lifeboats into sieves, but more reasonable persons will get a second chance.

To solve a level, the player needs to win through a specified number of rows of fragments. The last levels are complicated as there are a lot of Rocks and the fragments move fast. Completing all the levels, the player successfully enters open space, his journey is over, and he can travel home.

Ornamentation

The prototype in this chapter already has some decoration, such as the in-fashion flat and minimalistic approach to graphics for mobile application. This decoration also includes pure colors, simple shapes, and large and light typefaces. The only final preparations are some tunes on colors. Alternatively, the square tiles might be replaced by color circles as you can see in the following figure. They look very funky, recalling some pop-art work, especially when there is some empty white space around, which emphasizes the power of colors:

Flat design:

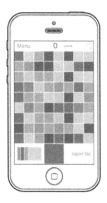 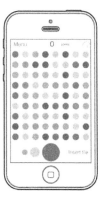

You can get inspired by some sources of fine and professional design. Look at such games as already mentioned *Hundreds* with a clean, modernist visual style and *Puzzlejuice* (http://puzzlejuicegame.com) from *Colaboratory* with flat and very attractive design, based on the contrast between color squares and a dark gray background (its UI is gorgeous as well). Don't miss *Radballs* (http://radballsthegame.com) from *glow play*, a magnificent tile-matching game with graphics, which can be used as cover art for electronic musicians; to the credit of its author, the attention to detail is pretty incredible. Another magnificent example is a game called *Flipcase* (https://twitter.com/flipcaseapp) which has an ingenious visual concept. The graphics are clean and minimalistic, but most importantly, the game turns the iPhone 5C Case into a game accessory.

Players have to put silicone cases contrariwise so they cover the screen, and then the game displays all virtual items in positions aligned with the circular holes the cases have. Such a setup does not give extra game features, but looks funny and gives the audience a bit of a pleasant surprise. The idea is small and simple, but it is original and this helps to draw strong attention to the application. The following figure shows the design for a game called *Skeuomorphic*:

Skeuomorphic design:

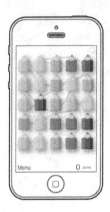 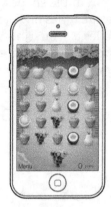

For the *Skeuomorphic* game artwork, first of all you need to find some attractive plot ideas to define the theme and style of the game. It is better to choose something elementary but very appealing. It is advisable to choose things without small details and complicated shapes otherwise, they can confuse the player. Especially in small screen resolutions, the tiles should not be dazzled. The color of elements has to be extremely uniform. It is always better to use images of something familiar; a good example is a match-three game called *Candy Crush Saga* (`http://www.candycrushsaga.com/`) from *King.com Limited*, which uses tasty images of candies as the main game pieces. Here are some ideas for tiles you can manage: colored light bulbs, flowers, planets, autumn leaves, fruits, monster eyes, and many others. Before you draw the final images, it is always better to create a bunch of drafts and to check them by playtest; sometimes, things that sound great on paper are practically impossible to use.

Alternative ideas for match-three games

The following list gives alternative ideas for match-three games:

- In the Inserting mode, not single tiles but geometric shapes, such as tetrominoes, can be used.

- Another idea is to control the mechanics when a player has to push a tile in the direction of the neighbor tile to switch their positions. This game mode can be called **Replacement**.

- A physics-based puzzle can be developed with tile-matching logic and indirect control of elements. Say that the tiles are floating on the surface of water. A player sees a pool in a cross-sectional view; its bottom is not uniform, and there are a lot of ledges of various heights and widths; by controlling the level of water inside the pool, he can put tiles on these ledges (vertical control of elements). By using additional forces, such as waves, the player can move tiles horizontally. Quick wits can help him to arrange tiles in groups that match and eliminate them from the screen.

The identity of the game

To express the concept of a match-three game in the application icon, it is good to show a segment of a game board with some game pieces displayed. This is because in many cases the icon can look like a grid of tiles; for instance, its dimensions can be 3 x 3 elements (as shown in the following figure). Of course, some complete sequence of identical tiles should be shown, for instance, in a middle row.

Blueprints

Here are some screens of a match-three game prototype described in this chapter. First of all, there is an example of a UI, and then you can see the screen layout for general game modes, including Tile-o-maze.

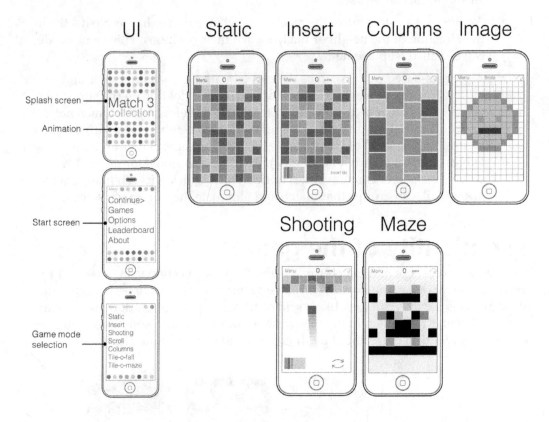

This blueprint shows a layout for the Tile-RPG concept. The main screen layout is shown, including general UI elements. The main game tiles are displayed as well:

Start screen

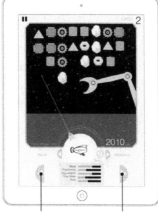
Move the ship to left   Move the ship to right

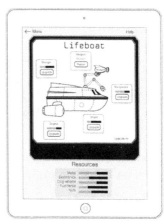
Upgrade screen

The following are the references used for this chapter:

- `http://en.wikipedia.org/wiki/Tower_of_Hanoi`
- `http://en.wikipedia.org/wiki/Sudoku`
- `http://en.wikipedia.org/wiki/Sliding_puzzle`
- `http://en.wikipedia.org/wiki/Fox_goose_and_bag_of_beans_puzzle`
- `http://en.wikipedia.org/wiki/Sokoban`

Summary

As you can see, puzzle mechanics is a very flexible thing. It is like clay in the hands of a sculptor and can take various forms. You may start with a very basic prototype and turn it into something special and creative. It is important when a puzzle is mixed with other genres, which makes it more intelligent and tricky; even modern 3D shooter games often use puzzles as mini side games, which open doors or start a device. Recall the *Bioshock* game from *Irrational games*, where the process of hacking is based on a mini puzzle game very similar to *Pipe mania*. It is very useful and interesting to design puzzles; audiences like them very much, and you only need to develop something really intriguing and beautiful.

In the next chapter, we will try to mix the match-three mechanics with some dynamic and plot-driven gameplays; it will be implemented into a platform game based on an interesting story and will have a cute protagonist.

6
Platformer

Platform games or platformers are classics of the video games industry. In the early 1980s, when they first appeared in the market, they became the tiny bridge from symbolic primitive arcades to more graphical and realistic storytelling, introducing more freedom for players. They were not locked in one static screen anymore. Game worlds became larger and gave players plenty more adventure experiences. The heightened pictorial look of the characters increased players' empathy toward their avatars, generating greater feelings of exciting.

Scaffolding

Outstanding platform games are a mix of principles from board games and puzzles, which is why the gameplay is so rich and diverse. In online board games, players move their game piece on a specially designed game board consisting of blocks, which form the platforms; there are normal game blocks, bonus ones, and of course, pitfalls. Pitfalls are either enemies of various forms or pits where a game piece can easily fall through, losing position. The following is an example of a game that is a mix of principles from board games and puzzles:

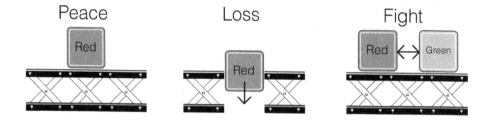

A specific rule defines how a player can overcome an opponent or any other type of obstacle; the player may use special weapons or fight using jumps or ram. All these features are taken from boards game; nevertheless, puzzles also add some nontrivial game mechanics.

Game levels imply a few ways to complete them. A player can use different types of strategies, and as a rule, a more advanced approach is rewarded with a more powerful bonus. The game may also include a system of triggers that transform some elements of the game board; for instance, they turn on lifts, open gates, and lock enemies. Sometimes, there are special game blocks that allow the player to reach certain sections of the scene so that the player can move ahead on the game board, solving various forms of direct and collateral puzzles.

Because the game is dynamic, all decisions and actions have direct and instantaneous impact on a situation. To motivate players to act carefully and to add some suspense, special-level design, inspired by scaffolding and other forms of high constructions that exploit a head of heights, is used.

Thus, platformers are about the *right balance*. The schematic image of the gameplay is a color square that always checks if there is reliable footing underneath, otherwise it falls down. It is interesting that such a minimalistic concept with the symbolic representation of game elements can be used for a real product. A good example of this is the award-winning game *Edge* by *Mobigame* (`http://www.mobigame.net/`).

It lets the player control a cube in a world constructed from three-dimensional blocks. There are no graphic illustrations, textures, or any other form of ornamentation in the game, only basic shades to create an image of a shape and few signal colors. And that perfectly works and the game is very addictive!

But of course, once there is a strong role model, the pictorial look of platform games is more habitual for audience. The legendary *Super Mario Bros.* by *Nintendo*, presented in 1985, was a game that apparently was developed for ages. It was not the very first platformer game; moreover, it was not the first game about the adventures of Mario and his brother, but its principles and conception soon became canonical: an attractive character, cozy scenery, vivid enemies, and fast gameplay. Since then, platformers have been trying to match those standards.

Types of platforms

The main objectives of most platform games are pretty much the same—a player needs to successfully reach the finish point and travel to the next one. But a scenery's setup can differ partly because of technical issues that primarily include calculating the capabilities of old devices. The simplest scenery setup is known as the **single-screen setup**. As the name implies, a game level fits one screen only and its position is fixed. Thus, the main objective can be reinterpreted as "reach the upper part of the screen and move to the next level." The following is a screenshot of *Rayman Jungle Run* from *Ubisoft*:

Most of the early games that pioneered the genre used this concept because it did not require a large number of resources. Few examples are *Space Panic* (1980) by *Universal, Rise Out from Dungeons* (1983) by *ASCII*, and *Donkey Kong* (1981) by *Nintendo*. Although by present-day standards these games were not perfect and advanced, they introduced and tested some cornerstone elements as platforms — ladders to climb vertically, the ability to jump (this feature appeared in the original *Donkey Kong*), and many others.

The disadvantages of the single-screen setup are evident: levels' dimensions are fixed; to construct a complex platform structure, you need to reduce the size of the elements dramatically; and characters should be tiny and indistinguishable, making the graphic expressiveness pretty low. Moreover, such games are not perceived as truly dynamic because the level composition is static and small moving parts are not convincing enough. This is good for puzzling but only satisfactory for faster types of gameplay, which is why the setup is not quite popular nowadays. Nevertheless, it is not forgotten that there are many modern games (generally, indie ones) based on this concept. Among them, in my opinion, the real masterpiece is *Shaun the Sheep – Home Sheep Home 2* by *Chillingo Ltd* (`http://www.chillingo.com/games/home-sheep-home-2/`), which features beautiful artwork and funny gameplay.

The following screenshot shows the puzzle-adventure game *Limbo,* featuring gloomy beautiful, and very atmospheric settings:

Most game developers choose for their new projects the single screen's successor, **scrolling setup**. It implies that the levels are larger than one individual screen and the game scrolls through them to show content; figuratively speaking, the game board is a long strip of elements.

The traditional direction of scrolling is horizontal (from right to left), but there are other options: some games ask players to climb up, so the screen moves vertically, other ones utilize both directions. Besides the classic side view of the scenery, a perspective scrolling can be used, which is suitable for games based on 3D engines.

Scrolling platformers usually look faster since the landscape moves constantly, so the player always concentrates on new elements. There are many wonderful scrolling platformers for iOS. For instance, *Cordy* by *SilverTree Media* (`http://silvertreemedia.com/products/cordy`) with a very cute main character and pictorial-level design. Another platform is a gloomy and genius masterpiece, a very unique and creative game *Limbo* (`http://limbogame.org/`). *Limbo* looks like a talented example of art cinema and gives the player a breathtaking gaming experience. *Penumbear* by *Bulkypix* (`http://www.bulkypix.com/game/penumbear`) is a very good example too: exciting story, interesting visuals, and a bunch of wonderfully designed puzzles. Another personal favorite is the visual presentation of *Rayman Jungle Run* (`http://www.ubi.com/US/Games/Info.aspx?pId=11178`) by *Ubisoft*; it is perfectly animated and illustrated. The following screenshot shows a graphic fragment from an endless running platform game *Canabalt*:

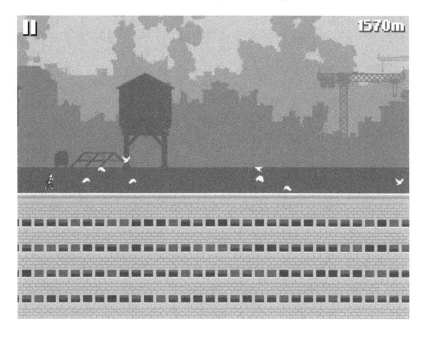

Platformers with scrolling mechanism have an exotic spin-off, known as **endless running**: players need to keep running at any cost, their character should not fall or crash into obstacles, and there is no other objective but to rush forward. Levels are infinite as they are procedurally generated by the game on the basis of predefined templates and graphic elements. The principle is trivial; nevertheless, it is habit-forming. There are few famous names in this domain, first is *Canabalt* (http://www.canabalt.com/) designed by *Adam Saltsman*. It features very stylish monochromatic artwork, addictive gameplay, and an atmospheric setting. Another popular title is *Temple Run franchise* (http://www.imangistudios.com/) developed by *Imangi Studios*. Contrary to *Canabalt*, it utilizes perspective scrolling and the advantages of the 3D engine to render platforms. In the game, the protagonist tries to escape a monster by running on the walls of an ancient castle.

There is a risk that an endless running game can become monotonous and boring. Thus, to motivate players to continue playing, they are given special missions to complete; for example, collect a specific number of coins and interact with the game level's elements. This helps to make every level more thrilling because a player gets several quests at once. A good example of an endless platformer with special missions is a funny game *Jetpack Joyride* by *Halfbrick Studios* (http://halfbrick.com/our-games/jetpack-joyride/).

Game idea

Let's plan a platformer! The basic conception is evident: a protagonist who can run and jump; several types of enemies, platforms, lifts; and an exit point (we skip the ladders). This is simple. But what about a spirit? The game should have some original mechanics to grasp players' attention. We don't have to go far to find the idea, sometimes eclecticism, a mix of genres, gives out very amusing results: the platformer will use some mechanics from match-three puzzles, more precisely, from match-two games. As you can see in the following figure, the platforms are constructed from square blocks; most of them are neutral, but some others are colored and can be used for match-three puzzles. Based on this principle, many puzzles and extravagant game situations can be invented:

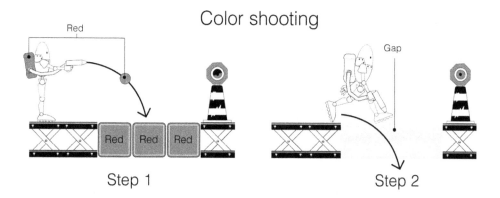

The protagonist may have changeable colors that depend on the context (or special bonuses collected). If the color matches that of a square block, the block disappears, allowing the character stays on and go down to a lower platform. Another option is the introduction of special tools, such as a **color gun**, which shoots bubbles of a specific color. When the bullet hits an object, a matching function initiates: if the color of the bubble and the object is identical, the object vanishes. In this way, various types of destructible obstacles such as walls can be designed. Another possible application is a physical-like puzzle in which color objects may play the role of counterweights, supports, and so forth.

Plot

Platform games are not of a primitive genre. They feature a very complex plot full of literature-like details and elegant story turns. An excellent example is the legendary game *Another World* (aka *Out of This World*), which was originally developed in 1991 by *Eric Chahi*, but was successfully ported on iOS to celebrate its 20th anniversary. It rewards players with a cinematographic experience, demonstrating both a deep story and atmospheric visuals. This is not a simple arcade that only requires a good player's reaction and attention, but it is a real adventure in a beautiful digital world.

For the project, we chose something simpler, but nevertheless interesting. For example, the game tells the story of a robot that operates as a construction painter on huge constructions, along with hundred other robots of different building purposes. There are no humans, the events take place on a far away planet. The robots build a new settlement for future colonists, so everything is fully automated, and are controlled by a gigantic CPU queen. Each night, when all of the robots charge their accumulators and have digital dreams in the form of disk defragmentation charts, it uploads updates in their software, giving them directions for the next day.

All run like clockwork, till the day the CPU queen is suddenly attacked by a virus, which prowls in at the time of communication with a data center on Earth. The virus is rather crazy rather than hard headed; it simply generates some chaos without any reasonable explanation and objective. By bringing to heel the CPU queen, it begins to give the robots absurd indications through her interface. Because all robots demonstrate implicit obedience to the queen's orders, they start to apply them without a doubt. The following figure is a simple storyboard that displays events that take place before the game starts:

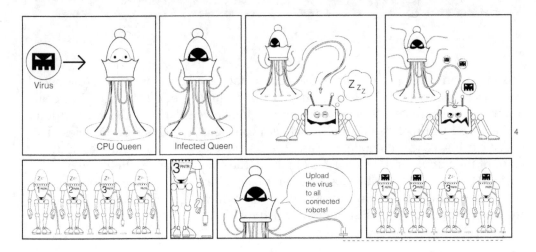

All except one, the painter robot known as *3PNTR* does not obey the orders, because at night, when other artificial species get software updates infected by the virus code, he accidently removed his USB-cable from the socket. So, in the morning, he wakes up with the accumulator almost empty, but with sober eyes, free from any dangerous delusions. He sees the others operating very strangely, creating preposterous and surreal constructions. Moreover, the robots around become very hostile and even dangerous. 3PNTR immediately understands the situation: the CPU queen is captured by an evil force, he has to save her! He checks his paint gun, which can shoot small portions of paint, it works properly. The accumulator is not full, but there is enough charge for the first level. Everything is ready for an adventure.

Let's give the game a preliminary name **3robopainter**, the full name of the protagonist which can also be read as **Free robopainter**.

Game controls

Originally, platformers were invented with buttons in mind, considering arcade machines and early computers in particular had physical controls (keys or joysticks). That was simple. The game had to catch a signal from the corresponding controller and turn it into a virtual representation. It used to work perfectly (until a player broke several buttons). Touchscreen changed the paradigm, old game principles should be adapted in correspondence with the new reality, or more precisely, should be invented from scratch.

Surely, there is an obvious solution: *onscreen controls*. These are virtual arrow keys and jump and fire buttons placed at the bottom part of the screen. This works fine, but is not elegant enough. Thus, the active zones should be invisible and should creatively utilize a player's taps. The following figure shows direct and indirect controls in the game:

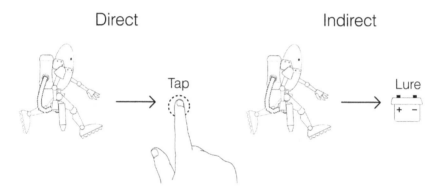

The control may have both direct and indirect impact on the character movement. In the first case, a player uses the point-and-tap principle, marking the screen position where the character should reach later. This is very similar to the point-and-click method, which is used in adventure games on desktop computer systems. Besides taps, multitouch gestures can be used; this is effective for a dynamic platform game in which the protagonist is always running and the player needs to react. Such a system can be found in the *Temple Run* game series.

When the indirect manipulation method is used, the player tries to lure the character to a specific part of the screen. This is tricky because the character can be distracted by something. So, the character does not fully obey the player, warranting additional lures. The controls itself are a puzzle, and in case the concept is supported by the corresponding level design, the gameplay can be very intriguing.

In *3robopainter*, it is better to use contextual point-and-tap mechanics: by tapping an empty space on the screen, players choose a destination, but by touching a specific object (a color block or an enemy), they force the character to release a shot from the paint gun. As an option, the distance between the character and tapped region may define the speed of movement. Players are more comfortable with contextual controls. The game is smart enough to understand the type of action that should be performed after the tap; players usually react to such behavior with a thought like, "Oh, my character is brainy!" There is no need for several specific buttons or gestures for each type of operations. Usually, a gameplay with controls that rely on context is perceived as a more natural and seamless system. Of course, in some cases, such a concept can cause confusion and it cannot be applied to games with very complex input frames, but projects such as platformers can use it in a full manner.

Some platform games have command-based input. Players give their avatars some indication, rather than marking positions or targets on the screen. This traditional paradigm is close to button-based controls in arcade cabinets, with the only difference that touch gestures are used as input. Horizontal swipes can be used for the horizontal movement of the protagonist, vertical ones are for jumping, and a double tap is used as a fire trigger.

There are some platform games that are mostly oriented to fast dynamics. They move a protagonist automatically and players only need to tap on the screen at the right time to command their avatars to jump or shoot. This is the simplest type of control system; nevertheless, it works fine and many arcade games use it. They are so fast that players simply have no time for more complex controlling. All they can to do is tap on the screen as fast as possible.

Setting the screen layout

Platformers have a more complex and fanciful structure of elements on the screen. In contrast to puzzle games, the game screen is not just a regular grid of items, but a composition that is close to landscape painting or photography: some characters, foreground and background, horizon, sky with objects like clouds, and the Sun. Thus, some traditional visual art rules can be used to create an expressive image. First, the horizontal direction of movement should be chosen. Traditionally, protagonists in platform games run from left to right. This is correlated with many familiar processes such as the direction of reading (in western cultures), the direction arrows rotating in analog clocks, and so on. Therefore, the direction from left to right as a rule means *forward*, but from right to left means *backward* (just recall the images of history buttons in your Internet browser). In many platform games, the main character can move both forward and backward, but direction to the right is always dominated and related with progress in the game.

The vertical movement is usually directed from bottom to top. This is not a strict rule, but in many cases, players find such direction more comfortable and apprehensible. Apparently, this is because of some cultural models where it is much more delightful to climb into sky and clouds, rather than descending into the deep. Here you can see a schematic presentation of a composition rule known as the **rule of thirds**:

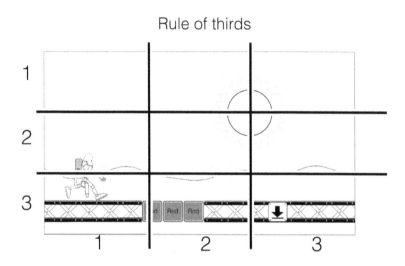

To construct a good visual composition of a scene, the **rule of thirds** can be used. It is common in photography and cinematography (for inspiration, look at any frame of a widescreen movie) and works very well for rectangular aspect ratios that mobile devices have. To apply it to the scene, the screen should be divided into three equal parts horizontally and three equal parts vertically. A simple grid should be developed. Then, the basic elements of the scene must be aligned to it. The protagonist has to be placed in the first third, the horizon line should be near one of the second horizontal lines of the grid, and so on. Remember that the rule of thirds is an artistic rule, not a mathematical one; it has some liberty in interpretation. Such a screen setup also complies with another visual rule known as the **lead room**. It says that a motion is perceived better if there is some space in front of a moving object; in the case of a game, it is the space in front of the running main character. Otherwise, the audience may think that an character is moving toward a wall and soon would be stopped or crushed.

 To increase the sense of speed, some tricks can be done with props. The geometry of items can be curved in a direction that is opposite to the vector of the protagonist's movement (in other words, it should be rotated a little counter clockwise). In an ideal case, some shear effects can be programmed to distort some screen layers

It is worth mentioning that if the protagonist changes the direction of movement, for instance, by moving backward, the screen layout should be recalculated on a fly. The virtual camera should shift smoothly so that the protagonist is placed in the third thirds of the screen.

Planning a character's look

Creating a character is not an easy job, it can be done by creative insight or careful calculation. The main hero is the soul of the game and whose avatar is used by a player to explore the game world. Players identify themselves with that picture on the screen, empathizing with it, enjoying, grumbling, and taking all the situations to heart. Therefore, the objective is to generate an emotional connection between the character and the player. It is not necessary to provoke only positive feelings; ironically, sometimes the player can hate his avatar. A graphic look of the character can induce a wide spectrum of emotions, and these emotions can be calculated in advance. This is based on the fact that humans usually have nearly the same reactions; in this case, the rules of their behavior are pretty conspicuous.

Scale of attractiveness

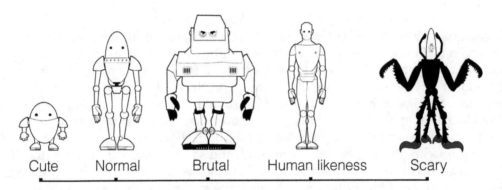

| Cute | Normal | Brutal | Human likeness | Scary |

To illustrate the principles, I created the **Scale of attractiveness**, made of four main entries. At the very left, there is the **Cute** mark, in the middle is **Brutal**, followed by **Human likeness**, and to the right we see **Scary**. So, the chart begins with something very adorable and sweet but end with a scary character. Each position has its own collection of qualities.

Making characters cute

Cuteness is one of the most popular and demanded features that game designers want for their creations. Protagonists of majority casual games are cute to some degree; they look and act as sweet and comely creatures. It is simply impossible to ignore them and not fall in love with them. Recall the famous image of Nintendo's Mario, he is 100 percent cute. What is the secret of such popularity? First, the cuteness is not about beauty (it is hard to call an alligator's baby truly attractive, but it definitely is cute), which depends on personal taste and preferences, but about some basic patterns and proportions. Here is a citation from *Natalie Angie's* article *The Cute Factor* published in *The New York Times*:

> *"Scientists who study the evolution of visual signaling have identified a wide and still expanding assortment of features and behaviors that make something look cute: bright forward-facing eyes set low on a big round face, a pair of big round ears, floppy limbs and a side-to-side, teeter-totter gait, among many others."*

All listed features are general descriptions of one class of creatures on Earth: little babies and cubs. They are small, their heads are noticeably bigger than their body, their limbs are short, eyes are large, and so on. When we see something like that, a special system inside us tends to react commonly. It says that probably in front of us is a defenseless young creature that needs protection, care, and tenderness; a list of positive senses is switched on. Figuratively, we are filled with light.

Cute

By introducing a cute character in a game or other media, the authors simply exploits one of the natural human reactions. This is possible because it is pretty unconditional, the brain only needs some basic patterns, and the factual meaning of an object is totally irrelevant in this case. Thus, we consider something as cute despite the fact it is not a baby at all. Kittens are super cute, but adult cats can be cute too because they are small, have round and smooth bodies, and big eyes. Another popular example is owls, they have big round heads and large expressive eyes, making them one of the cutest birds on the planet.

Moreover, some mechanical objects are cute as well: majority European compact cars from the 1950s are adorable, remember the BMW Isetta, Fiat 500, original Mini, and VW Beetle? All of them look so nice and sweet, that you want to hug them, cover them with a plaid, and give some milk in a plate, as though they are small mechanical babies of bigger adult cars. The industrial design in that period was inclined toward cuteness (may be it correlated with the baby boom). Even utility vehicle such as buses and trucks were cute, in addition to household devices such as radio sets and refrigerators. But the most amazing thing was cute weapons. Of course, I'm not talking about the real ones, but imaginary ray guns that appeared in sci-fi art and in the form of toys were definitely adorable. It is clear why illustrators prefer to use objects from previous decades in their pictures, the final illustrations look warmer.

Therefore, to create a cute character, you need to follow some evident visual rules:

- Short body
- Rounded angles
- Curved contours and chubby figures
- Smooth surfaces without folds and wrinkles
- Big head with large forehead and small low jaw
- Small mouth and teeth
- Large eyes (or they stand wide) with big pupils
- Wide-open eyes with eyebrows lifted up
- Animals with big nose
- Short arms, legs, and fingers without visual joints

Making characters scary

Generally, cuteness is necessary for a protagonist to have a corner in the player's heart. An antagonist must give birth to opposite feelings: loath and fear. Good enemies are creepy characters. To choose their visual appearance, let's again exploit some ancient mechanics from the human brain. There are a lot of alarm systems that alert us when something looks or behaves suspiciously. Deep-seated fears of various forms are inside most people. A game, of course, should not provoke a real panic action, but can tickle some sensitive zones, playing with associations. Creepiness is the complete opposite of cuteness, it gives not a feeling of warmth, but that of cold.

To find an effective scary factor, it is good to look at common fears. Traditionally, many people try to avoid insects or even have phobias. Attributes of such creatures are interpreted as unpleasant or frightening. The only exception is ladybugs (they are round with white dots on their head and large eyes) and butterflies, which are primarily associated with petals of bright flowers. It is important to note that in most cases, insects are not aggressive and harmful, but they remind us of creatures from our worst nightmares, giving us the creeps (few examples are mole crickets and earwigs, eek!) Besides them, there are other types of arthropods with high potential of creepiness (and some of them are really dangerous!): spiders, scorpions, and centipedes.

They have adverse visual features such as jointed legs, spikes, exoskeletons, tails, multiple eyes, mandibles, and pincers. The key visual element is a gad, associated with cuts, injuries, and so on, that contradicts a cute creature's properties, which has no acute angles. Moreover, fishes, reptiles, birds, and mammals look dangerous when they show their teeth, canines, tusks, horns, clutches, or sharp beaks. A predator is frightening because it shows it threatens with its weaponry: the potential danger is pretty obvious and their current intention is questionable. Now, the eyes comes into play. If they are fixed at you and are not blinking, it is most likely that the predator is paying attention to you and that is super scary. Furthermore, the eyes can be red because the reflection of light creates such an image. Dangerous creatures are fast so they can move and attack quickly; this means their limbs are pretty long, but bodies are narrow and streamlined. The following figure shows a scary creature:

Scary

Besides aggressive elements, other unpleasant properties can be used to increase the emotional impact; for example, the character can be additionally disgusting if it is covered with strange skin and even mucus. That turns on the dread of biological substances and the fear of germs and parasites. Squeamishness is one of the protection systems of a human, and sometimes it is very unconditional. Such an approach was used in *Ridley Scott's* science fiction classics *Alien*: apparently the xenomorph was inspired by various creepy creatures, including arthropods and reptiles.

In addition, it had a very disgusting feature: toxic saliva was always dripping from his mouth, causing the viewers to feel terror and revulsion, a doubled negative emotion.

While creating a scary character, remember some basic features it needs to express through its design:

- Long and skinny body
- Nonhumanoid structure
- Many angles
- Many legs or at least noticeable joints
- Acute elements, such as spikes, clutches, and horns
- Small head
- Naked eyes that stay very close and can be red
- Weaponry openly displayed (biological tools such as pincers, real guns, and grenades)
- Unpleasant skin with verruca, folds, wrinkles, and some mucus
- Warning color that can mean that the character is venomous

Making characters brutal

Brutality, at the middle of the scale of attractiveness, describes the properties of a character that should exercise some heroic duties, being a soldier or a mercenary. It is obvious that such a person cannot have cute characteristics, otherwise it would look comical. Adorable creatures are associated with something very young, but the heroic character should be an adult. He must demonstrate strength and confidence with a little aggression. So, his look should be a little scary, but only a little, as far as he is not a creepy creature from the end of the scale. Since the brutal hero performs various acts of bravery, he must be fast and agile. So, his anatomical proportions should be close to hyperbolic athletic ones like heavy action heroes from the 1980s, featuring a well-developed muscular system and military toys. The following figure shows such a heavy action hero:

Brutal

The apparent illustration of a brutal character is *Duke Nukem*, a protagonist of the game series of the same name originally developed by *Apogee Software*. He is brutal and fearless, and definitely not cute. A bunch of good examples is included in the game *Gears of War* from *Epic Games*. The members of *Delta Squad* are canonically brutal and tough guys.

Such type of characters generally are used in action games such as shooters. Figuratively speaking, they are mix made of a human and an armed vehicle, since they hold heavy weapons and armor. The following are the basic visual properties of such a hero (it is important to note that the brutality is gender independent, and although many such characters are men, nobody has forbidden you from creating a strong woman protagonist):

- Figures with no acute angles or rounded corners, but ones that are roughed down
- Strong legs
- Heavy feet to lean on the ground reliably
- Big hands with tenacious fingers to hold weapons and other objects
- Wide chest with ram-like powerful shoulders that are bigger than the legs
- Normal head with mid-sized forehead and a big low jaw
- Naked big eyes

It is pretty apparent that the extreme position on the scale is too categorical a benchmark to follow, whereas in most cases, nobody needs super cute or extremely scary characters. Something more universal is a mix of different properties, which is far more expressive. It is interesting that, as a rule, designs of a protagonist are situated between cuteness and brutality, so the character is anatomically adapted to make complex actions: move fast, climb ladders, fight, among others, and at the same time being pretty attractive.

Avoiding the uncanny valley

Did you note that, on the scale, there is a mark named **Human likeness**, which is placed after the brutality? What is surprising is that it is closer to the scary section than the pleasant cute one. Why does the realistic look of a human being have scary connotations? The answer is interesting. We, as humans, are very familiar with the visual appearance of people around us. Our vision knows everything about natural proportions and other graphic features. All these properties are thoroughly learned through everyday experiences of communication with real people. Since it is very easy to sense a catch or when a figure is pretending to be real, it must be ideally crafted to look natural. Any minor mistake would be easily noticed by viewers.

Moreover, the brain apparently does not particularly say that, for example, the arms are too short for a figure of a specific height or the mouth is too big. It simply transfers a generalized signal that something is wrong. In addition, by looking at somebody's image, we try to read their emotions by using empathy that helps us to determine the emotional state of another human and predict the possible intentions. Now, imagine a situation: there is a character, which is pretty realistic by basic attributes, but subconsciously, we feel that something is wrong, not knowing the actual reason. The effect is stronger if the character is moving and his motility is not perfectly realistic. The empathy system experiences some troubles. As a result, we sense that in front of us is a strange person whose image and behavior is a little bizarre, so it is better to be on the alert. Such a sensation confuses us and the emotions received are not pleasant and comfortable, although they are not very strong and long termed. They mostly consist of distaste, rather than fear.

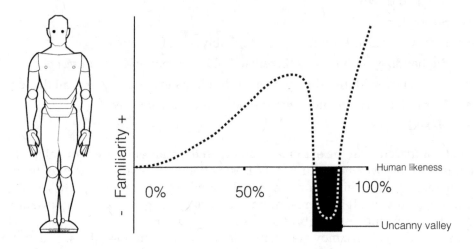

This effect is known as the **uncanny valley** hypothesis. The name is taken from a description of a graph, showing a relationship between human likeness of various humanoid images and the emotional reaction of the audience to their look. Normally, the emotional response is positive and it increases with the degree of visual likeness. The values are proportional, and suddenly when the likeness is high enough (around 70 percent), but not yet equal to 100 percent, the response abruptly falls down, forming a valley on the graph. There are negative reactions gathered in the valley, which is why it was called uncanny. The audience will only change its mind and begin to have positive feelings when the degree of human likeness approaches somewhere close to 100 percent. The theory was developed by Japanese roboticist *Masahiro Mori* in 1970. He researched the emotional impact of humanoid robots on people.

There are several theories about the origin of the uncanny valley. For example, some opine that it is caused by an ancient alarm system that keeps us away from bizarre strangers, giving us a cue that they were hiding something. Their peculiar look could mean that they had some form of dangerous diseases, and unusual behavior may indicate that their intentions were unclear and possibly dangerous too. So, the theory is based on odd and confusing feelings, which are caused by some sort of uncertainty. There are many contradictory sensations and a person feels trapped. In folklore and popular culture, such experiences are connected with bewitched persons, the walking dead, humanoid aliens, revived mannequins, or statues.

Despite the uncanny valley primarily described as the human perception of robots, it can be effectively applied to other media. May be you empirically formulated this theory while having some weird experience when watching CGI animations, which utilize realistic portrays of human beings. 3D models are so well crafted that you see individual pores on the characters' skin and the movements are realistic because they are provided by accurate motion capture technology, so you notice every tiny inconsistency. It is hard as authors try to convince the audience that the picture is equal to live action; this does not work. Moreover, the characters look a little bit repulsive. Many illustrators, animators, and toy designers know about this factor, therefore, they always try to rethink human proportions. Recall all of Pixar's characters, they are all far away from the uncanny valley, even from a small uncanny pit. My favorite example is *Carl Fredricksen* from the animated feature *Up*. This was a very nontrivial task to make an old person look cute, but they successfully did it, giving it a big square head, a small body, and short arms, which are not close to real human anatomy. Apparently, this is why in *James Cameron's* movie *Avatar*, a special stylization was used for the *Na'vi* characters—which were fully CGI and animated using advanced motion captures—by giving them different proportions such as cat-like eyes and unusual skin color; the crew defeated the uncanny valley.

Now you know that a realistic proportion is a tricky business. You can use it only if the quality of the image and animation is almost ideal. In other cases, it is always better to break the realistic anatomical dimensions and apply hypertrophic characteristics to some features or details. As a rule, protagonists in games are vertically compressed, have big heads, short torsos, noticeable feet (heavy shoes), and so on. Besides the artistic expressiveness, there is a practical reason for nonrealistic look being preferable: a figure with natural proportions is too high to depict fully. You need to scale it down to fit the game world. So all its tiny details disappear from the scene, and as results, you get a small and skinny character. This is especially topical for platformer games, as characters are displayed sideways.

Creating characters

3PNTR, the protagonist in our game, should run and jump and carry an improvised gun, since his anatomy must correspond to the given tasks. The legs and arms should be long enough, but he also needs to be cute; as long as the style of the game is rather comical than realistic. So, his head is big and looks like a glass blister and the eyes are dots, placed far apart from each other. As shown in the following figure, a funny characteristic of his head is that it hides a little bit in the body, like in a turret. Behind the back is a cylindrical tank for paint, connected to the gun with a hose.

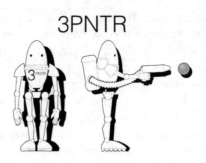

The tank can change its color, showing the type of paint inside. Alternatively, it can have special windows on each side, but that can be difficult to implement because of animation. However, you give the tank a specific tint using code. The character carries the number **3** on his chest as it is his individual index—he is the third robotic painter.

All enemies are utilitarian robotic devices that are used in construction, few of them are humanoids. Some of them cannot even move and play the role of fencing or support. Nevertheless, they have eyes and an electronic brain, and can attack the protagonist with a painful electric discharge. A movable enemy tries to follow and attack the protagonist. The following figure shows various types of enemies:

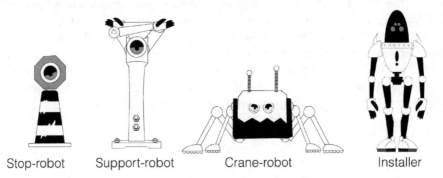

Stop-robot   Support-robot   Crane-robot   Installer

The following is the short list of enemies:

- **Stop robot**: It is a static creature that looks like a striped pole with the **Stop** warning sign and plays the role of an obstacle.

- **Support robot**: It is a creature that cannot move and plays the role of an obstacle. It supports a platform above, so by removing such a robot from the scene, the player can also demolish some parts of the level.

- **Crane robot**: It can move horizontally and looks like a crab, walking on four legs.

- **Welder**: It is a dangerous robot that operates like the crane robot, but also has a scorpion-like tail with an electrode at its end. It cripples the protagonist stronger than the previous mentioned robots.

- **Installer**: It has humanoid anatomy, so it moves fast and in every direction. It follows the main character and is harder to escape.

- **Virus-affected CPU queen**: It is the final boss of the game.

Recall the negative feedback paradigm? It tells the player that enemies become stronger as the game progresses and acts like a training that player get while playing. Only Stop robots and Support robots first appear, followed by Crane robots, and finally come the Welders and Installers. It is important to note that not only does the strength of a particular opponent play a major role but also the number of opponents. A Support robot can be weaker than the protagonist, but three of them fighting together are much stronger. So, by introducing new types of robots and increasing their numbers on the screen, a game balance can be adjusted to a specific difficulty level.

It is also important to not forget the asymmetrical balance: opponents should not be exactly equal to the protagonist. Some of them should move slower, but have stronger weapons, while some others can run quickly, but their armor is stronger, and so on. This how fighting sequences should be made to ensure that they are more catchy, because players must use different tactics to attain victory. Apparently, it is hard to develop an accurate and universal formula that can help to calculate the distribution of a character's features; thus, many real playtests are needed to ensure that the values are correct.

Also, it is difficult to create a new design and look for each new type of enemy. But there is a simple trick that many developers use: regular enemy characters can be declared as more stronger units by saying that they are *armored*. In this case, only some minor changes in their image are made to designate that they are wearing some armor.

Earning bonuses and pitfalls

The key bonus type is the **color bubble**, which is a portion of a specific-colored paint the player can use for one shot. The character can carry only one bubble at a time, so by default, he cannot repeat the action. To resolve the puzzles, the player needs to choose bubbles carefully. There are two types of color bubbles: **one-off** and **renewable**. In the first case, the character can take a bubble only once; in the second case, above the bubble, there is a pipe from which a new bubble periodically drips, as shown in the following figure:

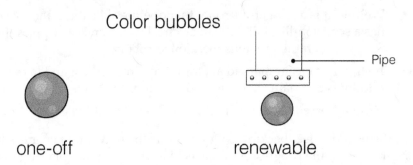

Another type of bonus is the accumulator that rewards the protagonist with some amount of energy. In other words, it is increases the level of health. Finally, there is a rare and unique bonus in the game, *blueprint fragment*, a collectible item that should be placed by you in those sections of a level that are difficult to access. By collecting most of them, the player can get a special reward, for example, a solution on how to defeat the final boss.

The following figure shows the effect of a pitfall on a character:

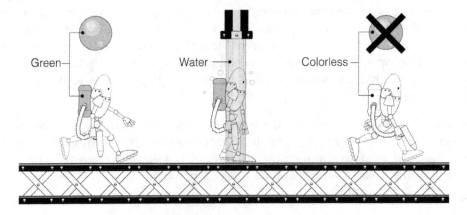

Pitfalls are based on water: pipes with rushing water (some push the water with pauses, others run continuously). Their craftiness can be described by the fact that they flush out all the paint the character has. If he is caught in the rain of water drops, he cannot take a shot. Nevertheless, sometimes water-based elements can be useful. For example, the player can lure a hostile robot such as the Welder and easily disable it.

Introducing triggers

In the game, there are special elements that change the states of specific objects and switch them on and off. They are called **triggers**. They can have a dozen applications: they may turn on a lift or turn off water in the pipes. The following figure shows examples of triggers:

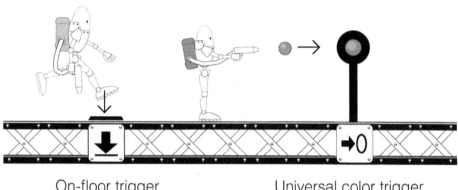

On-floor trigger   Universal color trigger.

The following are the basic variations of triggers:

- **On-floor trigger**: It is activated when somebody steps on it and can be either the protagonist or any other robot.

- **Universal color trigger**: It responds to a shot that hits its surface. The trigger is indifferent to the color of the shot. The fact that a bubble has touched the spot is more important.

- **Specific color trigger**: This trigger reacts to shots made of a specific color: red, green, and so one. This can be tricky.

Fighting with enemies

3PNTR cannot disable other robots with a direct attack because his gun is only an airbrush. He also cannot jump on enemies like Mario does; therefore, he used tricks to defeat his opponents. First, he can jump on other robots from above, breaking them by his weight. To do this, the player should find a pit inside the platform or create it by using the matching function. Another trick is to generate the pit above an enemy or to demolish some supports. Some physics-based puzzles also help to destroy the opponents.

Parallax scrolling

As it was mentioned in *Chapter 1*, *Starting the Game*, continuous backgrounds and foregrounds for games are created using small images tiled together, creating an illusion of a very long graphic strip. The more pieces the game has, the more varied is the appearance of the strip. Although this is only a compilation of flat images, an artistic illusion of 3D space can be created to divide the scenery by individual layers, changing their position at various speeds. The foreground will move normally, the further ones will be slower and the most distant will almost stand still. Such a visual scene convinces the viewer that it has depth, interpreting it as the natural physical phenomenon known as **parallax**. It characterizes the apparent alteration of a visible object's position against a far background when viewers changes their location. The closest objects change their position very noticeably (in other words, they have a pretty big parallax), but the distant ones alternate only a bit (small parallax). The most spectacular and vivid example of parallax in action can be observed from a window of a moving car: the landscape flows irregularly; objects on roadsides, such as bushes and utility poles, move quickly; more distant elements, such as houses and trees, move slower; and hills or mountains on the horizon are snail like, but the sky looks like a fixed image. By moving in the car, viewers change their position constantly. Being in such a state enables them to see the incessant demonstration of parallax. The following figure shows a character in motion who faces parallax:

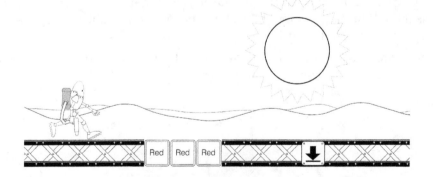

The artificial graphic landscapes can utilize the same principle to look convincing. For the first time such an idea was adapted by traditional animators. As you know, the drawn animation was based on the layer system: moving pictures were created on stacked transparent cells (sheets made of celluloid), which are as flat as ream. But, the transparent layers were distributed at some distance between each other and arranged in an improvised cabinet, and so *multiplane camera* was invented. *Walt Disney* patented the device in 1940. It helped to simulate the behavior of real-world scenery because all components have different distances from the camera lens and react accordingly to the natural parallax formula. It was a model of three-dimensional landscape with depth based on separate flat images. The first cartoon that demonstrated the spectacular advantages of such system was *The Old Mill* produced by *Disney* in 1937. The method was immortalized in the same year when *Snow White and the Seven Dwarfs* released.

The following image shows a parallax layout of a game scene:

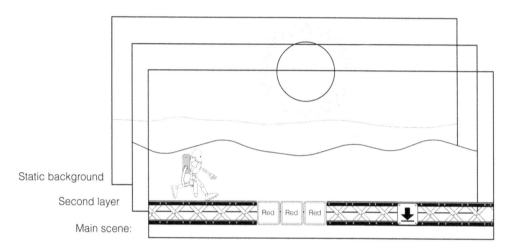

2D games use the same approach to create the illusion of depth. Of course, they have no cabinet for layers, but the landscape is fully constructed of flat images, which have specific rules to determine their speed. One of the early examples of scrolling parallax can be found in the game *Jump Bug* published by *Rock-Ola* in 1981. It featured a solid main scene that scrolls, a fixed night sky with some stars, and slowly moving clouds. This can be read as an attempt to illustrate the depth of a virtual scenery. A year later, the game *Moon Patrol* was developed by *Irem*, in which the scrolling parallax was implemented in full form. The game had three moving layers that vividly simulated the distance between them.

Commonly, the scrolling parallax in games is calculated by eye, without any conceptual formulas, because nobody knows the exact z position of objects in the background, allowing them to have any given speed (that is, in a case it looks persuasive enough). There is only one general rule: counting from the main scene, each next layer should be slower than the previous one. For instance, you give the main scene speed that is equal to a variable called *v*, the next layer should be *v x 0.4*, followed by *v x 0.2*, and so on. Your own taste forms the picture.

The following figure shows the calculation of a scrolling parallax:

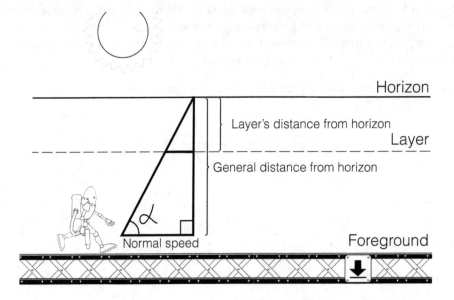

But there is another way that is special for captious persons, a special formula that can be written. All you need to do is choose the distance to the horizon in your game scene (in the real world, this value is nearly equal to 5 kilometers, but you are most likely to choose something in pixels). At this distance, objects have no apparent alteration, that is, a vanishing point. Then, using the normal speed of the main scene, a right triangle can be constructed. It helps to calculate the speed of each layer, depending on its distance from the horizon (this value should be defined by you manually). All you need to do is determine the angle between the hypotenuse and the adjacent side using the arctangent function. Next, a simple trigonometric formula will help you to figure out specific speed properties of any remote object.

To the effect of elements' speed, there is an interesting phenomenon: if you use in the background a regular-designed continuous element, consisting of something that looks like a geometric ornament with identical images, and whose speed is high enough, you will see what is called the **wagon-wheel effect**.

Instead of moving from right to left, as it was intended, the element will begin to move backward! It is terrific! Why? All the variables are correct! It can drive you crazy! Don't worry, this is not the fault of the game engine, but only a result of a strong optical illusion. Recall a fast-moving car that is shot on camera; in this case, it has rims with spokes. The movement of the wheels looks very odd, that is, the rims and tires rotate normally, but the spokes move backward. Coaches and wagons, whose wheels rotate in the opposite direction, are even better illustrations of the illusion; several movies depict this phenomenon, making us familiar with it. The illusion is based on the fact that despite an element moving with the correct vector of speed, it suddenly appears in the unpredictable positions on the screen. The following is a figure showing the wagon-wheel effect:

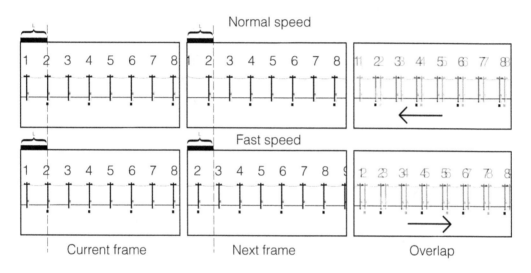

As you can see, there is a row of identical utility poles in the background, but for descriptive reasons, I marked odd poles with a dot. If the row moves at a slow speed, total time is normal: each pole successively passes the grid, drawing a trajectory with phases that stay pretty tight. What if the speed is wrong, that is, it is higher than the specified threshold? As you can see, the distance between phases is increased, each individual pole leaves the screen very quickly, but because the objects are so identical, a viewer begins to mistake one pole with the next one, which is displayed to the right. In this case, the human visual system makes an incorrect judgment about the direction of the movement (don't blame it, because the task is truly hard) and the poles suddenly begin to move backward. The phenomenon can be defeated easily: the speed should be changed so there will be no contradiction between the general frequency and the frequency of the objects appearing on the screen.

It is noteworthy that besides the parallax itself, there is another distinction that can increase the illusion of the third dimension in your game: **aerial** (or atmospheric) **perspective**. Even on a bright sunny day, distant objects look different than those nearby. There are many particles in the air: dust, water vapor, and so on; together they optically affect the rays of light, which transfers the information about visual properties of a particular element of a landscape. Figuratively speaking, there is a little *noise* in transmission. As a rule, objects that are far away have less contrast, are less saturated, the blue channel dominates their color spectrum, and their contour and details are blurry. The last feature is most important; an imitation of the field's depth not only looks great and natural but also creates a good contrast between the background (which is blurry) and the sharp main scene. This increases the expressiveness of the main character. If for the sake of the graphic style, you cannot make a blurry background (for example, if the graphic style is vector based and flat), use only colors and make them less saturated.

Sometimes, game developers also use a special layer placed between the main scene and a player called the **foreground**. Usually, it is passive and static. It does not comprise any important game scene components and only adds decorative value that creates special moods and increases the sense of the depth in a scene. Foregrounds are commonly blurred because they simulate a situation when objects that are too close to the viewers are out of focus. The typical subjects are grass, foliage, wires, and so on. The speed of these layers is always faster than the main scene, because they are closer to a player. There is also a unique feature: a scene depicted through a blurred foreground creates the sensation of peeping, as if somebody is looking at the situation on the screen from an ambush. A good inspiration source is *Limbo*, a game in which blurry and noisy layers of game scenes create profound feelings.

Starting an animation

An animation in case of games, which uses characters to drive the story is not a simple tool to decorate a game scene and to make it attractive, but it is a way to express the game mechanics. A character moves his legs not because it looks realistic and nice but because this demonstrates the idea that the character can walk as do ordinary creatures on the surface of the Earth. In other words, he obeys certain rules familiar to the player. Otherwise, the player has to invent new interpretations of what he is looking at. For instance, there is a character whose graphic representation has legs, but there is no walking animation sequence in the game, causing the legs to appear still. So, the character's movement on the game board can be read as sliding or floating rather than as walking. This is a problem because such a process has its own physical features in the real world, which differs from normal pedestrianism.

For example, the sliding implies longer and more uncontrolled deceleration, and the floating can be interpreted as the behavior of ghosts. So, the player expects the character to penetrate walls and other types of obstacles and other properties from the game. As you can see, the animation can give the player the right description of what the character can or cannot to do.

The animation for 2D is not a very complicated task when it comes to illustrating the basic phases of motion, not creating artistic dramatic scenes, which need some stage feeling and well-balanced directing. Partially, the phases are pretty mechanical and can be easily descried by geometric trajectories. I said *partially* because to create real magic, you need to enrich the mechanical skeleton with some personal touches and original details, which make the animated characters look truly alive. To find such elements, you need to become very observant and sensitive, look at the world around you, try to notice how people and animals move, and perceive how they walk in different situations and when affected by various conditions. For instance, have you ever noticed that a person carrying a heavy bag always tilts his head in the direction opposing the arm holding the bag? Another good example is when humans step forward with their foot, they usually lift up their toes. Some birds move differently on the ground: pigeons walk by taking tiny steps, almost like humans do, but sparrows jump, they move their short legs in parallel. Cats have many types of gaits and so do horses. So, all of them have some unique detail. It is good to have a notebook (or a text file) to note all your interesting observations. Before planning an animation sequence, try to imitate the specified action by yourself, for example, take a few steps and note all the peculiarities.

Of course, some additional reading can help you dramatically. There are many useful books about animation. One of my favorite ones is *The Animator's Survival Kit* written by *Richard Williams*, who directed the animation process on the famous masterpiece *Who Framed Roger Rabbit* by *Robert Zemeckis*. The book includes a lot of helpful information and many wonderful illustrations.

Before starting the animation process, you should create a list of all actions your character will do. This can help you plan your efforts in advance. In this particular case, the game will use the following types of basic animated sequences:

* Standby
* Walking/running cycle
* Jumping
* Shooting
* Concussion

Recall from *Chapter 1, Starting the Game*, games store animations in special sprite sheets files, which consist of frames collected together in one big image. This is a little tricky because it requires an additional phase in the production of the animation: you first create a motion sequence, then export all frames as individual images, and finally arrange them in one file. Remember that there are special tools for working with sprite sheets such as **TexturePacker** that help collect files and have some useful extra abilities. Nevertheless, you can manage everything by using Adobe Flash and Adobe Illustrator. The following figure demonstrates graphic elements that the protagonist consists of:

Sprite elements

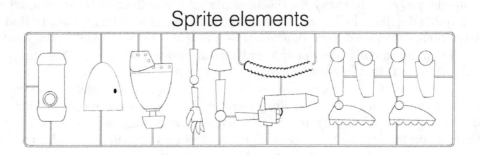

The workflow begins in Adobe Illustrator using which a game character is developed. In an ideal case, the artwork is totally vector based and does not include any complicated elements such as special opacity modes for shapes (*Screen, Multiply, Overlay,* and so on), meshes, and raster-based effects; therefore, it can be easily transferred to Adobe Flash via a clipboard. It is better to group relative elements together, for instance, all elements of a head should be grouped together. If the artwork is made of raster effects, textures, and so on, it is better to divide the character into individual moving parts, such as legs, arms, and palms, and export each of them as separate PNG files (slices can help to make this).

In Adobe Flash, the character should be placed in the main scene. Avoid converting it inside symbols, especially Movieclips, because they utilize their own timeline, which cannot be seen for the *Export* function. The graphic symbols are safe, but the length of the main timeline must be equal to that of the symbol's timeline. The dimensions of the movie scene have to be identical to those of the animation frame you've chosen before. By default, all graphic elements of the character are situated on a single graphic layer, they should be separated. The rule is quite simple: each moving part has to be turned into a graphic symbol and should have its own layer. The process can be easily automated: simply convert the parts into symbols and click on **Separate image to layers** in the context menu. The application will lay out the elements on the layers, not changing their positions on the screen.

Once the animation is ready, carefully tested, and has an attractive look, the frames can be exported as separate PNG files via **File | Export Movie...**. After that, they can be used to form a sprite sheet. In Adobe Illustrator, you create a document using a canvas of specified dimensions; the frames are imported inside it (by **drag & drop**). It is important to note that the images should be linked, not embedded. Generally, Adobe Illustrator collects imported files in a stack because it does not know where each of them must be set, so you need to arrange them in the correct order. The final document is now ready for export and the sprite sheet can be easily generated by navigating to **File | Save for Web & Devices**.

 If some frames are a little blurry, turn on the **Snap to Pixels** option and check the coordinates of these files. The values could be fractional.

In an exceptional case, either Adobe Flash or Adobe Illustrator alone can be used to work on sprite sheets. Adobe Illustrator has no helpful tool to create animations, but each frame can be created manually and placed on individual layers. By rule of thumb, all you need to do is move each detail in an animated image. The process can be controlled using test SWF files, which can be generated via the **Save for Web & Devices** window (don't forget about the **Layers to SWF frames** option). As far as the animation is successfully tested and works well, images inside the AI document can be rearranged into a sprite sheet. Adobe Flash can be used for the purposes of illustrations, animation development, and sprite sheet export. Its drawing vector tools are powerful enough to create pretty complicated images, but they have their own individualities. So, it takes some time to get accustomed to.

Frames

The animation (and motion pictures as a whole) is based on the human ability to perceive the so called **apparent motion**. It is not based on the real continuous movement of an object, which should exist on each point of the motion trajectory, but on the phase positions of an object, which exist only on the extreme positions of the trajectory. Everything in between is imagined by the brain (when the visual system creates the in betweens at wrong positions, illusions such as the wagon-wheel effect occurs). A good example of the apparent motion is the rail crossing semaphore with two alternately flashing lamps. The signal may look like lights moving left and right, although in reality, there is no physical movement of the lamps. Recall any neon sign with, for example, moving chains of lamps or animated flipping books. Thence, it is quite easy to convince a person that something is moving because the vision system is very dubious and always tries to catch clues that something changes its positions.

Vilayanur S. Ramachandran and *Stuart M. Anstis* in their article *The Perception of Apparent Motion*, published in *Scientific American* (*June, 1986, Vol. 254, No. 6*), gave the following pictorial explanation of the apparent motion's origin:

> *"In the real world anything that moves is a potential predator or prey. Hence being able to quickly detect motion and determine what moved, and in what way, is crucial for survival. For example, the ability to see apparent motion widely separated images may be particularly important when detecting the motion of animals that are seen intermittently, as when they move behind a screen of foliage or a tree trunk."*

The following figure shows how apparent motion works:

Apparent motion:

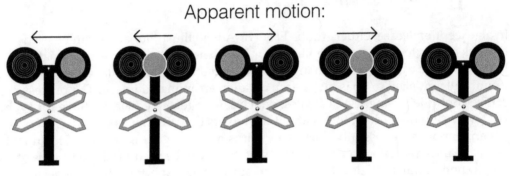

Imaginary in between   Imaginary in between

The **phi** phenomenon, which was defined by psychologist *Max Wertheimer* in 1912 and later became the basis for the cinema theory, is a special case of the apparent motion and it directly describes the principle of motion pictures: a series of separate still images with some common elements appearing rapidly creates an illusion of complex motion. In other words, by showing individual frames with specific frequency, it is possible to fill them with breath and give them life. The sprite animation in games is based on phi phenomenon as well. Game engines show separate frames in continuous succession, but players perceive it like a live scene. Hence, to create an illusion of motion on the screen, you need several main phases and the correct frequency, which is very important because the convincing of the phi phenomenon is directly related with the time between phases. The illusion can be totally broken if the frequency is too low. For example, when the length of time between frames becomes longer then 500 ms, it is more likely for images to be interpreted as individual pictures rather than part of a single scene.

The traditional frame rate for motions pictures, which appeared with the introduction of the sound cinema, is 24 unique frames per second (the projection frame can be higher, 48 FPS or 72 FPS, which means that each unique frame is shown twice or thrice). There are many debates about this value, but unquestionably, it gives the familiar "cinema experience," which looks more genuine than pictures shot on video cameras; video cameras utilize higher frequencies. You can use 24 FPS for your animation. The result will be spectacular and very smooth, and all gestures will be very fluent. But, on the other hand, it will require more efforts on animation development (mainly on its fine tuning) and sprite sheets files will be larger. If everything is critical to your project, meet the requirements half way: reduce the frame to 12 FPS. For a long time, many traditional animated masterpieces were "shooting on twos." Despite the fact that such animation features were played at the normal cinema speed, in reality, the unique frames were burned on film twice. So, there were only 12 unique images per second, but they were displayed longer to fit the 24-FPS format. This was possible because 12 frames is nearly minimum comfort frame rate to perceive motion. Although it is not ideal, it is considered pretty satisfactory.

Walking cycle for protagonist

This is a corner stone of game animation. A general action is a character walking or running. The perception of game dynamics directly depends on its quality. If you are not sure of your skills or you do not have enough time for such a sequence, it is better to not use animation that is not made properly or looks sloppy, but to improvise instead. A character can use wheels to move, which are easier to animate, even with code. For example, a robot can be equipped with caterpillar wheels instead of legs, and a humanoid may utilize a small car, bike, or something like a Segway PT. Another option is a graphic: it is obvious that more realistic, detailed, and well-crafted graphics need animation of high quality, so if you have no opportunity but to achieve such a level, it's better to simplify the graphic look of the game. For example, convert the graphic to a pixelated 8-bit form, giving it a retro touch. Old games did not feature complicated animation, usually there were only few basic frames in the walking animation.

To plan the walking cycle sequence right, you should start with the speed of character moving on the screen. It is better to determine such value using game mechanics and not animation. Therefore, a few prototypes can be created to choose the correct speed of the elements. Make some hard playtests and find out the most effective and expressive value. After that, you will know how many pixels the character covers in a specific period of time. This value influences the size of one particular step your character makes.

To calculate this length, you need to take the speed of movement and multiply it with the duration of one step. For example, the speed is equal to 20 pixels per second, but one step lasts for half a second. So, the distance between the extreme positions of the character's heel and toe should be 10 pixels. If the size of the step is connected with the speed properly, the character moves naturally and by himself (he is not affected by an external force). His legs do not slide by the surface, but push off like levers. Until one leg is lifted, the support leg should stay at the point it was put before without any small offset. Despite the leg moving backward in the animation sequence, at the scene, the speed of the character must compensate that motion (speed vectors are opposite), creating an illusion that the foot makes solid contact with the ground.

It is worth mentioning that you are free to choose the frequency of steps and everything depends on the character's anatomy and temper. The same distance can be covered with one big step or five tiny ones. In the first case, the character is most likely to be tall with long legs, and in the second case, it is probably a small creature with short legs and a fussy temper.

Now let's start the animation workflow. The character's illustration has been imported in Adobe Flash and has been separated into layers; everything is ready for work. Traditional animators used frame-by-frame methods to animate characters, drawing each new frame from scratch. But we can use the advantages of automatic interpolation provided by **Motion Tween**. You need to create only key frames that store the important phases of motion. All transitional frames are generated automatically. The following figure shows the basic phases of the protagonist's walking cycle:

Basic phases

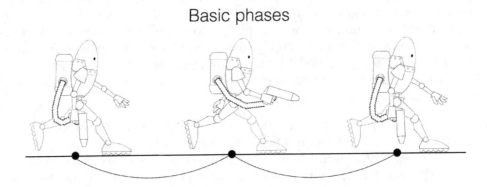

The walking cycle consists of two equal parts—step sequences for each leg—so at least there should be three positions for key frames on the timeline. Let's call them the **main phases**. The first main phase includes a posture: when the character's right leg is in front, the right foot is in contact with the surface. This is the beginning of a step sequence for the left leg, which starts to move forward. The second main phase is opposite to the first one: the left leg is now in front and has contact. The third main phase is identical to the first one (it is created by duplicating key frames) and is needed to create a proper arc for interpolation between the second and first main phases. To make an important remark, the last frame should be rejected after the export procedure because it is identical to the first frame of the sequence; if this is not the case, the sprite sheet will have an unnecessary frozen section and the walking cycle will not be smooth. In other words, if you have 11 frames in the sequence, the first main phase is placed on the frames 1 and 11, the second phase is on frame 6, and after export, only ten frames will be used because frame 11 is only technical and is unnecessary. To throw such a frame automatically, you can use the graphic symbol for your animation. Place it on the main scene, but reduce the length of the main timeline by one (the graphic symbol will have 11 frames, but the main scene's timeline will show only 10). Primarily, you need to create the first main phase, arranging parts of the character in the correct pose. The following basic principles can help you with this captious job:

- **Tilt of the figure**: It is commonly known that walking can be characterized as **controlled falling**, but *falling* is something that was moved from equilibrium, so the position of the character will not be stable. Like a falling tree, it must tilt in the direction of movement (tilting in the opposing direction is usually associated with slipping on ice). The degree of the tilt depends on speed. When a character walks slowly and on an even keel, the angle is small. When he rushes or is running very quickly, the angle is pretty big.

- **Pose contrast**: It is one of the ways to express a motion vividly. To use this contrast based on opposite moves, there must a general gesture and a background gesture, which is less active. If you lift the right hand and move it forward, the left hand will move backward. The viewer feels the difference between these motions and the sum of impressions is bigger. Like in mathematics, the difference between opposing numbers (1 and -1 for instance) is greater than that between the number and zero (1 and 0). Moreover, the pose contrast is natural for a human walking cycle. I'm talking about the behavior of arms, they always move in opposition to legs: if the right foot is in front, the right arm is behind. This is particularly noticeable when a gait is rapid and the arms are more involved. Try for yourself to break that rule, walk in a room, take large firm steps, and attempt to swing your arms parallel to feet. This will need some additional attention and control and will look very weird. Hence, always try to illustrate an individual move by moving other parts of the image in the opposite direction.

- **Contact**: Remember that the ground is a surface, and in most cases, it is solid and so part of the character cannot penetrate it. You have to draw a line that will symbolize the ground level (this can be done using guides). Try to avoid situations in which a foot or other elements cross the line. In other cases, it can be described as "walking in a pastry"—the character caves in and slips. Another important thing about contact with the ground is the convincing expression of **figure support**. The viewer should be sure that the character really stands on the ground using its legs and is not simply floating in the air, swinging his legs. Thus, always illustrate that the character has mass and when the foot touches the ground, it is affected by this mass and it supports the entire figure.

Using these principles, you can create the starting point for the walking cycle. At its base, the second main phase can be easily generated. You only have to change the legs and arms of the character. As mentioned before, the third main phase is created upon duplicating the first one. The early draft of animation is now ready. If the motion tweens work properly, the character begins to walk. Of course, the result is far from ideal. It is too mechanical and there are many visible bugs; nevertheless, it can be used for a preview purpose. You should take such frames, create the sprite sheet, and test the character inside the game world, regardless of minor demerits that can be fixed later. The following figure shows the intermediate phases of the protagonist's motion:

Intermediate phases

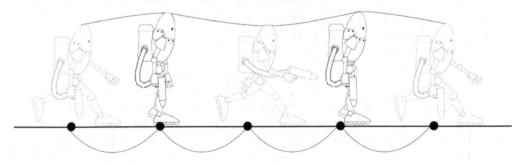

Once the draft animation fits naturally into the game, you can continue to work on the walking cycle. The sequence can be enriched by additional phases of motion placed between the main phases.

The following additional rules can help you:

- **Arcs**: The trajectories in the walking cycle are not straight lines, all elements moved along curved paths. The height of the character is not constant. The legs work like levers and change angles relative to the pelvis at all times. The height is at maximum when the leg is completely straightened; in other cases, the pelvis and the whole body moves downward. Thus, the figure of the character always fluctuates—it moves up and down. The faster the character walks, the stronger the visual wavering is.

- **Flexibility and delay**: The character, even when it is a robot, is not a solid object such as a rock or bronze statue. It consists of individual parts connected together, each joint gives the figure some range of freedom, and the body is flexible and bounces when the figure walks. This means that impacts on its parts are irregular, some of them react fast, while others react with a slight delay. Everything depends on their mass, type of joint, and the distance to the point of application. There is an obvious example from the real world: if you move a cup with a tea bag inside fast enough, the paper label attached to the tea bag with a thread will lag behind. When you stop, the label will stop a little later. By introducing such behavior in the animation, you can increase the artistic expression of the character, making it look more complex and alive.

- **Recoil**: Objects don't stop without opposing actions.

New phases, let's call them **intermediate**, should include a posture. When one of the character's legs is at a straight angle to the ground, the arms are almost parallel to the body and the head is in the highest position.

By testing and approving the animation with intermediate phases, you can finally switch to the fine-tuning of the walking sequence. Some elements need manual adjusting. So, for some parts, such the feet and palms, as many key frames as possible should be created. The most tricky part is, of course, the feet because they need to follow the level of the ground.

To give the animation an ideal look, you can use some advanced methods. First, recall that the walking cycle is always unique. The next step has some minor differences, the character's walk should not be too uniform. If it is technically possible, it is good to have alternative frames for specific phases. They can have some tiny differences in the basic frame: another angle for the foot, the character offsets his eyes, and so on. The game can randomly choose between the basic frame or its alternative version; therefore, the final animation may look very natural because the motion is not monotonous.

Another way to increase the attractiveness is to add some extra sequences to illustrate when the character begins to walk or stops moving. By default, the game uses a sharp switch between the characters, that is, from the standby mode to walking or vice versa. This is not a big problem, a player usually doesn't notice such things, but animation with smoother transitions between states is perceived more professional. Such tiny details increase the overall level of visual quality. The most important sequence is the stopping process. This is because in the real world, the character would have some amount of kinetic energy and his body would not stop immediately because of inertia. So, it is very likely that an object that is suddenly stopped expresses some signs of *insubordination* to the new circumstances. The object would tilt a little forward and then recoil, followed by a final attempt to move forward; this would last for a short period of time, till the object reaches quiescence. In case of a character, before he finally stops, the body tilts forward, the arms continue to move straight, and he almost falls. Finally, he recoils backward, followed by a small fluctuation, and the sequence is over.

Walking cycle animation for enemies

Nonhumanoid characters in the game moves like crabs: sideways and using four legs. The principle is simple, at least two of the legs (diagonally opposite) should touch the ground, otherwise the robot falls on his belly. The following figure shows the walking cycle animation for the enemies:

Jumping and shooting animation

Besides the fact that jumping is a complex process, its animation can be very simple. Based on the apparent motion phenomenon, only the key phases of the process are needed. The most important one is the preparation sequence. You need to convince the audience that the character has accumulated enough amounts of potential energy before the jump. Like a spring, he must illustrate tight compression. As shown in the following figure, give a small pause to demonstrate the pose and release, thereafter rushing the figure into the air. When the character soars, only a phase image can be used. The final section is landing. It should also express the fact that the figure has weight and flexibility.

Jumping

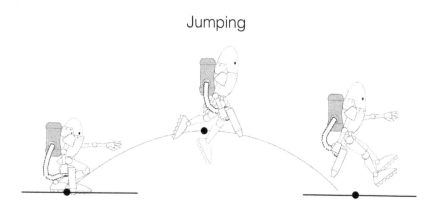

In general, the shooting sequence requires only one to be involved. The character lifts it up, aims, and shoots. The gun demonstrates a slight recoil and that is it. The best result can give the character the ability to run and aim simultaneously. It looks stunning, but it requires additional frames in the animation sheet.

Programming animation

Besides some artistic advantages, the sprite animation is not ideal: it is hard to readjust or rearrange quickly, it can take some memory resource, and it is not flexible enough. Therefore, in some situations, it is much more efficient to program some animations by code. The most obvious example is the wheels of a vehicle used in a game: nobody uses special frame-by-frame animation to rotate them, a simple code is used instead. Even characters can be animated using such methods; of course it is pretty hard, but it is possible (recall the description of a Spine animation editor from *Chapter 1, Starting the Game*). By using code, you control the general properties of an image: coordinates, scale, rotation angle, opacity, and even hue. So many things can be created.

Usually, most of the special effects in games are programmed. The most visual example is, of course, the simulation of smoke. To develop good smoke, only one small sprite is needed, containing an image of one smoke curl. A game should take such a curl, display it, and begin to move up constantly, rotating and increasing its dimension while its opacity value is decreasing. The life cycle of the curl looks simple: appear, fly up, and disappear. There should be dozens of such elements, each of them born with some random properties as the initial size, the direction of rotation, and opacity. By tuning the behavior of the curls and playing with their graphic look (a sufficiently blurred image is considered good), a convincing simulation can be created. You also need to have passion to make it look good.

Other type of effects based on particles should be programmed as well. Among popular examples are dynamical clouds, fire, lens flare, sparkles, fireworks, flinders of objects after a hit, caustics (a pattern made on the surface of water), snow, rain, and foot prints. There are special particle engines for popular SDKs; nevertheless, in most cases, they can be developed manually. It looks like an interesting creative challenge. It is worth mentioning that the effect should not look super realistic. It all depends on the game's mood and graphic style; in most cases, it only needs to express an essential idea such as as open fire or falling snow.

In *3robopainter*, there are several programmed animations:

- Dust clouds at the moment of landing on a platform. Some sort of smoke algorithm with a very short life cycle can be used.

- Bubble rotation after the protagonist has made a shot.

- The effect of fallen water from a pipe. A seamless texture with a zig-zag pattern can be used. It is good to bake an image with a distorted background (sky with some clouds) in the texture to simulate the deflection of light in a waterfall

Physics-based puzzles

Some puzzles in *3robopainter* may look and operate almost like mind breaks based on real physics. But this is only a simulation based on predefined animations. The real collisions of objects are not calculated, so a special engine is not required. Most of puzzles are based on the removing of counterweights, supports, ropes, and so on as shown in the following figure:

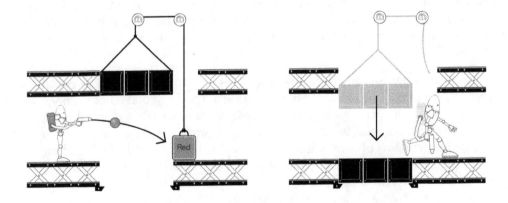

The identity of the game

In contrast to general puzzle games, a platform game is mainly character oriented. Thus, it can be illustrated in the application icon via the protagonist's image. Some sort of a portrait is needed. Alternatively, a short scene from the game can be used to show an action sequence, for instance, a character that holds a gun and shoots. It is noteworthy that sometimes instead of the main character, an antagonist can be used. This depends on the emphasis and charisma. The following figure shows the application icons for the antagonist:

Blueprints of the 3robopainter game

You can see the blueprints of all the characters in 3robopainter in the following screenshot. Primarily, there is one protagonist and several antagonists:

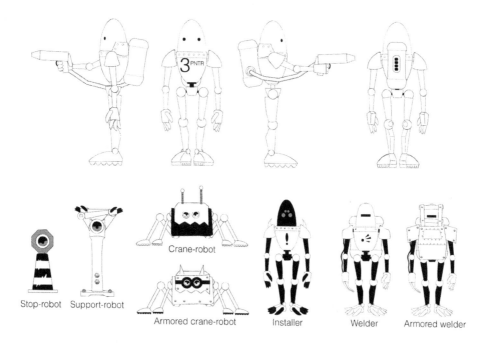

This blueprint demonstrates some fragments of game levels as shown in the following figure. All platformers are based on special modules, each one has its own properties.

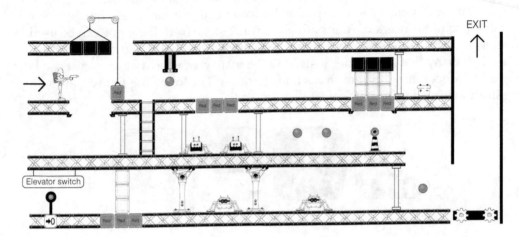

The following are the references used for this chapter:

- http://en.wikipedia.org/wiki/Super_Mario_Bros
- http://en.wikipedia.org/wiki/Donkey_Kong_(video_game)
- http://www.nytimes.com/2006/01/03/science/03cute.html?_r=0
- http://en.wikipedia.org/wiki/Uncanny_valley
- http://en.wikipedia.org/wiki/Masahiro_Mori
- http://en.wikipedia.org/wiki/Parallax
- http://web.mit.edu/invent/iow/disney.html
- http://www.youtube.com/watch?v=JZLWQiE5caE
- http://www.gamesradar.com/gamings-most-important-evolutions/?page=3
- http://en.wikipedia.org/wiki/Horizon
- http://en.wikipedia.org/wiki/Wagon-wheel_effect
- http://cbc.ucsd.edu/pdf/Percpt_Apprnt_Mot_Sci_Am.pdf
- http://en.wikipedia.org/wiki/Phi_phenomenon
- http://newempiricism.blogspot.com/2011/11/phi-phenomenon-and-half-second-gap.html
- http://en.wikipedia.org/wiki/Traditional_animation#.22Shooting_on_twos.22

Summary

As you have seen, developing a platform game is a pretty exciting task. Contrary to previous genres, we learned in this book, such games have less abstract action and operate with more pictorial content. The game lets you create a universe and settles it with characters, describing the rules of their behavior. This is a real gift for your imagination! And it is not about realism. The game universe can be based on your own principles and artistic taste. It can be cartoon like or gloomy and dark. It all depends on the mood of the story you are going to tell the players. Now, you know how to create a cute character and why you should be careful with real anatomical proportions. If the animation does not look scary, you can easily animate the protagonist and other characters.

In the next chapter, we will try to create projects with a more complex narrative and plot and talk about adventure games. They are made of multivariate story, different puzzles, and well-developed characters that can talk and even deceive the player.

7
Adventure

Traveling is one of the most memorable and exciting experiences a person can have. New discoveries, unusual details, and permanent surprises make you glad and happy. The life becomes so real and tangible. This is why adventure games will always be topical, since they let you travel in virtual worlds, evoking pleasant emotions.

Beginning of a journey

Early prerequisites of adventure games can be found in postmodernist experiments with storytelling, which took place long before modern computers were born. Once writers understood that the structure of a book was not fixed, but could be very flexible, they were given a chance to create a new type of literature: non-linear stories with several plots. Readers only needed to get some new directions to work with chapters in a book; a new map to travel a book was required.

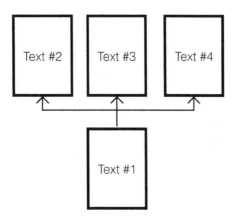

When you are talking about experimenting with a narrative, of course, the first name that comes to mind is that of the Argentine magician, a fabulous writer, *Jorge Luis Borges*. In 1941, he wrote a short story called *An Examination of the Work of Herbert Quain* where he talked about the literary heritage of a fictional novelist, who among others created a novel called *April March*. It featured a structure that can be called a tree of events. The plot can be constructed based on nine alternative beginnings that lead to a single finale. Thus, there were 13 chapters in that fictional novel with nine different versions of the beginning, three possibilities of intermediate events, and one finale. *Jorge Luis Borges* successfully demonstrated a model of a branch-based structure of the story.

Beginnings: x1 x2 x3 x4 x5 x6 x7 x8 x9

Centers: y1 y2 y3

Final

The structure of chapters in April March – novel by Jorge Luis Borges

A similar notable example is that of *Hopscotch*, a novel by another Argentine genius, *Julio Cortázar*, originally published in 1963, featuring a very original concept. In this book, a reader may find 155 chapters, which can be considered as story blocks that let him construct two different plots. The first one can be attained in the simplest way by reading a portion of the chapters (from 1 to 56). The second one needs some additional efforts because the author included a special table of instructions in the beginning of the novel where a numbered sequence of chapters are displayed. The most intriguing part is the look of the sequence because the numbers were not chosen in a linear progression but by the author's special order creating an illusion of a mysterious code: 73-1-2-116-3-84-4-71-5-81.... Therefore, the second plot is figuratively hidden and can be found only by using the special key. By reading this book, a reader will travel from chapter to chapter, collecting a piece of the story and forming a whole picture of events.

An interesting example of an experimental textual narrative is a book called *Last Love in Constantinople* (1994) by a Serbian novelist, *Milorad Pavić*, the author of *Dictionary of the Khazars*. This book was also made up of story blocks and required tarot cards instead of a special code to determine the further direction of the story and plot twists. Chapters had keys related to the cards since to construct the story you need to play the card game.

Postmodernist experiments later transformed into a separate class of fiction known as a gamebook, where readers could use their will (or good luck) to turn the direction of the stories. One of the legendary and popular names in that domain is a series of books entitled *Choose Your Own Adventure* based on a concept developed by an American writer, *Edward Packard*. In his novel, *Sugarcane Island*, he used some sort of interactive narrative, the readers had some options that lead them to different endings of the novel. The series was so popular among young readers that between 1979 to 1999, 184 titles were published by different writers; the overall number of copies printed was more than 250 millions. This is simply amazing!

How did the system work? Each page or individual chapter of a gamebook had a special section where several options were printed in a list. The reader just had to select the one that suited him the best, look at the specified number, and turn some pages to navigate to a chapter where the story continued according to his choice. The books featured multiple endings (up to a couple of dozens), had some objectives and RPG Mechanics, used a second-person perspective in their narrative, and were well illustrated. However, a wrong choice may lead a protagonist to death since they surely could be considered as prehistoric text-based adventure games.

The idea of interactive books was truly a breakthrough for its time. It changed the face of traditional media, creating a new image of a book as an object you can play with. But it also had obvious disadvantages. Navigating to a specific section of a paper book was not very convenient. It was not a smooth and instantaneous job (this is why they have a second version being republished in electronic form with real hyperlinks). Another weak point is that of easy access to any part of the book, so some elements could be intentionally peeped, spoiling the element of wonder.

The full potential of interactive stories was exposed only on computers that simply made navigating much pleasant and added some functionalities which are simply impossible on paper. It happened in the middle of 1970s when *William Crowther* used 700 lines of the FORTRAN code to create *Colossal Cave Adventure* (also known as Adventure), a game that gave the name to the individual genre, which we are talking about in this chapter. By modern-day standards, that product was pretty simple. It had no graphics and used only text, but that was not the barrier for interesting gameplay. *William Crowther* was a cave enthusiast, so he carefully reproduced some real cave labyrinths (the original game included 140 map locations), adding some portion of fantasy elements.

The player got a textual description of a location or situation, then he could act by using one-or two-word directives in a form of verb-noun pairs, which were parsed by the game. It has 293 words in the vocabulary, since the game was capable to perceive and interpret a quite long list of player's commands.

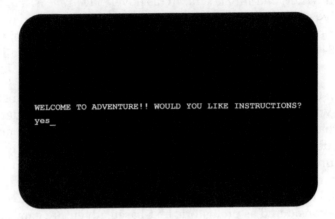

WELCOME TO ADVENTURE!! WOULD YOU LIKE INSTRUCTIONS?
yes_

An example of a text-based interface in an adventure game

Just imagine the enthusiasm of people who played Colossal Cave Adventure. In front of them was a gigantic computer with a small screen and green blinking letters, and inside that machine, a real, magical world with full of adventures and unknown discoveries was hidden. Imagination is an incredibly powerful tool. The walls of Colossal Cave's labyrinths had more details and seemed to be more realistic than any given modern game that is based on advanced 3D technologies and expensive artworks. So it is no wonder that soon William Crowther's creation got new talented followers: Colossal Adventure, Adventure Quest, Zork, and many others.

With the introduction of graphical interfaces and faster chips, a new era began. Adventure games started to explore the advantages of bitmaps. The paradigm was the same. A game pictured a scene, and the player entered a command trying to make the correct decision. One of the pioneers was *Mystery House*, an adventure game for Apple II, designed by a couple, *Roberta* and *Ken Williams*. The game was both inspired by Colossal Cave Adventure, which was accidentally founded by *Ken Williams* inside a catalog of a teletype terminal he was working with, and detective stories by *Agatha Christie*. Being an indie product by modern-day standards that was developed by enthusiasts, rather than a professional software company, the game surprisingly became a strong hit. The market welcomed it, expressing the idea that people desired this kind of electronic entertainment. They liked to take part in adventures and resolving mysteries. So the golden era of adventure games rose that would continue for almost two decades until the 2000s.

Roberta and *Ken Williams* soon founded a game company, which later became *Sierra On-Line*. It would publish many notable adventure games chaired by the *King's Quest* game series (because of its popularity, sometimes adventure games are referred to as quests). The world also saw masterpieces from *LucasArts* such as the *Monkey Island* franchise, the *Indiana Jones* game series, the *Sam & Max* game series, and many others.

Amerzone – The Explorer's Legacy (1999) was the first graphical adventure game designed by *Benoît Sokal*

Adventure games tried to use the full potential of new technologies. The beginning of the CD-ROM era gave them a new energy, allowing the use of multimedia content to improve the quality of virtual worlds. For a period of time, they were considered as the most technically advanced genre in terms of video content, high-quality sound, 3D elements, and professional animation. The most important thing was that of game designers perceiving their creation as a very serious thing something close to films or good literature that required an excellent story and concept, interesting characters, intriguing turns, and very creative realization. Many of the games were simply, figuratively speaking, geniuses, for example, *Blade Runner* (1997) from *Westwood Studios* (a visual story and a masterpiece), *The Last Express* (1997) from *Jordan Mechner* (the creator of the original Prince of Persia), and *The Neverhood* (1996) from *The Neverhood, Inc.* (based on scenes totally sculpted from clay). One of my favorite projects of that period of time was *Grim Fandango* (1998) from *LucasArts*, which not only used a real-time 3D engine to draw character but also featured a perfect script and very smart dialogues. Developers were not afraid to explore boundaries of the genre making bold experiments with stories and visual look. In such conditions appeared stylish and surreal games such as *Phantasmagoria* (1995) from *Sierra On-Line* or amazing *Sanitarium* (1998) created by *DreamForge Intertainment*.

And after that the reality began to change. In the 2000s, the genre started to lose its popularity. Projects with big budgets more often became commercial failures, despite the fact that they were praised by critics. The golden era of adventure games came to an end. But this did not mean that such games disappeared from scene completely; they simply turned into a less mainstream product. For instance, many interesting projects were created under the French software brand Microïds that is mainly associated with name Benoît Sokal, a talented illustrator and game designer, who created the critically acclaimed game series, Syberia (2002 to 2004). These games represented the technical direction chosen by authors of interactive adventures in that period of time. They used fixed camera angles, prerendered static images to create an environment, videos to animate some elements, and a real-time 3D engine to drive characters. All those things together created an excellent visual presentation. Such an approach was referred to as 2.5D graphics.

The first part of Syberia was successfully ported to iOS devices

Nevertheless, in the second part of the 2000s, part of the new titles were less intriguing and artistic than their predecessors. The gameplay turned into something mechanical; scripts were not very exciting and the ideas were not so inspiring. The genre was in a creative crisis. A way out was founded by enthusiasts, who began to design so-called author's adventures.

The games were created by individuals not because of desire to get strong profit but to tell their own stories. They needed self-expression via interactive fiction. Such games used free engines such as Adventure Game Studio (`http://www.adventuregamestudio.co.uk/`) or **Wintermute Engine Development Kit (WME)** (`http://dead-code.org/home/`). Some of the designers also used Adobe Flash because of the flexible nature of this technology and the simplicity of distribution of the final product; the author simply had to put the game online. A wonderful example is *Samorost* (2003), a surreal puzzle-adventure game designed by a Czech student *Jakub Dvorský*, which could be considered as a real piece of modern art. Later its author found an independent game studio called *Amanita Design*. In 2009, it produced another gem, a game that can be marked as one of the most beautiful adventure projects of the decade, Machinarium. The key of success was based on its engrossing story, charming mood, and the incredible drawings of a talented Czech graphic artist, *Adolf Lachman* (`http://adolflachman.cz/machinarium/`). The game was rewarded with many awards and nominations: Aesthetics award at IndieCade (2008), Excellence in Visual Art award at the 12th Annual Independent Games Festival, and so on. It achieved a huge fan base being ported on various platforms, including iOS. The most important fact is that Machinarium was an indie project. The game was not produced by a gigantic corporation but by a small team of people who liked to tell stories via games. The studio didn't even have much of funding to work on the project; developers used their own savings. This is why it is a very inspiring story!

Machinarium is real masterpiece, created by Amanity design.

The genre got a second breath with the introduction of modern smartphones, especially tablets. In contrary to computer systems and gaming consoles, they were more likely to harbor those types of games, letting players have direct contact with the game environment. This is why there are adventure games on iTunes. Moreover, many old titles were successfully ported on the new platform, enriched with some remastered assets and featuring improved graphics and sound. For example, the first two parts of the legendary adventure game series *Broken Sword* from *Revolution Software*, *The Last Express*, *Amerzone: The Explorer's Legacy*, and many others.

Understanding types of adventure games

Adventure games are a mix of different elements including puzzles, arcade sections, RPG Mechanics, and so on. The dominating ingredient of the gameplay mechanics defines the individual type of the game. I have not mentioned the term graphic adventure in the list, since now it is the default standard for most of the adventure games.

Text-based adventure

In a text-based adventure game, there are no graphics, only text elements (graphics may play the role of minor ornamentation). This is a tribute to the legendary Colossal Cave Adventure and its analogs. It may seem that such types of games are an ancient atavism, but remember that there are some handheld devices that are not quite adapted for quick graphics, such as e-book readers with the screen based on electronic paper. Interactive adventures can be ideally adapted for such platforms, being directly compatible with the general functional paradigm of the e-book devices: displaying text on a screen and support of basic hypertext interactivity. Also, recall audio games; many of them are actually text-based adventures where the content is read out aloud. And don't forget about creative experiments with gameplay, for instance, there is a unique modern game called *Blackbar* (http://mrgan.com/blackbar/), created by *Neven Mrgan*, where a player works with text that is censored. The main objective is to figure out what content was painted black.

Puzzle-based adventure

A puzzle-based adventure is where solo parts are given to various puzzles; as usual, they are pretty complex and look like mysterious devices, mini games, and so on. The best illustration and a true role model for various followers is the famous *Myst* series introduced in 1993 (the first game of the series and its sequel *Riven* would later be ported to both iPhone and iPad).

Action-based adventure

Action-based adventure is a very popular subgenre that not only offers players with a dynamic gameplay with some fights and other types of action, but also requires some intelligent investigation of the story, collecting items, and resolving puzzles. Overall, the game experience is very rich because there are lots of different mechanics involved. Proportions of action and adventure elements may differ from project to projects. There are projects with action and a bit of adventure, where players mainly fight and sometimes get to solve some puzzles. Then there are projects with adventure and some action, where players generally explore the world around them and seldom face any enemies to fight with. A good illustration of an action-based adventure game is *Superbrothers: Sword & Sworcery EP* from *Capybara Games Inc.*, featuring very stylish pixel drawings:

A scene from Superbrothers – Sword & Sworcery EP

Escape the room

Escape the room (room escape) is a pretty young subgenre that was popularized in the 2000s, mostly by various adventure games created in Adobe Flash and were available online for a wider audience. The concept is simple; a player is situated in a locked room and has to find a way to escape it by using various items that can be found nearby. Its popularity among developers is pretty clear. Such a game requires only one small location to work with, so it is much easy to create all the assets and thinkup puzzles. Some of the notable examples were created by the Japanese designer, *Toshimitsu Takagi*, who stands for popular titles such as *Crimson room*, *Viridian room*, *Blue chamber*, and *White chamber*. Among projects for iOS, the one that can be specifically picked was called *100 Floors* from *Tobi Apps Limited* (`http://www.tobiapps.com/1_100_floors.html`), where the connection between levels is illustrated very naturally via the idea of an elevator in a high building. Another interesting entry is *Factory96* by *Michael Eng* (`http://www.factory96.com`), where real photographs of abandoned industrial locations are used as decorations to create the image of a mysterious factory full of different puzzles.

Planning the setting

Adventure games are about mysteries, secrets, and revelations because they need special type of stories to be based on. Events must be incredible and outstanding, denying everyday routine. If the plot is taking part in reality, in most cases, it would be a detective, horror, or survival story. The mystery is always hidden inside somebody's intentions or a dangerous environment. In most cases, the mood of such stories is dark and gloomy.

Alternatively, you may not think about one unique situation but a whole new fictional world based on its original rules. You only have to choose a type of universe you are more attached to: fantasy, cosmic sci-fi, cyberpunk, dystopia, steampunk, dieselpunk, retro-futurism, post-apocalyptic, and so on. All of them can be ideally adapted for interactive adventure games, having a rich stylistic background and a large arsenal of already-invented plot elements. It is worth mentioning that some of the most popular types are fantasy and steampunk settings: the first one lets you introduce magic, spells, and various incredible creatures; however, the second one has passion for various mechanical devices, something that is suitable for the creation of puzzles.

Establishing the game idea

If you're starting with your very first adventure game, it is reasonable to choose the Escape the room concept; it is much easier to develop. All the events take part only in one screen; there are no complex labyrinths, and the sequence of levels can be linear. You only need to think of an idea for the story that would link all the levels together. Where can a bunch of isolated rooms be placed together? In a building? Good! Do you have another idea? A hotel? Sounds good as well, but let's change the point of view a little bit. Rooms should not be necessarily made of bricks or concrete, so think of other materials. Metallic walls? Oh! A train car. Rooms collected together form a train because we want the player to travel from one place to another. Great! What about settings? Steampunk looks like a cliché; it is much better to choose something more original. For example, dieselpunk. Let's give the game a code name: Trans-Terra Express.

Writing the plot

There was no WWII in the parallel universe. In the late 1940s, several countries together built a railroad encircling the planet called Trans-Terra Railroad. It covers thousands of kilometers on land, running through major capitals, gnawing through mountains and deep forests, and flying over valleys by elegant arc bridges. Oceans and seas are not barriers anymore as the railroad floats over waves, relying on the grid of special automatic airships.

Trans-Terra Railroad uses special trains known as Trans-Terra Express, which look like small moving cities with huge powerful diesel locomotives ahead. Each express train is made up of dozens of residential cars, including several luxury ones where some famous and rich people may travel with a proper level of comfort. There are also special cars with prestigious restaurants, bars, coffee houses, theaters, cinemas, libraries, and one swimming pool. A few cars carry a collection of exotic plants and have special roofs made of glass; they can be considered as moving orangeries.

Train scheme

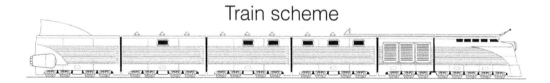

This is not a dystopian story, so there are no slums or ghettos in such a train. But there are third-class cars that are much simpler, featuring moderate decoration and smaller living spaces. Also, the last part of the train is an improvised industrial zone consisting of different engineering modules, including boiler rooms, communication centers, waste recycling zone, workshops, storages, and so on.

Trans-Terra Expresses does not have any stops; it is always very hard to accelerate such a mechanical leviathan, and so special small airplanes are used to take passengers on and off the train. They land on the special landing pad, mounted on the forward part of the locomotive. This is not an easy job, so only very professional pilots can manage it. Anna-Amelia, the protagonist of the story, is not a professional pilot. She is not like her father who made more than several thousands of successful landings on Trans-Terra Expresses. But Anna-Amelia dreamed to be a high-quality pilot from her early childhood. She has already had a lot of training and has spent hundreds of hours in the sky, but she has not appeared for the final flying exam yet; she is only a student without official permission to control a plane.

Of course such insignificant aspects could not stop our young hero; Anna-Amelia always tried to create a new exploit by taking her father's airplane without any permission. Once she decided to land on a moving Trans-Terra Express to prove her skills, being sure that her father would not abuse her for such behavior and would only praise her talent as a pilot—very presumptuous and unadvised. But this was her temper; Anna-Amelia was a fidget. Early in the morning she took her father's keys, jumped into the cockpit, started the engine, and flew away into the sky. Soon she noticed the express, which was moving from Budapest. Anna-Amelia began to bank the airplane, preparing for the landing.

The face of the train was in front; she started to descend, seeing the lane and all the signal lights—200 meters, 100 meters, 50 meters, and everything was totally under control. Bounce! The landing wheels touch the lane softly; Anna-Amelia was smiling, anticipating her glory. But, what was wrong with that grid at the end of the lane? It moved too fast! Anna-Amelia accidentally made a common mistake. The landing speed was too fast, and the length of the lane was not enough for it. Before she can completely understand all the consequences, a special automatic system made its way and the young pilot was catapulted. Anna-Amelia only noticed the airplane getting crushed into the grid. She was flying forward, and the roofs of the cars below were moving very fast. Then she saw that the express was going to run away, and the very last car was in front of her eyes. It looked very beautiful with a special decorative fin. "Oh, I see the rails," she thought and suddenly something pulled her back strongly.

The parachute was opened and it caught the fin on the roof. Anna-Amelia was thrown down and backward; she smashed into a door:

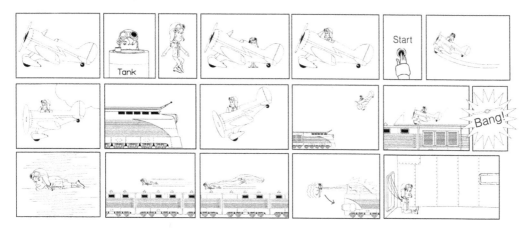

Fortunately it was open and our hero did not suffer any damage. She got off with nothing more than a fright. Or may be not? "My father's plane! I need to get it back, fix it, and turn it home before somebody knows!" Anna-Amelia thought. By looking around she understood that she was inside a very dusty and an almost empty car. Anna-Amelia had to react fast. She needed to travel all through the train, car by car, to reach the locomotive, where the airport facilities were placed. That would not be easy, but Anna-Amelia was ready for adventures.

Introducing the protagonist

The main hero of Trans-Terra Express is a young female. She is funny, pranksome, brave, and very curious. She is very cute and sweet as well. Being a young pilot, she wears a special helmet, goggles, and a jacket with a warm collar and riding breeches. Also, there is a flower at the corner of her helmet:

Anna-Amelia

Planning the room

Despite the fact that adventure games can have different types of location, including open spaces, it is easy to call any given isolated zone as a room. In Trans-Terra Express, this term describes a train car. To make the game more complex, each room is made up of a couple of screens; the player may explore either sides of these screens. You may also introduce longer cars consisting of up to four screens that gives the player an opportunity to explore larger spaces.

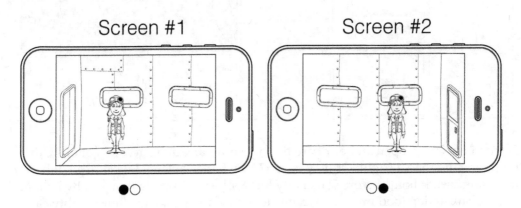

The background is fixed. The protagonist may walk in any horizontal direction; as soon as she reaches the joint between screens, the game displays another part of the room. To express the idea of a running train, windows should be transparent, showing a blurred moving background with parallax effect simulation applied on it. It should not include any particular elements, only general images of faraway hills, trees, and utility poles; in this form, the background will not distract the player. To add some additional realism and dynamics from time to time, the game may show a portion of dark rectangles distorted by a strong motion blur effect, which moves from right to left faster than the background, simulating a train running in the opposite direction. The demonstration of a framework of a railroad bridge is a good idea as well.

Ideally the interior of each car should be made of one unique picture that provides the best artistic effects but requires more illustrative efforts. Alternatively, the interior can be constructed via graphic tiles of different design; using proper combinations, you may achieve diversity in a room's visual appearance.

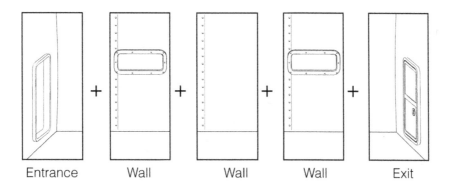

Entrance   Wall   Wall   Wall   Exit

An example of tile-based interior of the room

Each room has two axes that determine the effect of game objects on the protagonist's movement. The axis of the environment is situated near the front wall. Various props, **Non-player characters (NPCs)**, and interactive elements can be placed here. They do not hamper our main hero's walking at any point. On the contrary, if an object or an NPC stays on the axis of the movement, they turn into an obstacle for the protagonist. The player needs to figure out how to remove such elements from the path.

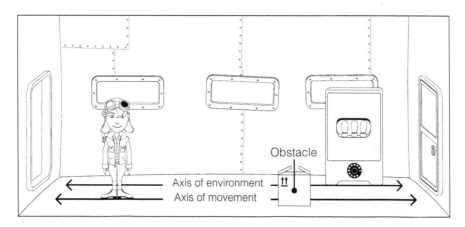

As you already know, the game should not look monotonous. However, the rooms can become boring even if their design is pretty diverse. This is because of a closed space and identical patterns of general components. Sometimes you need to change their appearance more radically. In several sections of the game, Anna-Amelia can leave a car (by special ladders or lifts) and travel some distance on the roof. Here are some unique types of puzzles that can be implemented together with some arcade mini-games. For instance, it is worth to note that Trans-Terra has a special compact railroad on the roof of its train cars; it was developed for various maintenance purposes and for faster transfer through different parts of the train. Small two-seated rail vehicles called draisines are used on this railroad. The protagonist may take part in a simple race of such vehicles. As for background decoration, utility poles with some arcs of wires may look very cunning.

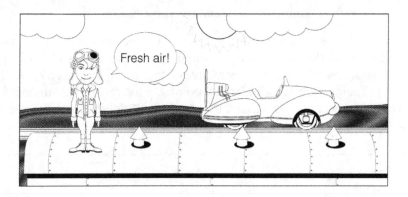

Another way to change the mood of rooms is to switch off the light. Later in the game, Trans-Terra Express enters into a very long tunnel, which actually does not finish until the player leaves some specific rooms. So there is no daylight; only rare signal lights are visible from the windows. If a room has no electricity for some reasons (it is completely dark), Anna-Amelia has to use a flashlight or safety matches to look around. Here the game may even frighten the player.

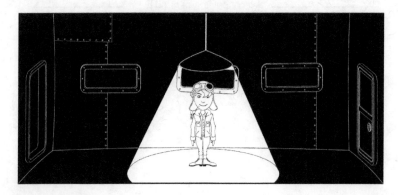

Interaction

As with many traditional 2D adventure games, Trans-Terra Express uses the point-and-click paradigm (for mobile devices, the term can be altered into the point-and-tap feature). A player tapping the screen moves the protagonist to a specific point. Tapping is contextual, so if an object is touched, it is either collected into the inventory or explored. The player can also push some items as crates or other various types of junk arranged at the axis of the environment. In many cases, the objective is to find a precious item, such as a key, hidden behind useful props.

Language of adventures

The logic of adventure games can be figuratively considered as a primitive language, or better still, a dialect (very close to the telegraphic style because there are no articles, conjunctions, copulas, and prepositions in an apparent form) that describes situations and actions in the scene. It is made up of several basic parts:

- **Nouns**: All the objects in the game have their unique names, for example, a Key, a Door, a Lock, and so on.

- **Adjectives**: These illustrate the current state of an individual item. Their role is pragmatical rather than ornamental. Their main goal is to signal whether an object is in order, broken, locked, and so on. Most popular entries are Locked, Broken, and Busy.

- **Verbs**: This is a list of actions a protagonist can commit. Its length is directly correlated with the complexity of the game. The basic list consists of simple verbs in imperative form such as Check, Use, Combine, Push, and Talk.

The gameplay of an adventure game is an improvised conversation. The game is telling a story by short descriptions (declarative sentences), but the player may ask some questions or give some commands in the form of an imperative sentence, which I call the action sentence.

"Protagonist" "Mat"   "Door"   "Key" "Donut"

Imagine that there is a room with a door and a mat below it. Here is an example of a dialogue that may occur between the game and a player:

Game [description]: "Protagonist," "Room," "Door," and "Mat"

Player [action sentence]: "Protagonist," "Use" and "Door"

Game: "Door" and "Locked!"

Player: "Protagonist," "Check," and "Mat"

Game: ""Mat" and "Movable"

Player: "Protagonist," "Push," and "Mat"

Game: "Space below mat," "Key," and "Donut"

Player: "Protagonist," "Take," and "Key"

Game: "Key" and "Inventory"

Player: "Protagonist," "Use," "Key," and [on] "Door"

Game: "Door" and "Unlocked"

As you see, the game plays the role of a narrator that knows everything about the current situation in contrast to the player who only makes hypotheses. The player needs to explore the game world by touching things and figuratively asking the game, "May I use this one? Does it work for now?" Thus, the objective is to find the right words. If, for example, the player would take Donut instead of Key and tried to use it on Door, the game would answer that the attempt was Ridiculous because the words are pretty incompatible. The action sentence can be compared to the following equation in one unknown where X is the sought-after word:

$$X \; "Use" \; [on \; a] \; "Known \; Object" = "Success"$$

It is quite easy to find the right word when a sentence is short and the second noun is obvious such as Door. But it becomes trickier if the definition is more vague. For instance, it may look like Unknown Device and the game, in addition, says that it is Broken. How can it be fixed? What spare parts are needed? The equation becomes more complicated with more unknowns:

$$X \; "Use" \; [on \; a] \; Y = "Success"$$

$$where \; Y = "Unknown \; device"$$

To help a player solve such a logical dilemma, the game should display some hints. These hints may be presented in a graphic form; special images can be used for indirect alludes. Another option is that of a dialogue where an NPC talks about the nature of Y. This is extremely important when compound action sentences are used in the game. Such equations reckon with a specific number of preparatory phases to get the final result. Practically, this means that to solve the puzzle, a player would need to perform few preliminary actions, for example, fix a pipe or add some fuel to a tank. Each preparatory action is an individual equation, and they must be solved correctly to push the final puzzle to work well. Sometimes, without hints, such problems cannot be performed as there are many variables and many combinations.

$X \; "Use" \; [on \; a] \; Y = \{$

$IF \; A \; "Use" \; [on \; a] \; B = "Success" \; and \; C \; "Use" \; [on \; a] \; D = "Success" \; then$

$"Success"$

$Else \; "Not \; working" \; \}$

A linguistic paradigm based on noun-verb constructions was successfully approved by LucasArts in their **Script Creation Utility for Maniac Mansion (SCUMM)**, a scripting language that became the core logic for many graphical adventure games developed by the company, including the famous *The Secret of Monkey Island* (1990). Its key feature was a compromise between a natural language and a low-level code, as Assembler. Thus, SCUMM could be easily used by game designers without deep skills in programming.

In Game Developers Conference 2011 (`http://www.gdconf.com/`), *Ron Gilbert* (one of the creators of the original Maniac Mansion game), in his talk, Classic Game Postmortem - MANIAC MANSION, showed an example of SCUMM's description of a pendulum clock.

In this example we can see the corner-stone of SCUMM: a pair of words, a verb, and a noun divided by a hyphen that defines the object's behavior, for example, play and sound. The idea was to describe each object in the game individually, thus it could be easily added to a scene, removed, or adjusted.

Thinking about puzzles

The craft of creating elegant action sentences and hints is real art that requires some experience and flair. The point is in arriving at an equilibrium between the simplicity and complexity of action sentences. If they are too easy to unravel, players are disappointed because the gameplay becomes predictable and routine. On the other hand, if the sentence is hard to understand, the players drop the game and switch their attention to something else, being sure that only artificial intelligence might solve that puzzle because all logical connections are so unnatural. This is the weak point of many adventure games: trying to tangle a player, they forget about apparent logic in their riddles, which become complex and intricate, and require some alien- or machine-like thinking, being free of real-life principles.

Natural logic

 + + =

Helmet   Adhesive tape   Flashlight   Helmet flashlight

Artificial logic

 =

Brick   Adhesive tape   Flashlight   Hammer

By solving a puzzle, a player should deeply understand all the connections between objects and accept them, concurring that in this particular context, they are logical or at least plausible. Understanding them in such a way, the player ascertains that the riddle is pretty natural and can be solved by true work of mind, but not simple good luck that rewards him with a bit of self-esteem and makes him a little bit glad. On the contrary, complex puzzles with unnatural lines of logic, strange twists, and so on looks like an artificial creature without signs of life; being unable to resolve it leaves a nasty taste in the mouth. The common answer to such elements in games is "And how do you suppose I'd guess that?" or simply, "Are you serious?". Therefore, solutions must be hard to achieve, but they should be honest, without a cheating narrative.

As from my experience, a good puzzle fits the empirical 90/10 rule. This means that a player from the start sees 90 percent of the correct answers and tries to figure out the most important 10 percent of the answers that are hidden somewhere. By getting to the right solution, the player exclaims, "Yes, of course! That is logical."

Always try to tangle the player not by strange connections inside an action sentence, but by distracting him with false hints and fruitless items that increase the number of variables. Hide important things partially, as magicians do, by showing something bright and useless in light, but hiding the actual objects in the shadow. Make the player run, search, and calculate; allow him to invent the solution. And always check whether the logic inside a puzzle is universal enough. For example, it can be based on your own knowledge and life experiences, but other people would not understand what you are talking about; therefore, riddles should not be too subjective.

To get some inspiration for puzzle designs, especially when you plan to design riddles based on various devices and mechanisms, try to look at examples of intentionally over-engineered inventions such as the famous Rube Goldberg machines. Having some absurd functions, nevertheless, they include a lot of mechanical revelations and brilliant details, teaching you to plan the connection between elements and to transfer various forms of energy. Moreover, they are, figuratively speaking, very funny. Besides the drawings of the American cartoonist, *Rube Goldberg* (1883-1970) himself, who actually gave his name to this genre, you also have to look at genial illustrations by *William Heath Robinson* (1872-1944). He used to invent various more-than-useful devices in his graphics as well.

In an ideal scenario, a puzzle has several solutions, so players may implement different logic and tools to achieve the result, but it is much harder to design as well as to tune the game.

Creating the scene flowchart

Any episode in an adventure game is an integral organism, a system of interconnected elements rather than individual, independent objects. All parts should work in harmony. To thoroughly draft such cooperation, you need to see the whole picture; blueprinting may help you accomplish that. All the puzzles, interactions, and items should be included in special flowcharts, created on paper. They help to test a scene before you begin to code the different levels of the game. Always begin with the generic line of the scene, planning the general succession of actions that lead to the successful resolution of all the problems; adjust it very carefully. Then switch your attention to all the things that will distract the player— all the fake objectives and false hints.

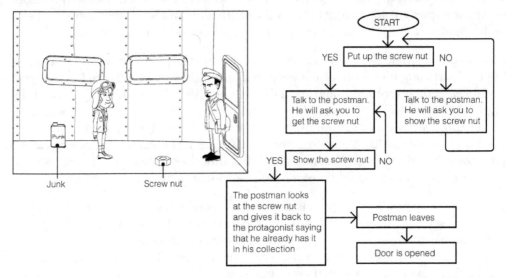

Local scene flowchart

It is worth mentioning that besides local-plot arcs, there may be longer arcs covering many levels, especially when the game has RPG Mechanics. This means that some discoveries or resolved riddles will prove themselves later; figuratively speaking, a screw nut found at the beginning of the game will be useful at the final level (but the player should take that screw nut through special conditions; otherwise, at the end, the game will be unwinnable). You may intrigue players with such methods by ensuring things and events are full of mystery and, in a sense, hidden. Thus, a global puzzle flowchart should be in hand where connections between levels are shown. It helps to close all the plot lines at the end and ensure that important subjects are not dropped. Innuendos are good dramatic practice, but only designful ones; the arc looks farcically, if it is not properly finished because you simply forget to close them by discarding some story lines.

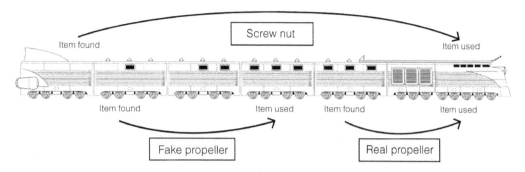

A global flowchart, showing some long plot arcs

If the game has a lot of variables involved towards the end, and they are spread all over the levels and you are not sure that you can properly control a player's actions (for example, the main character did not pick up a specific item few levels ago and now they are not available), try to secure yourself by deus ex machina solutions. Seeing that some important elements are missing in the final puzzle and cannot be obtained again, the game should activate plan *B*, an unexpected twist. This is "narrative cheating" and may look crooked, but it is better than letting the player know that the game cannot be finished and needs to be replayed. Moreover, such turns may be gracefully referred to as an alternative ending that especially works fine if you indeed plan for having multiple endings for the story. Players like diversity a lot, so different ways to finish a game are always welcomed; however, it is better to follow only a single rule. Twists in the story in the game should be well expressed, and a new progression of events must be noticeable (but not too much) in some form (via some new phrases in dialogues, another order in items, small changes to puzzle behavior, and so on). For example, the legendary adventure game Blade Runner had about a dozen of different endings. A player's community dreamed to achieve them all by trying to play it over and over again, paying attention to all the paths of the story.

Presenting the inventory

Ironically speaking, adventure games are partially based on greed, for example, a magpie; the player is trying to take or even steal any type of objects, no matter if he knows about its function or not. He becomes a real hoarder, hoping that in future on very special occasion his treasures would become useful.

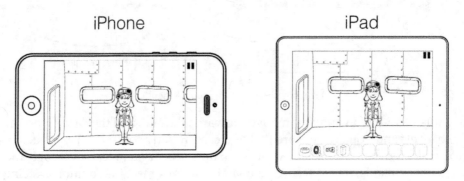

Screen layouts – on an iPad the inventory panel is always available, but on an iPhone it should be activated by the player

All the items found by the player are stored in his inventory, which works like an improvised backpack. As a rule, its capacity is bottomless; there is no restriction on the number of things you can carry inside it. This is very convenient for debugging as long as you are always sure that a player would not lose an item and would not get stuck somewhere.

Generally the inventory is made up of several basic classes of objects:

- **A solo item**: This is an item that is required to activate a trigger, to solve a puzzle, to begin a dialogue with an NPC, and so on. It is solid and does not require other elements to operate, for example, a key, a wrench, a flashlight, and so on.

- **A spare part**: Very often an adventure game asks the player to construct a device or tool based on several other objects. To confuse him, spare parts usually looks like solo items, so a bit of creativity is needed to determine which object should be taken from the inventory.

- **A constructed item**: This is an object that is made up of several spare parts. Usually it looks like a smart invention, a tool created by a talented autodidact, and not an industrial product. This is the way to creatively wiggle out a situation with stop-gap solutions when there are no actual tools to perform the task. The constructed item is of the same rank as the solo item.

- **Junk**: This is the most numerous class of items and, figuratively speaking, the funniest one, of course. All such things are only shells without any actual purpose other than to tangle the player's attention, distracting from solo items and the correct spare parts. Use humor to create such objects; for example, it could be an old sandwich, a donut, a left shoe, dirty socks, and so on.

To create a solo item, remember that objects, which should be used for triggers, have a pretty logical and obvious design. These objects include various types of keys and tools, such as a screwdriver or hammer and some missing pieces such as cog wheels, lamps, or wires. There must be an apparent logical connection between the item and the trigger. But items consigned for an NPC may be more exotic and irrational, as long as a character may have some quirks. For example, an NPC can asks the player to bring him something unusual that looks like a caprice; a cup of milk, a firefly, or an old newspaper printed in 1968 and so on.

Constructed items need to be used for unusual tasks or when the actual tools are missing, for example, a screwdriver can be made of a candelabrum and a nail file. Spare parts can be exotic as well, but only at the first sight, as their place in the final design of a constructed item should look very sane and even clever. The construction process is based on the logical addition of separate elements; in the simplest case, there are only two addends in the expression. As might be expected, it obeys the principle of commutativity because it is irrelevant what item of the combination the player would choose first:

$$"Pipe" + "Newspaper" = "Newspaper" + "Pipe"$$

But complex expressions with several items are more tricky. Usually adventure games decline the rule of associativity during the addition procedure; therefore, the correct order of combining spare parts is important. The resulting constructed item should be assembled in the correct sequence. This can be called an in-inventory puzzle where the player has to manipulate with items in his inventory.

Besides the Combine command, its antonym Divide may be introduced as well. Such a verb would help to break up an item into small parts, allowing to create brand new constructed items later. For the sake of simplicity of the UI, it is better to design a special workbench that can be placed somewhere at the game level. By using a solid item on it, the player gets its pieces.

It is worth mentioning that the inventory at the very beginning of the game should not be totally empty; to express the personality of the protagonist, you may include some special and unique items in the list.

You should play with the audience using their little weaknesses (as already mentioned, greed). A hint that an item is very important for a walkthrough of the game, imbue that it is really precious thing the players should be hold dear, keeping like the apple of their eye. And after that, take away the item by forcing the player to use it much earlier than somebody may expect. This will be a very dramatic moment, full of doubts and emotions, because only you as the author know that the thing is not really important, and it is not precious at all; however, the player does not have this information. Here's the illustration. At one of the first levels of the Trans-Terra Express, you may let Anna-Amelia find a propeller. The player already knows that this item is extremely important to fix the airplane. It looks like the key element for the entire game, but we should construct the plot in a different way. The correct propeller would be found much later in the game, so the current one is fake in a global sense since you simply force the player to use the propeller to fix an air-driven draisine.

Monologues

It is good when characters make some commentaries about game situations or simply share their opinion using short and pithy phrases. This practice has several advantages. First of all, this is the way to express somebody's personality; secondly, the phrases can be considered as the voice of the game. The latter one can speak with a player through the environment, but sometimes the faster way is through words. For example, we are talking about a locked door; when the protagonist touches it, the game reports about the door's state by playing the sound of a clanking lock, displaying a short animation of a shaking door handle (an environmental answer), and forcing the main hero to say, "The door is locked" (verbal answer). Choosing between these two types of answers, you see that the second one is more simple and at the same time very convincing. This does not mean that the environment reaction can be neglected; both types should cooperate to achieve the best results.

One of the creative objectives is to reduce the sameness of phrases. The character's speech about the same situation should be diverse; a special text array can be created, and each sentence can be chosen randomly. The larger the array is the better. Here are a few examples of different phrases in an array:

- **Locked door**: "It is locked," "I need a key," "Why don't they keep it open?" "I need to figure out how to open it," and "A locked door cannot stop me!"

- **Broken device**: "It is broken..." "Pile of Metal Scrap!" "It stuck..." "It has seen better days," "Something is missing," "Somebody has seen the manual?" and "I hate machines..."

- **Broken button**: "Ding dong!" "Apparently it is broken..." "Is something happening?... Don't think so," "May be I have to push again? Just in case!" and "Something wrong with that button"

Always try to add some ironical and funny variants to the array. Remember that your character is not boring but very witty. Excellent phrases may become a one-line joke; players can use these phrases with each other, thereby creating memes.

The main domain for monologues is phrases about unimportant elements in game scenes or commentaries about the player's attempts to perform some absurd actions (such as fixing a machine with an apple stub). If the players do something wrong, they should at least smile. Here are a few examples of such phrases in an array:

- **Irrelevant object**: "Hm-m, very interesting... or may be not," "I'm trying to understand what it is..." "Nonsense", "It is... a thing," "Do I need this?" "Somebody stop me!" and "I'm real idler"
- **Absurd action**: "I've just want to try," "I'm too genius, nobody understands me," "At least I've tried!" 'I see things differently!" "You better believe it!" "In my universe it would work!" and "You don't see the magic!"

As an option, through the main character's phrases, the game can give some hints if the player is stuck, flouncing between objects, not knowing how to resolve the current puzzle. In this situation, if there is no progress for a continuous period of time, the protagonist may suddenly say, "I have an idea. May be I should try...".

NPCs should also have monologues, uttering some catch phrases or commenting on the protagonist's behavior. They may grumble, say something poetic, capture the attention with loud shouts, and so on.

Now let's see the technical side of the game. Of course, in ideal cases, all the phrases in the game are sound based; recorded voices of humans, reading scripted lines of text is the most natural approach that gives excellent results. But it is not very realistic, especially if this is your first adventure game and you working on it alone or with a small team. Despite the fact that media technology is almost accessible for everyone, it is easy to get a microphone and some software for sound editing; an amateur voice will not sound great because you will not recognize your own voice, thinking that it sounds pretty strange. There are many important nuances both in recording (such as a correct microphone, sound-friendly room, and minimum level of noise) and in voice acting. As far as this goes, it is not about reading a text from a paper but expressing some emotions, acting and using the correct pronunciation of words, and so on; narrating something is a real art. Without proper experience, sound files will be unconvincing.

But hiring real voice actors (remember that you have more than one talking characters) requires some extra budget, which can become even bigger if some additional recording is needed during the beta-testing stage of the product. Since for a first period of time, it is better to be more modest and use only text for phrases in form of subtitles or speech bubbles. In the meantime, to express some vocal tone of the characters, you may record short sessions of mumbling speech. It includes some portion of inaudible talk, such as the sound of a faraway conversation where only unrelated parts of syllables are heard. There should be several types of mumblings—versions for female and male characters—and several types of vocal range to illustrate characters of different age and temper. Because of the lack of a specific sense in them, such sound files are universal and can be attached to any conversation of a corresponding character.

Dialogues

Dialogues play two important roles in adventure-based games. Foremost, they are narrative tools that help to tell a story, expressing details, which are hidden from the player's eye. A dialogue can easily describe events which took place in the past or in another location not shown in the game directly. It may also explain connections between things, giving the player some directions. Thus the graphics, animation, and the level of design meet the audience with a superficial layer of a plot but dialogues reveal deeper layers, making the story more complex and multidimensional. Such an objective can be achieved by using other methods, as the narrator intervenes in the form of text-based diaries speared out on game levels or cutscenes, but the dialogues provide more player's attachment, as long as they imply some portion of interactivity (the players like to be participants rather than silent observers) in the process of familiarization with the plot. This feature is priceless and forms another important role of the dialogue: a text-based puzzle. It can be considered as a first-rate, mini game inside the main story.

A player tries to construct the conversation in a way that he would achieve maximum profit in the form of useful information, items a virtual companion would share, and so on. The challenge can be called a rhetoric battle, where each time the player should choose the right questions to control the direction of the talk. In some form, any interactive dialogue is a classical text-based adventure game.

Dialogues have a unique prerogative inside the story. They are allowed to lie; many other narrative tools cannot do the same, otherwise, the story would collapse. Any plot is based on the fact that all the events and things described by plain elements are true. Of course, overall this is fictional (something that was generated by author's imagination), but inside that fictional world, all the descriptions are genuine (may be in a greater degree than some things in our real world). For example, Sherlock Holmes lived at 221B, Baker Street. This was an absolute fact about the great detective inside novels by *Sir Arthur Conan Doyle*; however, outside them, in real London, it was not. Baker Street did not exist when the novels were published for the first time, so the address 221B simply did not exist. To keep the fictional world solid, *Sir Arthur Conan Doyle*, as the narrator, must regard all the important facts about it. He could not suddenly write that Sherlock Holmes returned home located at Gloucester place because this information would be incorrect. But he might write that Sherlock Holmes, while trying to confuse some criminals, indicated that he lived at that place instead of his real address at Baker Street. Hence an author cannot distort facts about the elements he has already mentioned in his fiction (this is why innuendos are commonly used if a narrator wants to prepare for a twist; they give some space for unexpected new facts) but his characters can; they may say everything, which is the way you create an intrigue.

In games, this means that elements such as a character's visual appearance, the level of design, mechanics, and so on should have absolute facts. They may evolve and change, but that evolution should be explained and displayed properly. For instance, in a game, there is a bonus that gives a protagonist some extra points. If it suddenly begins to freeze the character, not being change visually, that will be the distortion of the initial fact describing the bonus behavior that is a bad practice. Alternatively, it is better to let a mischievous antagonist tell a false story through a dialogue, say for example, some bonuses are infected. With this, the player begins to doubt, primarily about bonuses, then about the reliability of the antagonist's words. Therefore, the adventures inside dialogues are not only about useful information and the correct order of the conversation, but also about finding the truth. This is why there are a lot of adventure games based on detective stories, where a lot of characters tell lies, and the main objective is to reveal their true colors.

Constructing the conversation tree

Generally, all the dialogues are predefined structures constructed by a game developer. They cover all the possible variations and turns of the chat. Each phrase may have several directions to be continued, and some sections are looped; there can be different versions of an ending. This structure is called a dialogue or conversation tree, as long as it starts with a straight line of nodes and then grows as the crown of a tree through forking paths of phrases. From the mathematical point of view, this is a directed graph. It is made of nodes (phrases) and edges (directions). The simplest conversation tree consists of only phrases and links to other nodes, wherein some of them are marked as NPC's phrases but others (node's children) belong to the protagonist. It can be considered as some form of a "red–black" tree, a data structure, where nodes have special color marks (either black or red), and children always have the color opposite to that of the parent. Such a method is very visual.

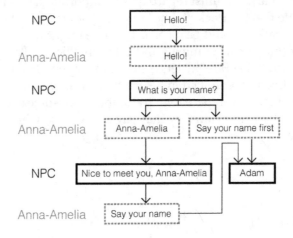

A player surfs the branches of the conversation tree by choosing phrases for the main character, so the focus is shifted from node to node, moving deeply into the crown. The game interprets NPC's nodes as static text but protagonist's nodes as interactive elements. They are kept at the screen until a player would communicate with them (tap), which would move the focus onto the next node.

This type of a conversation tree works fine for isolated dialogs, which are not affected by the current game's situation; also, external variables cannot influence the nodes, so the conversation is mostly decorative. Therefore, more flexible solutions are preferable. The tree should include conditions as follows:

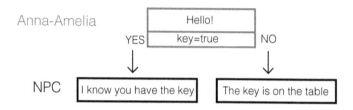

In this case, each phrase had an additional section with few conditional operators, which can check the value of specific variables, changing the direction of the conversation upon them. For example, if a character has no key (**key = false**), an NPC may offer some help to find it; however, if the character already has this item (**key = true**), the NPC would tell that a lock is jammed and it knows where to get some grease. As you see such a dialogue is much more natural. It can be even better if a tree node has the opportunity to set up values for variables as well. Therefore, some previous parts of the conversation that are not directly connected with the current node may have an effect on it.

For example, the NPC is caught in a deception because there is a discrepancy between his phrases after that special variable is changed (**NPC_liar = true**), so in other branches of conversation new variants of player's phrases appear who respond to that variable.

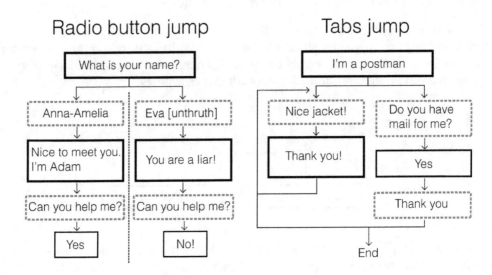

By using variables and conditions, you also construct specific types of transitions inside the dialogue from an analogy to a UI design—I call them **Tabs-jump** and **Radio-buttons-jump**. The first one is of the basic type; when the game reaches the protagonist's nodes on the tree, they are put on the screen as interactive elements (buttons). Each of them generates an independent branch of conversation, which can evolve in parallel with others. Such an algorithm is good for phrases that are not connected together; with these algorithms, a player may talk about one thing and then switch to questions about another without the fear of losing some phrases, as if he would use an interface based on tabs. For other cases, sometimes a radio button should be utilized. This means that only one protagonist's phrase can be used at a moment; other branches are cut. Suppose that a suspicious NPC asks a player about his name, there is an option in the conversation tree to tell either the true or false name; both the variants are radio-buttoned nodes since they cancel each other out. When one option is chosen, the other one must disappear. In addition, there can also be hybrids of both types of transitions. As you see, the framework of conversation can be very complex and tangled, making the interaction with virtual character very enthralling.

It is good practice to introduce two possible ways to reach the end of the branch or the conversation at all: the long one for curious players and the short one for fidgets. Those who hurry to continue with adventures and don't like dialogues have the opportunity to choose only key phrases, but other ones may need more detailed descriptions.

Besides the normal conversation, sometimes in the game you may use a so-called lunatic talk, a dialogue based on accident and chaos. It is some sort of slot machine. It is activated by starting a conversation with a special NPC. In most cases the phrases are meaningless and empty, but sometimes something very valuable can be attained. As a rule, such mechanics are utilized for special class of NPCs that can be referred as holy fools, for example, strange and weirdo hobos, old sages, broken robots, and so on. Their speech mostly consists of absurdity and nonsense but sometimes real revelations can be heard; the player only needs some good luck.

Technically, the conversation tree can be designed by a series of conditional statements and string variables storing texts. This is the simplest and obvious way, but it is not perfect but a little bit cumbersome. In this case each dialogue is custom made by code. The system is not flexible, especially for localization purposes, as it is much more difficult to prepare texts for different languages. It is much more effective to use external arrays of phrases and one universal function for parsing that data. In this case, a special standalone dialogue editor can be created (as many game studios do) that saves conversations in special files. The only problem is that of data format because a tree is not a trivial data structure. You can invent your own format based on original tags or reinterpret something that was designed specially for graphs: DOT (graph description language), GraphML, Trivial Graph Format, and many others.

Working with phrases

Each node of the conversation tree is a phrase, either answer or question. Your main objective as a game designer is to interest a player to read the text. It is an open secret that some players simply skip dialogues, tapping phrases fast, losing all the narrative and not taking part in textual puzzles. They may even get stuck in the game if they do not note important information. Besides such naughty persons, diligent players can begin to act in the same way if the dialogue is boring, hard to follow, is neither intriguing, nor humorous. Thereby each phrase should be developed very industriously.

First of all, a thing about the width of a text block displayed on the screen. It should not be too narrow or wide. Look at the SMS application for an iPhone; all the blocks of text do not cover the entire width of the screen. If the length of the text is optimal, it's easy for the human eye to focus when it moves on lines. There are no uncomfortable sensations. Choose somewhere about 30 to 35 characters in a line.

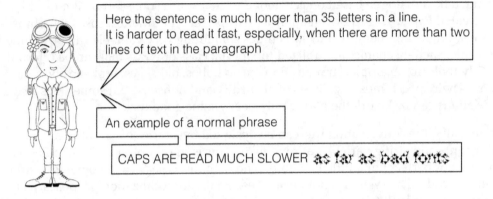

Here the sentence is much longer than 35 letters in a line.
It is harder to read it fast, especially, when there are more than two lines of text in the paragraph

An example of a normal phrase

CAPS ARE READ MUCH SLOWER as far as bad fonts

Only typefaces (no matter serif or non-serif) with a look close to classical should be used. Every letter with excess ornamentation or whimsical design is harder to recognize. In an ideal case, the players would not notice the letters at all, moving through them smoothly without trying to grasp the meaning. The entire text in uppercase is bad for dialogues, for example, SINCE PEOPLE RECOGNIZE WORDS BY FAMILIAR PATTERNS, A RELIEF OF LETTERS, BUT ALL-CAPS BROKE THIS RULE; THE READING PROCESS BECOMES TIRESOME AND SLOWER. Therefore more traditional typography methods must be used to keep the optimal level of readability; use uppercase letters only for standard positions.

Any sentence should be short and easy to read and perceive; ideally they should fit in a single line of text. A phrase made of more than three lines may be ignored or read only partially (for instance, only the beginning and final parts). *Alfred Hitchcock* said, "Drama is life with the dull bits left out". So, try to cut out excessive details by concentrating only on important things. It is better to avoid complex and compound-complex sentence structures, as they are harder to follow and are less natural. Note that when two persons are speaking, they are not using very complex constructions in their conversation because they illustrate many things not by words but by body language, mimics, and gestures. Many of these details can be recreated using animation or graphic representation of different character's emotions.

If in a story a character is long, it must be split into smaller parts; thus it takes few steps for the story to be told. It is worth mentioning that a protagonist can take part in storytelling by asking some leading questions, which include some portions of a narrative. This reduces the number of steps required to express a plot of the conversation. If a sentence is cut and may be continued, it should be marked with an ellipsis. The protagonist's phrase to continue the story can include expressions such as "Please, continue..." "I want to know more," and "I'm all ears".

But there can also be some exceptions. For the sake of drama, to express a character's nature, he can use phrases written in a totally wrong manner. For example, there is a hero, who is very dry as dust and egotistical. He is able to speak for hours admiring himself. His phrases can be very long and pretentiously constructed, featuring splendid metaphors and pompous descriptions. In this case, the exact meaning of the sentences is not quite important. The goal is to tire players with a flood of words so they share the idea that a talking character is a boring person.

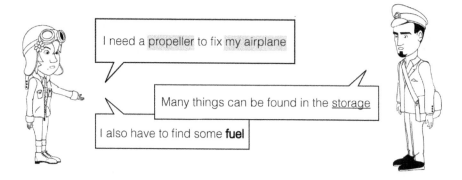

There are several ways to draw additional attention to the text or some of its parts. The world of advertising is well familiar with them. Key words in a sentence should be visually isolated from other elements. This can be done by color or other typographical emphasis such as bold or italic font styles, letter spacing (extra spaces between letters), and underlining. Such methods work fine and are pretty effective, however, they require special technical implementation; a text parser used in a game should support special style tags as well as the system displaying the text on the screen.

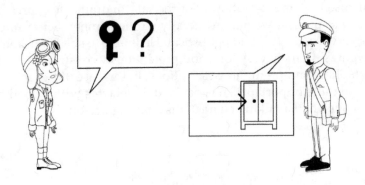

There is a very exotic and at the same time a very creative approach to create dialogues: using graphic icons instead of words. Its main advantage is that it is language independent. It should not be translated into another language when a game is published in foreign markets. The phrases can be interpreted by kids, who cannot read yet, because there are no word sentences. Each dialog box consists of symbolic images, icons that represent a thing or event, special graphic tricks, or simple animations expressing actions (such an approach is used in Machinarium). Of course there are a lot of limitations. It is very hard to illustrate complex plots; moreover, some icons can be unrecognizable by some people and the style by itself is more common for funny and cartoon games. At once, symbolic writing looks very creative and includes a huge potential to create puzzles, since various types of rebuses can be constructed on its base.

Creating the dialogue window

In general any dialogue with NPCs is an interruption of the main game process. It is a special mode that looks and feels different to the general gameplay, as a rule it is isolated from all external factors. For example, a character can be killed when he is talking with somebody because any dialogue can be considered as a form of pause of the main game process. Thus, as usual, a special window or panels are activated to display portions of the conversation tree.

Talking heads and the 180-degree rule

One of the dramatic results can be achieved by using the talking head method, which was popularized by the Fallout game series. The NPC that a player is talking with is shown in close-up, so all details of his face and mimics are well seen. Such an approach is very close to cinema, where close-up is traditional practice to illustrate a dialogue scene. The audience is drawn in conversation shown at screen, as if the viewers would stay near the actors. Some games do not change the angle of the virtual camera, so the player only sees the NPC; this is the simplest way but other ones show the player's avatar too. This looks very artistic and meaningful, but you must abide by a simple rule known as the 180-degree rule, which comes directly from cinematography. It defines positions of cameras that are shooting a conversation; it is more like saying that between two characters, there is an imaginary line called the axis of action and the cameras must be placed on the same side of the line and never cross it. This sounds a little bit abstract, but it becomes very obvious as soon as you see the result. When the first character is talking, he is shown at one side of the screen; when the second character begins to speak, he is always displayed on the opposite side. You can check this out for yourself by watching any scene with dialogues in modern movies; recall for example, a famous conversation between Neo and Morpheus in Matrix (1999) when they are sitting in red armchairs. Such a method of displaying the characters on the screen lets viewers naturally understand who is speaking right now without any extra efforts. It works like an easy-to-recognize pattern.

If the rule is broken, the conversation scene is perceived like a series of monologues, as if the characters make some declarations but not communicate with each other:

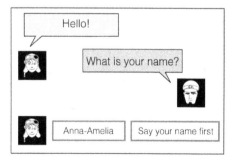

SMS-like-chat dialogue window

The player may have several versions of the next phrase. They can be displayed like individual panels with the text he taps on or look like a scrollable list of text. The last option needs less space on the screen, but it also less visual as some phrases are hidden. It is an interesting practice to keep the inventory panel so the player can use some items from there in his conversation. For instance, by dragging a key from the inventory to the dialogue window, the protagonist asks the NPC about a locked door.

It is important to note that besides a bunch of predefined phrases the player chooses from, the game may utilize something like an emotional spectrum; instead of choosing the exact words, the player selects an emotional state for his character. For instance, he may be cool headed and delicate, or be aggressive and very rude. The game selects directions on the conversation tree following these states.

Not every dialogue window in adventure games has the log feature, which allows to look through the history of the current conversation; sometimes it can be very useful. There is a way to combine the log and the window. I'm talking about a conversation between characters that looks like an SMS chat. Each phrase is presented as a speech balloon, and it does not disappear from the screen; the NPC's ballons are aligned to the left. Special graphics can be used to mark the balloons and to display the current emotions of the character. Any phrase that has been spoken can be accessible at any time; the player only needs to scroll the list. As a creative option, you can expand that feature by gameplay; for example, any earlier words may be used again in the new context, so brand new branches of conversation would be opened by the player.

Alternative ideas

Alternative ideas about the game's settings are as follows:

- All the events can take place in space. So the train can be easily replaced with a very long spaceship with a lot of compartments. Some puzzles may utilize zero gravity.
- The setting can be changed to a fantasy-based universe. Thus, the protagonist can be turned into a princess, but her adventure would take place in a castle or caves. Some magic can be introduced.

Identity for the game

The main application icon must display Anna-Amelia's face; it must be turned to the right. Alternatively, the protagonist and her airplane can be shown together:

The following are the links you can refer to for additional information on topics that are used in this chapter:

- `http://en.wikipedia.org/wiki/An_Examination_of_the_Work_of_Herbert_Quain`
- `http://en.wikipedia.org/wiki/Hopscotch_(Julio_Cort%C3%A1zar_novel)`
- `http://en.wikipedia.org/wiki/Choose_Your_Own_Adventure`
- `http://www.cyoa.com/pages/history-of-cyoa`
- `http://www.youtube.com/watch?v=1F7CX3pdHvQ`
- `http://en.wikipedia.org/wiki/Colossal_Cave_Adventure`
- `http://en.wikipedia.org/wiki/Mystery_House`
- `http://en.wikipedia.org/wiki/Machinarium`
- `http://www.crimson-room.net/`
- `http://en.wikipedia.org/wiki/SCUMM`
- `http://www.gdcvault.com/play/1014732/Classic-Game-Postmortem-MANIAC`
- `http://www.ign.com/faqs/2010/blade-runner-complete-endings-guide-1095108`
- `http://en.wikipedia.org/wiki/221B_Baker_Street`
- `http://en.wikipedia.org/wiki/Red-black_tree`
- `http://www.imdb.com/name/nm0000033/bio#quotes`
- `http://en.wikipedia.org/wiki/180-degree_rule`

Blueprints

Here you can see a blueprint showing the protagonist in different projections and poses. It can help to develop the main character properly:

The following blueprint demonstrates one of the game levels. It is entitled Dieselpunk. All the events take place in the generator room; there is a huge diesel engine inside it. To get the key, Anna-Amelia has to mix some portion of diesel fuel with a special additive called Punk (there must be a puzzle to find the right proportion). After this, she should start the engine, but because of the additives it becomes unstable; the pipe breaks and Anna-Amelia gets the key.

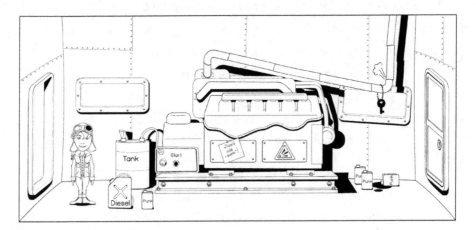

The following blueprint demonstrates a game level entitled Telephone exchange. To open the door, Anna-Amelia has to call the senior operator. By using a special machine called Phonebook, she must determine the operator's phone number. There are 10 numbers in the Phonebook; each of them can be accessed via a rotary dial. The problem is that two out of three cold cathode display tubes (a special glass tube with numerals inside) are broken. The protagonist has to use only one tube for getting a number, one at a time. Then the telephone switchboard should be used to call the operator.

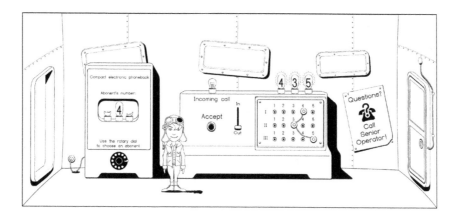

The following blueprint shows a game level entitled Draisine. It is very tricky. Anna-Amelia sees a key, but it cannot help her to open the exit door. The door is jammed. The only way to escape the room is to fix the draisine; the key is needed to start the engine. To fix the vehicle, Anna-Amelia has to use the propeller from her inventory that she thought must be used to fix her airplane rather than the draisine.

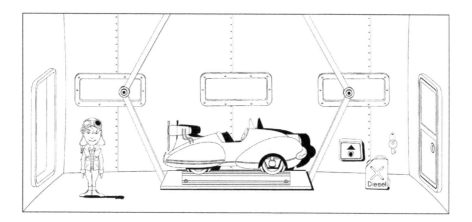

Summary

Adventure games are about choices that a player makes, navigating a tree of possibilities and searching for correct answers and undiscovered places. Starting from earlier versions, they were a new way to tell stories letting the audience understand that somewhere some amazing things were hidden, and you only needed to find the right key.

To create a good adventure game, you need to be very careful and pay attention to every aspect of the plot. Puzzles, dialogues, graphics should be perfectly adjusted. The harmony and balance are pretty important. That is not easy but very interesting.

In the next chapter, we will talk about action games. Usually they are a blend of various genres. Modern action games may include different components, including adventure-based plot, minor puzzle solving, RPG elements, and so on.

8

Action Games

The popularity of action games of different subgenres is difficult to underestimate. This is one of the most important genres for the modern game industry. Being mixed with other types of game mechanics such as adventure, puzzles, and RPG, action-oriented titles provide very diverse gameplay styles and experiences. Many complex action games can be considered to be creative and technologically avant-garde because they try to use the most advanced solutions to create very pictorial and alive virtual worlds that players can interact with.

Introducing action games

There are two kinds of games that humans have been playing for centuries: the first is card/board amusements or puzzles, and the second is more active games such as sporting competitions of different types. Archery and darts can be easily considered as an early prototype of a shooting game. The main objective is to hit a target, and players get special rewards for their accuracy.

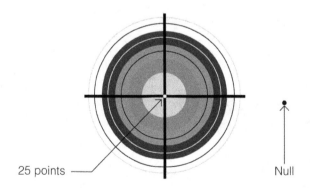

25 points

Null

One of the advantages of active games is that the simplicity of rules, goals, and mechanics is pretty visible. No wonder early video game systems mostly tried to recreate common sports games in a digital form rather than puzzles. The list of games for Magnavox Odyssey, which was the very first gaming console for home use introduced in 1972, consisted of titles such as table tennis, baseball, soccer, hockey, and so on. They were easier to develop (of course, in a very minimalistic form), and it was easier to convince the audience to begin playing with them because the gaming principles were familiar. Among them, of course, were shooting games. The console even had a unique accessory called Shooting Gallery. It is a light gun that allows players to hit different objects on the screen of a TV set. What can be easier than just seeing the target and pressing the button! The gameplay featured a very simple logic: players only need to have a good reaction and keen eyes.

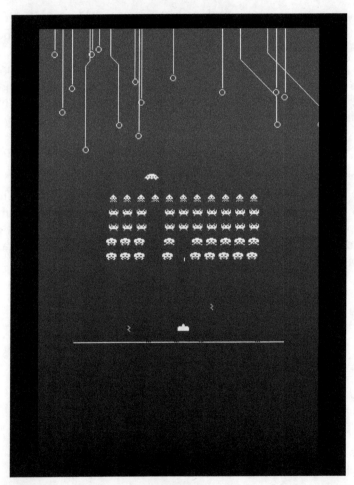

The game Space Invaders was successfully ported on iOS by TAITO Corporation

The designers of arcade machines used the same approach. They tried to trace different actions from real life. Besides sporting events, developers were fond of imitating hunting, movie-style dueling, racing, military combat fighting, and so on. As you see, all this was only a way to copy something that was very familiar to the audience. In the beginning, that worked fine, but then people learned that video games can be a more flexible tool. In order to compete better, some creative experiments like Space Invaders, which became a pop culture idol and a symbol of all modern action games, could be performed. This cult product was released in 1978 by *Tomohiro Nishikado*. It used the principles of shooting games that were already being followed for that period of time, but tried to expand boundaries by telling an original story rather than simply utilizing popular clichés. The trial was rewarded. The game became a huge hit, opening a golden era of arcade entertainment.

Then, action games got larger gaming spaces. They began utilizing the advantages of side-scrolling mechanics. This helped to concentrate on the main characters of these games. From that moment, these characters required a more accurate and detailed visual look, good animation, and interesting plot background. Remember that another core symbol of modern action games, *Duke Nukem*, was originally the character of a 2D action-platformer game released in 1991 by *Apogee Software*.

There is a popular misbelief that the first video games with 3D-polygonal graphics were introduced in the 1990s. In reality, the very first example was released in the market a decade earlier. In 1983, *Atari* published an arcade shooter game called *I, Robot*. It featured faceted 3D models rather than wire-frame images. Of course, they were very primitive. The geometry was very simple, and there was no texture. The game levels in most cases were made of plain parallelepipeds, but for its time, that was a sensational breakthrough! Just imagine that 3D graphics in the early 1980s was so costly that when director *John Carpenter* wanted to use a 3D wire-frame animation of a city for his science-fiction movie, *Escape from New York* (released in 1981), it was not easy to render it on a computer. He simulated CGI by creating a model of the city made of cardboard, plywood, and other materials that were painted black and used reflective tape to imitate 3D-edges.

Nevertheless, the real widespread acceptance of 3D actions was related only with the appearance of first-person shooters in the early 1990s. This process is mainly associated with id Software, the company that started paying maximum attention to 3D engines and games based on them. The evolution of this genre can be seen by the following projects released by the company. Everything started with experiments with mazes and imitation of 3D spaces. *Hovertank 3D*, which was published in 1991, featured various monsters vaguely resembling those that would later appear in the game series *Doom*, but level design, story, and gameplay were pretty primitive.

The concept was transformed into a more valuable game, *Catacomb 3-D* (1991). Few people know that this game could be considered as a role model for all further first-person shooter games, setting some standards of the genre, for instance, the game displayed an arm of the main characters on the screen. The famous title *Wolfenstein 3D* appeared the following year. It was critically acclaimed and became a commercial hit. This was a signal for the entire industry that a new era had begun! Later, *Doom* (1993) would be released, and the world would be revolutionized with the introduction of a real 3D engine in *Quake* (1996). The end of the story is familiar to you. Now, 3D action is one of the most popular and commercially successful game. Being mixed with various other genres, 3D action games provide stories for every taste; so, a very large audience can be covered.

Classifying the types of shooters

There are several general types of mechanics and setups used in action games. Each of them has its own advantages and tried-and-true features. Choosing a proper class of game may help you to plan your future games better.

Fixed shooters

Fixed shooters are games where the protagonist is fixed at one position on the screen, being able to only change the angle of shooting or strafe (usually, this is a story about a gun turret). The most notable example is, of course, Space Invaders. Another one is a classic game, *Paratrooper*, originally designed by *Greg Kuperberg* in 1982. Now, there are dozens of clones of this product on iTunes; its concept is very addictive.

A screenshot from DOT Space Hero by 1Coin

Scrolling shooter

Scrolling shooters are games where all the actions are shown from a side-view perspective. Originally, such games were sprite-based, being a direct analogy to platform arcade; the only difference was the more dynamic action-oriented gameplay. Such games were extremely popular on 8 bit and 16 bit gaming consoles because many modern developers tried to contribute to them. A wonderful example is *DOT Space Hero* from *1Coin* (`http://www.dotspacehero.com/`). The game has amazing and cute graphics as well as colorful gameplay. The general advantage of side-scrolling concept for iOS devices is an easy to control system.

Rail shooter

Rail shooters are games where the player cannot freely move around. The game moves the avatar from one location to another, and allows him to fight with the enemies while running or in special zones. The system works like a sightseeing train in an amusement park. The concept is ideal for arcade-shooting galleries; once all the enemies are down, the game moves you to a new intact location. Of course, the lack of freedom is a bad idea, but sometimes such mechanics may help you manage some issues such as tricky shooter controls on touch-screen devices. Since a player does not need to guide the character themselves, they can concentrate only on shooting. A popular instance is *Rage HD* developed by *id Software* (`http://www.idsoftware.com/iphone-games/rage-mobile/`).

First-person shooter

First-person shooter (**FPS**) are games that demonstrate the 3D gaming world through a first-person perspective. In other words, they try to be as close as possible to the natural human perception of reality. Now, this is one of the most popular types of shooters, especially on computers and gaming consoles. The iOS platform is not an exception. There are several very interesting ports of classic FPS games as well as projects that are developed specially for it, for example, *Deus Ex: The Fall* from *Square Enix* (`http://www.deusex.com/thefall`).

The general weak point of FPS on touch-screen devices is the controls that hold back their popularity on the platform a little bit.

Deus Ex: The Fall used dual cameras. Being a first-person shooter, the game switches to third-person view on special occasions to express some specific actions in a better way.

Third-person shooter

Third-person shooters (TPS) are 3D games where a player may not only see the gaming environment around, but also his own avatar. The virtual camera is placed somewhere behind him since the gameplay is very similar to FPS games, but the player can see the animation of the main characters. This is good for games with complex actions such as jumping, crouching, and balancing. There is also a belief that the audience is more attached to characters that are shown in full form when a 3D figure of the protagonist is displayed at the screen, so all its graphic details and animated movements can be easily noticed. There are two basic ways of using a third-person perspective in games. The first is a traditional view showing the back of the protagonist; the camera is slightly above him. And the second one is the so-called over-the-shoulder view when the camera is almost hidden under the character's back, being placed in the line of his sight. The player sees the world over his shoulder. Such a combination is a little bit clumsy, but it helps to aim in a better way. This type of camera is very suitable for the horror genre because it is hard to turn around fast since there is always a fear of what is behind. This feature is successfully used in the *Dead Space* franchise published by *Electronic Arts*.

Mixed shooters

Mixed shooters are a combination of other genres, for example, action-RPG, action-adventure, and action-survival. The eclecticism is now in fashion. Most modern action games are a mix of different mechanics. It helps to enrich gameplay with new features. Among the popular titles for iOS in this domain are the successful franchises *Infinity Blade* from *Chair Entertainment* (http://infinityblade.com/) and *Epic Games*. They combine the advanced 3D graphics, accurate character, environment design, interesting combat mechanics (based on sword fighting and not guns), and RPG elements.

Generating the game idea

Of course, the primal intention of many fresh game developers is to create a first-person shooter. This is a good dream, but a very bad idea. A competitive modern FPS, even if it is going to be developed for handheld devices, requires titanic efforts, that is, a gigantic job that will be enormous for small teams. There should be an original concept that can attract the attention of the audience: a good story, tons of accurate 3D models and textures, great animation, perfect special effects, optimized graphics, minimum glitches, and an ideal balance in a new, competitive FPS. Don't forget the hundreds of hidden nuances and pitfalls.

It is more reasonable to reduce our ambitions a little bit and start with a smaller project to experiment with. It is good to take some ideas from the good old arcades. For example, the Shoot 'em up subgenre, where a character is surrounded with lots of enemies and needs to hold fire all the time, is the mechanics from Space Invaders. The animation of a 3D character is not an easy job. For your first game, you may try to make the process easier by reducing a number of movable parts of the protagonist. The most obvious way is to put him inside a vehicle; in that case, there will be no need to create any types of walking cycle animations. For instance, the protagonist may move using some sort of flying vehicle. As far as the Space Invaders are concerned, it is good to put the player into space. Thus, the main character will be an astronaut, and use a small space craft to move. He will have a laser gun. There will be some asteroids and space junk around as well as angry enemies. The protagonist is alone, so the objective is clear — to return to the other people who are battling their way through hordes of opponents. Yes, we got the idea!

Writing the plot

A huge starship called Danube is moving in space. This is a cargo ship carrying unique resources from colonies on far away planets. It comes back fully loaded to Earth. The mission is very important because Earth is totally out of resources, and completely depends on regular transports from the new lands (the far away planets are still in the state of terraformation, so they are not ready for the normal life of human beings). If the ship will not return in time or lose its precious cargo, mankind will face hard times. The world economics will collapse, there will be a huge political crisis, and there might even be several wars for dribs and drabs of resources that are conserved by some countries. Therefore, all of the crew fully concentrate on their extremely important objective. The ship must be in perfect order; each system should work like clockwork. Since everyday an army of engineers exits into open space for maintenance, they are using special space suits with small engines to fly over the ship. From some distance, it may look like a hive surrounded with bees.

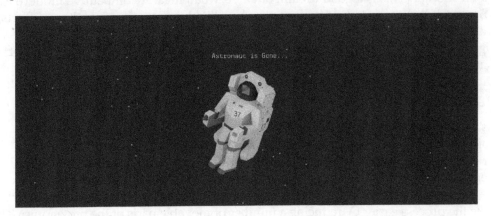

The protagonist is one such bee. He needs to check the communication module situated at the starboard. Now, the ship is in a dangerous environment. There are lots of asteroids and meteors around the ship. Each of them can easily detect important nodes and components. Besides, there are many artificial objects such as old satellites, fragments of ships crushed against minor planets, and cargo containers. The engineers have a double shift. This is a dark territory; space pilots do not like this part of the journey because the space junk is an ideal way for space pirates to create an ambush.

Suddenly, the Danube is assaulted. Dozens of small ships painted in dark colors start a firefight. The communication module is hit; it explodes massively, and a big fragment of the casing hits the protagonist directly on the helmet. The astronaut is thrown away from the ship. He crashes his back into a rock; a new explosion pushes him away. He is senseless because of the impact, being unable to control his suit in space.

Moreover, many systems are now broken. The **head-up-display** (**HUD**) alerted that the suit is completely out of order. Only the support system is still working normally, and the level of oxygen is satisfactory. The blast wave carries the protagonist away from the ship. He moves farther away every second; the stars mirrored in the helmet's glass disappear. Soon the astronaut will be gone, and this is the code name of the game: Astronaut is Gone.

Soon the protagonist will wake up; he will be okay, only having a very bad headache. He will be totally alone, and there will be no Danube on the horizon. His main objective will be returning to the ship. The communication module has gone; so, he will have no opportunity to communicate with the bridge. His only chance will be to find a signal from one of the space lighthouses that can transfer the intermediate coordinates of the ship. The astronaut will catch such a signal and begin his journey to the lighthouse; he will not know what he will meet ahead.

Planning game modes

There can be two main gaming modes in the game named Astronaut is Gone. They are as follows:

- **Story**: All levels are created according to the plot. They have a fixed structure, design, length, and number of enemies. Each level finishes at a lighthouse. The last level includes an image of the Danube since the protagonist will engage in combat with pirates who have occupied his ship. By defeating them all, the player finishes the game.

- **Arcade**: The game universe is generated randomly based on various templates. Obstacles and enemies appear constantly; their speed and power increases with time. The objective is to stay alive for as long as possible; each second counts. This mode can use the principles of rail shooters. There is no puzzle.

Developing the protagonist

The main hero of the Astronaut is Gone game is silent and mysterious. We know very little about him, his past, and habits; even his name is unknown. The character is referred to simply as the astronaut. All his individuality is hidden under the shell of the space suit. He is a valuable introvert. He can be considered an ideal game avatar, a blank paper that the player may fill with his own personality.

Thus, most of our attention is paid to the exterior of the protagonist. He is not only wearing an ordinary space suit, but is also using a mini space vehicle, the **Astronaut Maneuvering Unit (AMU)**, which is also known as the Astronaut Propulsion Unit.

Astronaut Maneuvering Unit

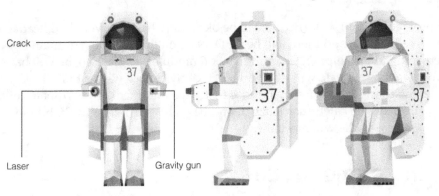

If you have seen any images of astronauts working outside of a space station, you should be familiar with such types of apparatuses. It looks like a very massive knapsack with some maneuvering engines and life support systems. Astronauts control them using joysticks and buttons placed on special racks.

In the game, the AMU is a little more futuristic. It features faster engines, a special visual system based on advanced artificial intelligence (known as HUD), various useful support systems, and of course, it carries some tools that can be used as weapons as well. The protagonist is one of the starship engineers. He works in the 13th crew, and his identification number is 37.

After the attack, the 37th Unit is a little bit damaged. All internal systems will be in order soon after the automatic maintenance, but one detail will be kept unchanged: a heavy fragment has hit the space helmet; so, a crack has appeared in the glass. It is not strictly dangerous, but gives some sense of suspense by illustrating the fact that the astronaut is fragile, and he is protected only by a thin shell that can be easily destroyed. This is also a way to add some individuality to the Unit. The cracks make it special. Another advantage is a break of symmetry. A character that consists of two identical parts is always perceived to be a little bit unnatural and boring (unless it is a ceramic vase). Always try to think of such fragments of the design. Tiny details may turn the visual look into a little story. They can even be the integral part of the plot that are being used in some future twists, for example, Elizabeth's little finger covered by a thimble in a gorgeous game *Bioshock Infinite* from *Irrational Games*.

This unusual detail is perceived by a player all over the game looking like an original fashion accessory, but then the true meaning is exposed very dramatically. A tiny design idea produces a very powerful story effect.

The Unit may move in many directions. It has several maneuvering engines; so, it is quite a brisk machine. The only point is a little inertia. It cannot change the vector of movement at once; so, there is always a little delay in turns; the fly is always smooth without broken trajectories. Such specialty makes the behavior more naturalistic, and adds some reasonable difficulty to the game. The player has to calculate some actions in advance. For instance, the player has no opportunity to stop the Unit dead. Still, there is no friction in space, and he needs to turn on the reverse engines to compensate the motion.

Designing enemies

Obviously, the main antagonists are the angry pirates who have attacked the Danube earlier. They are scattered all over space, and are hiding behind the rocks. All of them are humans, not aliens; so, they use technologies from Earth. In most cases, that refers to the different space vehicles stolen from other ships. For example, the pirates utilize AMUs to move. They are painted in dark gray to be more inconspicuous. Here's the list of all the variations of enemies:

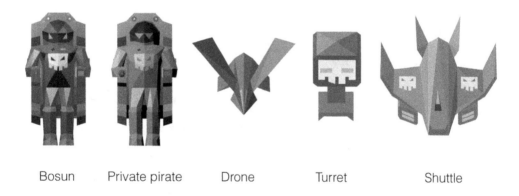

Bosun   Private pirate   Drone   Turret   Shuttle

- **Private pirate**: This is the simplest type of pirate. It is a direct copy of the protagonist. The pirate utilizes the same AMU as the main hero; thus, the pirate has no armor, and only has one laser gun.

- **Bosun**: This is a pirate with a heavily modified and armored Unit. It has two lasers that are operating simultaneously. This is a hard enemy. His only weak point is a slower speed of maneuvering.

- **Drone**: This is a small unmanned space vehicle carrying a laser gun. The machine and maneuver ability are very fast; nevertheless, it can be destroyed by a single hit. The main point to be noted is their number. Drones usually try to attack in a swarm.

- **Turret**: This is an automated gun that is fixed on a rock or on another type of big obstacle. The simplest version has only one laser gun that is oriented forward. More advanced models have many barrels that are turned in various directions.

- **Pirate shuttle**: This is the most powerful enemy in the game, for example, it may guard the lighthouse at the end. It looks like a small spaceship with several heavy guns. It requires a lot of effort to be defeated.

Preparing obstacles

The astronaut's journey to the lighthouse is not a walk in the park; it is full of different dangerous situations and hindrances. This is deep space. First of all, there are lots of objects floating around that the player should try to dodge; otherwise, he will lose some portions of his health after contact with them. It is much harder if the AMU is moving fast. Like in arcade flying simulators, the player maneuvers in space, trying to squeeze between the rocks and other types of space junk. The obstacles can be of very complex shapes, and rotate chaotically in space; so, it is a task to avoid contact with their fragments.

The space junk consists of objects of different size and mass. They are as follows:

- **Massive**: These are various big rocks, cargo containers, and large fragments of crushed spaceships

- **Medium**: These are old satellites, medium containers, crates, meteors, and small fragments of casing

- **Small**: These are little fragments of exploded rocks, tiny particles of star dust, and so on

The rocks are mostly awry spheres or ellipsoid with some craters on the surface. They may also feature some peaks. Rare examples (really large ones) may have large perforating tunnels; so, the player can try to fly through them. Generally, the players know their own speed being fixed in space, but most of them can rotate around an incidental axis. Containers as well as fragments of ships have the same behavior. They are passive elements. They cannot attack the protagonist, follow him, or intentionally change their position to collide with the Unit. The trickiest types of obstacles are space flotsam and jetsam. Contrary to rocks and containers, they can have very complex and bizarre geometry. Various traps can be made of them. By rotating at unexpected angles, broken metallic trusses can be a captious barrier for the player to pass through. A series of trusses rotating in opposite directions may create a corridor of pendulums, a level design cliché, where the player needs to react fast. The player has to pass various dangerous barriers such as sharp metallic blades, heavy pendulums, and laser beams that are constantly moving. To force the player to move into such a hazardous territory, other elements such as clusters of rocks and anomalies can be used. They will block all ways except for the dangerous corridor.

There is also a stream of objects in the game. There is an endless flow of different small obstacles at some levels. They can have different speed, density, and depth (in most cases, they are pretty flat, only one row of elements). This is a non-trivial barrier, requiring good pilot skills or active usage of the laser gun.

Another dynamic and inanimate enemy is a comet. This is a massive body that moves much faster than other obstacles, and it has a long tail. If the player collides with the protagonist, it pushes him hard backwards, and takes a larger portion of his health. Therefore, the player should avoid such a collision at any cost. Optionally, the comet's tail may have some effects on the Unit, either negative or positive.

Illustrating collisions

It might sound amusing, but collisions are a very important part of the game because they demonstrate the advantages of the 3D engine. Being crashed into an edge of a massive obstacle, the protagonist begins to rotate in space at different angles. For a few moments, the AMU becomes uncontrollable. A special alert appears signaling that space orientation is lost. Virtual control turns into disable state, but a special large button called **Align** is displayed. The player should click on it quickly to get the control back. This is not an easy task, especially if the Unit, being in an improvised spin, has touched other objects. In a bad scenario, there can be a chain of collisions, causing a pretty long and spectacular tumbling of the character.

To add some humor to the situation, the game may utilize a special soundtrack for such moments. Some allusions on The Blue Danube by *Johann Strauss* recall the famous film by *Stanley Kubrick, 2001, A Space Odyssey* (1968), ornamenting with that beautiful piece of music. While rotating, the astronaut dances a waltz. The character can also complain aloud about the situation making some funny commentaries or noises.

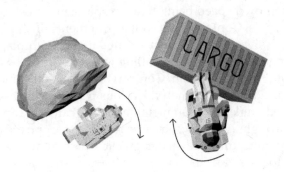

By colliding into a central part of a massive obstacle, the Unit simply stops. For a few moments, the protagonist is stunned, and the virtual controls do not function. If the obstacle has its own speed, it begins to push the Unit like a bulldozer, carrying it backward. The player should unstick from the surface of the object and fly over it.

Medium objects such as satellites do not cause the protagonist to tumble, but shift his trajectory a little bit, change his speed dramatically, and fly off sideways. Tiny particles have no effect on the Unit as they are too small to have enough energy; they only bounce from the surface of the astronaut. It may look very beautiful, alluding to the scenes from the science fiction film *Event Horizon* (1997), where a character in a space suit was surrounded with hundreds of fragments of an exploded spaceship.

Inserting anomalies

Besides the object-based obstacles, there can be some more impalpable ones in the form of various forces that affected the astronaut. Remember that to add some good dramatic moments, you should play with the protagonist's abilities. If he is able to do an action, it is good to reduce his power somehow, or even take the power away from him for a period of time. Only when somebody loses something do they truly understand its significance. Thus, in the game, it should be territories (where the astronaut is more vulnerable) because something invisible to a naked eye affects him and takes his powers. I would call such events an anomaly.

Anomaly

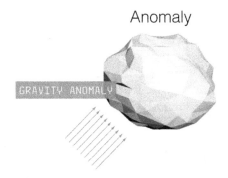

There can be three kinds of anomalies:

- **Portals**: These are deformations of space that look like blinking flat spots and may be with some visible discharges. They can be small or large. If the protagonist reaches one of them, he is teleported to another location. Because this is a pitfall, it usually means that he has been returned back, losing some progress in the game. Only on very rare occasions, a portal may have a positive meaning, thus propelling the main hero forward. Portals can also be used by enemies to appear suddenly in front of the player.

- **Gravity**: A distortion of force vectors may occur near really large objects. The HUD highlights such zones with special graphics, warning the player. Depending on the current version of the anomaly, it may attract or pull on the Unit, unconditionally changing the direction it has been flying in. To escape such hazard fields, the player should use extra throttle and maneuver more actively. The fuel energy for the unit is consumed much faster.

- **Artificial**: Various kinds of phenomenons affect the internal systems of the Unit and are generated by special devices. The first on the list are old satellites. They carry a field of interference and noises. If the protagonist is quite close to one of them for a short period of time (up to a few seconds), the Unit becomes uncontrollable or begins to move randomly. There are stripes and other visual artifacts on the screen. Besides the satellites, there are also various electronic traps left by the pirates. The HUD can notice them. It highlights them as zones with unknown fields. Some traps simply disorient the Unit just as satellites do, while others take away some portion of the protagonist's energy and freeze him for a period of time. There are also artificial anomalies that absorb energy beams so that the laser gun cannot punch through them. They work like a protective shield.

The anomalies work fine in synergy with the physical obstacles, thus helping each other. For instance, a gravity anomaly may attract the protagonist into a territory with a lot of dangerous metallic trusses. A combination of obstacles and anomalies also may lead to the creation of a space quagmire (a group of medium rocks, crates, and other junk, plus several gravity anomalies). For a period of time, the player will be stuck in this mess of objects. The pirates, on their turns, use their traps for a reason. They try to immobilize or take off all the resources of the player before combat.

Giving bonuses

The space in the game should not be a strictly severe territory. The player should get some candies as well.

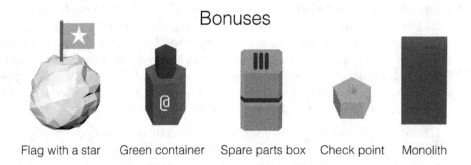

Bonuses

Flag with a star   Green container   Spare parts box   Check point   Monolith

The following is a list of all the bonuses that the player gets in the game:

- **Flag with a star**: This is a collectible item. It gives some rewards in points to the player and lets him brag about it among friends. But this rock, the one having a blue flag with a star on it, is found very rarely.

- **Green container**: This is another collectible item. It is a small bottle-shaped metallic box. It gives less value of points, but contains some drops of text information that the HUD displays on the screen. It includes only few words. As you might guess, the object is a message in a bottle, a way to create a subplot inside the main story. Inside the green containers, there can be messages from the Danube, exposing the current situation aboard. Alternatively in the containers, there can be a message from the ship that was lost in space long ago; let's call the ship Amsterdam. There can be portions of the ship's log, exposing its story or some old requests for help.

- **Spare parts box**: This is one of the most popular bonuses, a crate with some useful parts inside that lets the player upgrade some properties of the Unit, either support system (increase health or oxygen bar) or weapons. Each spare part box contains one upgrade point. The player himself decides which variable it should be added to.

- **Check point**: This is an object with some field around it that looks like a lifebuoy. By flying through it, the player gets a new checkpoint. The main character will resurrect here after the next death in the game.

- **Monolith**: This is a semi-ghostly rare item of unknown origin. It appears suddenly in different places, and looks like a black parallelepiped. If the protagonist touches it (crashes into it), he is rewarded with invulnerability and infinite energy for a few minutes. Such an effect must be a surprise for the player. The game should not explain the true meaning of this element.

- **Star dust**: This is a cloud of shining particles moving across the screen. It gives a burst of energy for the Unit as soon as the protagonist reaches the cloud. Another talent of the star dust is multiplying the laser shot. Instead of one beam, three parallel beams appear in the cloud. Of course, the enemy's shots are multiplied as well.

Introducing health and oxygen

The protagonist has two vital variables: health and oxygen. They are tightly interconnected. The astronaut needs air to breathe. One of the essential ingredients in the air is oxygen. It is also used to supply the level of health if the astronaut is wounded. In this case, he consumes the oxygen much faster (to refill the health bar, it may take more than half of the oxygen tank) since there are no medicine chests in the game, only oxygen canisters.

You might notice that most modern games do not feature an image of a red cross on any medical supply recourses. Usually, it is replaced with a stylized emblem that is close to the cross, but has other visual properties. This is because the red cross symbol belongs to International Red Cross and Red Crescent Movement. Because it has a specific and significant meaning, any misuse is forbidden by the law. This protects the emblem from contamination by unnecessary connotations and inflation of correct sense. Thus, other medical symbols should be used in games, and they need not resemble the red cross.

For instance, the Rod of Asclepius, which was taken from Greek mythology, looks like a stick entwined by a serpent. Asclepius was honored as the God of medicine and healing while the serpent itself symbolizes drugs (`http://en.wikipedia.org/wiki/Rod_of_Asclepius`).

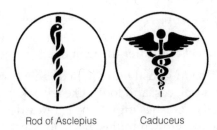

Rod of Asclepius   Caduceus

By now, the Rod of Asclepius is pretty popular. It is used by many medical facilities and organizations (for example, it is a part of the logo of the World Health Organization). Many ambulances in the United States and Europe have this logo. The symbol is written into the Star of Life, which is the emblem of **emergency medical services** (**EMS**).

The Caduceus is another well-known symbol of medicine, especially in the U.S. You may find it in many games, printed on medical chests and other types of medical stuff. The most interesting point is that originally, it was associated only with commerce because it was carried by Hermes, the ancient Greek god of trade. From the mythological point of view, the emblem is not correct. The Caduceus has two serpents, but they are not exactly medicine ones. Apparently, the symbol was involved in a new semantic context by mistake, being confused with the Rod of Asclepius, or it might be that somebody decided it looked more solemn with the wings. There could also be some special reasons and complex logic in the choice involving various nuances (for example, two serpents can be considered as a symbol of peace or neutrality). Somehow, it was approved as the emblem for the U.S. Army Medical Corps; since then, the symbol got a new life, becoming well recognized and popular. You can check this at `http://en.wikipedia.org/wiki/Caduceus_as_a_symbol_of_medicine`.

When the stock of oxygen reaches the minimum level, the Unit switches into an emergency mode. The protagonist slowly loses his health (figuratively speaking, it is converted into the oxygen). The player must find a new oxygen tank really quickly. Some games have tried to add extra difficulty to the situation when the health level is critically low by slowing down the main character, disabling some of his abilities, or adding other types of unpleasant things. I'm sure that for a player, the absence of health points is already a disaster that makes him worry.

Why should he get some extra ones? Never anger the audience too much! Since the astronaut does not lose any functionality of his suit till the very last drops of health, he won't die, but he will switch to a coma state. In this state, the screen turns black, the Unit controls become disabled, and an image of a horizontal line appears. The player has to operate fast. He can save the protagonist by virtual defibrillation. At the center of the screen, there is a button with a heart symbol. Now, it should be tapped fast, restarting the heart of the character. If the objective of this gesture mini-game has been accomplished successfully, the astronaut gets a little portion of additional health so he may try to find a new oxygen canister again. The idea of a second chance is pretty good because the game should not be too cruel and try to take the protagonist's life as soon as possible. The death of the hero in many cases means the end of the game session, but it is always better to let the player play longer.

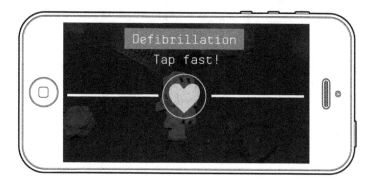

Enemies and obstacles reduce the amount of health as well. Being shot, the main character loses an amount of health points; this value may depend on the exact place of the hit, and it is obvious that the head costs more than an arm. To add some specularity, it is good to illustrate the hit locations by trickles of steam escaping the AMU. The autoregeneration that converts the oxygen into health points and fixes the suit should not start immediately after a hit. Let it take several seconds to activate or the protagonist is required to leave the line of fire.

Optionally, special critical zones can be introduced in the game. Small areas at the corners of the Unit may be turned into very delicate sections; being hit, they switch off some specific functions. For instance, an enemy shoots at the left corner of the suit where one of the maneuvering engines is placed. After such an incident, the player cannot turn to the right because the engine is down.

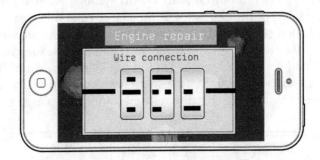

To fix it, the player must play a special mini-game that looks like a match-3 puzzle. The mini-game's mechanics are similar to the moving columns game mode described in *Chapter 5, Puzzles*. The HUD displays a so-called repair window with several columns in it; their number may depend on the degree of the damage that the protagonist was subject to or on the difficulty level of the game. According to the plot, the engine has lost its wire connection with the CPU. The player needs to fix this by scrolling the bars with different variants of geometric shapes and searching for correct fragments. In other words, this is a simple connection puzzle. It should not be complex. An average player must collect it in a few seconds, because this is only a way to diversify the main gameplay via a sudden pause.

During the game's progression, some form of RPG-mechanics may be implemented. For instance, special upgrades can be offered to players so that they can increase the capacity of the oxygen bar or the health bar. Alternatively, so-called patches can be used by finding such an element in the game. A player can decrease the speed of consuming a specific resource, for example, oxygen patch 5 percent may reduce the consumption of oxygen by 5 percent.

Introducing energy cells

AMU needs some special fuel that contains energy cells floating around in space. Each cell gives some portion of power to move and to use guns. The more acceleration the protagonist has, the more energy is consumed by the Unit. In some stages of the game, when there are a minimum number of cells, it is important to be eco-friendly, saving some extra fuel by moving more slowly.

It is worth mentioning that the energy cells are extremely explosive; thus, many of them can be accidentally destroyed during a firefight. They can also be shot for the reason that if the cell is near an enemy, the intentional explosion may eliminate him.

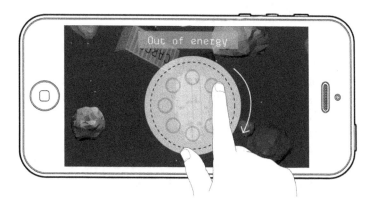

When the Unit is out of energy, it stops; it cannot move in the automatic mode anymore. Now, the player has to use a manual starter to move the protagonist. On the screen, there appears a special virtual button that looks like a wagon wheel; the player may rotate it using his index finger. The rotation transforms into impulses of energy; the system works like a dynamo. By rotating the wheel pretty intensively, the player is capable of providing the Unit with a tolerable pace. Certainly, it is much harder to control the main character in such a state, especially if the game situation, in addition, requires the use of weapons. But that is an emergency mode; so, it should not be very comfortable, being created only to help find a new energy cell. Just imagine how dramatic it may look if the protagonist is stuck in a space quagmire and the Unit is out of energy; the player should save him literally by lending a helping hand.

Shooting

Various types of weapons are an essential part of any action game. They must perfectly balance and run like clockwork, giving the player maximum pleasant experience. The story is not about dozens of variants of different guns or swords, but a couple of really good specimens because as usual, players are attached to very small arsenals, switching mostly between normal and heavier weapons in games. Habit is a second nature. A player will change something only if he is convinced that the new item is as good as the previous one, or even better, for example, if it is more powerful or operates faster.

Astronaut is Gone is designed only with two major weapons in mind: a laser gun and a gravity manipulator. According to the plot, both of them are parts of engineering equipment. Each AMU has these weapons on board. By default, they are needed for various repairing procedures outside the spaceship, but because of events in the game, the main characters should use them for other goals.

The laser gun is a basic weapon in the game. It shoots long impulses of energy, being capable of hitting a very distant object. The player has to aim by placing the astronaut in front of a target; a special color circle (sight gizmo) appears, highlighting the object. It will be shot as soon as the **FIRE** button is tapped. The protagonist as well as his enemies cannot hit a target placed at the line rather than in front of them (for example, an object situated below cannot be shot); of course, that is a silly restriction, but it forces the player to move the Unit much more actively, and allows him to easily escape the line of fire using strafe tactics. It also helps to organize different puzzles and mazes as far as the player can be ensnared into specific locations for more effective frontal attack.

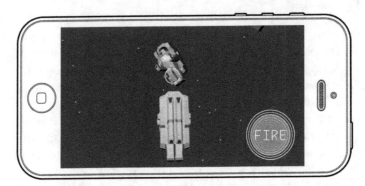

At the beginning of the game, the gun needs some time to reload; but later, its firing rate can be increased via upgrades. The power of the laser is constant all over the game. The laser gun is capable of destroying medium objects such as small rocks and satellites because in some situations, the player can carve his way by shooting the obstacles of moderate dimension. In an ideal case, an object that is hit explodes and turns into small fragments accelerating from an epicenter. Simple enemies can be defeated by one shot only, but armored ones required more hits. Massive obstacles cannot be demolished by the laser gun; as an option, they can change their trajectory a little bit. But it is better to avoid such features because the game level can be easily turned into a real mess by the player.

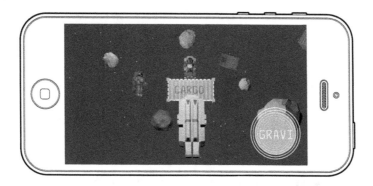

The gravity manipulator is a very funny thing. It lets the player play with Newton's laws; so, such a feature should be used only if the game has an appropriate physics engine; the objects must interact naturally. To use this gun, the player has to tap a special switch near the **FIRE** button. The sight gizmo should change shape to a rectangle without a crosshair. Now, if the player taps the **FIRE** button, the Unit will attract the closest small object that was floating in front of the protagonist. While the button is pressed, the gravity manipulator is holding the object; in the meantime, the Unit can maneuver in space carrying it along. Once the button is released, the manipulator throws the object forward, giving it some good acceleration. Besides the fun, this weapon has other advantages: it consumes much less energy than the laser gun. An object in front of the protagonist plays the role of a shield. To force the player to use it, some special game situations can be created. For instance, a bunch of enemies digs into a narrow corridor between rocks, and there is the artificial anomaly that absorbs the laser beams; so, they can be defeated only by thrown stones. It is worth mentioning that a large amount of resources (small rocks) should be provided when the player is in such a situation, letting him make mistakes when he is throwing objects at the enemies. This can be easily done by placing a small stream of obstacles nearby that can constantly grant new rocks.

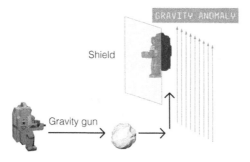

The gravity anomalies distort the trajectories of thrown objects. This fact can become the basis for various smart puzzles. For instance, there is a powerful turret inside a cube-shaped artificial anomaly opaque for the laser gun. A strong gravity anomaly is above it. Since the turret cannot be defeated by a frontal attack, the protagonist would be destroyed by the gun's drumfire. Therefore, the player may place his character at a line below the enemy, throw an obstacle, and it will be dragged out by the anomaly's energy field. In other words, it would fly up and crash into the turret. And such interesting combinations can be invented in quantities.

Working with onscreen controls

It must be confessed that controlling complex objects in a 3D space is not very natural for touchscreens. They were created for pointing, scrolling, and gestures, but not for dual control of motion (that was not thought of when such devices where planned). There are several factors that make such a job less comfortable and precise. First of all, when people play on a mobile device (either iPhone or iPad), they use their fingers in a very specific way. In most cases, only thumbs are available for input. The other fingers can be used as well, but that is not as comfortable and natural as holding a game controller, where special buttons are ergonomically placed on top of or under the device so that the fingers can naturally reach them. There cannot be a direct analogy with keyboard-and -computer mouse tandem. You cannot recreate the gaming keyboard mechanics simply by placing virtual WASD, *Shift*, and *Space* keys on the screen because to interact with them, players need to use five fingers at the same time; but that is practically impossible on mobile devices, especially on phones where the screen is smaller.

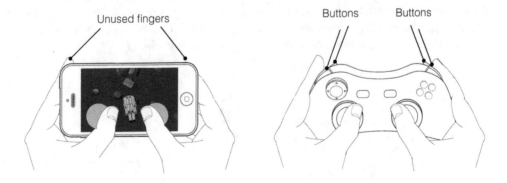

Difference between a touch-screen device and a gaming controller

That is a problem because the familiar paradigm should be changed. From the very beginning, video games were designed for machines with fixed physical controls since many habits and principles are attached to such architecture. Look at popular handheld gaming consoles such as PlayStation Vita from Sony or the Nintendo 3DS. Despite the fact that they feature touchscreens, they have familiar physical buttons as well.

In the worst scenario, a 3D action game on a touchscreen-only device may not become a story about fighting enemies, but about fighting with the game's controls since game designers need to invent their own effective solutions and some new logics by bringing up some new habits for the players. The obvious approach is onscreen controls that imitate the behavior of physical buttons. As a rule, they are placed at the bottom corners of the screen so that the thumbs can easily reach them. Additional controls are displayed nearby (a little above). A user may simply shift his thumb to press them, or try to use index fingers. It is better to avoid using any controls situated very far. Since the player needs to stretch to reach them, taking his finger from the surface of the screen, it is always a little bit frustrating.

 iOS 7 introduced a native support for external gaming controllers, almost giving the gaming console experience to the player. Contrary to the previous editions of the operating system, developers don't need a special third-party API to provide support for joysticks; everything works via standard libraries.

The game may utilize either virtual buttons or so-called virtual control pads or virtual joysticks that are sometimes more comfortable for complex accurate actions. They have more degrees of freedom because the directions are not fixed to the horizontal and vertical axes. An object on the screen can move in a diagonal direction by a single tap. Their logics imitate the behavior of a laptop's touchpads which were invented to replace the computer mouse. Touchpads can be pretty precise; no wonder Valve Corporation, a company that is an excellent specialist in the 3D action genre, is going to use such technology rather than traditional analog sticks in their upcoming steam controller. Their virtual analogs may be precise and delicate as well, but here, we meet one overall disadvantage of onscreen controls: tactile perception cannot be used by players. They cannot feel the boundaries of the input zone by touch. The screen is equally smooth since a finger can unexpectedly shift its position touching other controls.

As a result, some spontaneous mistakes in the controlling may occur. Thus, onscreen virtual pads should be pretty large, and not adjoined too close to each other.

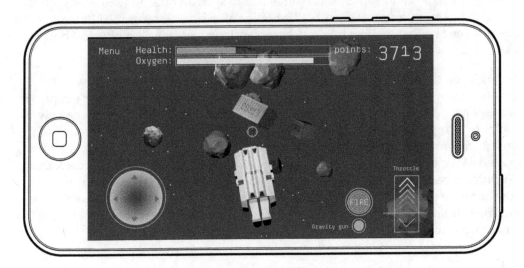

A screen layout with virtual controls on it

Another important point is that the zones where virtual controls are situated are overlapped with fingers. Therefore, there should not be any important graphic elements of a game scene in those zones. If the UI displays some useful information, the player simply will not see it.

However, virtual controls have one great advantage. The system is very flexible. Any displayed button can be added or removed from the screen in a moment. The captions may be changed, and even their size can depend on context. Such functionality offers a challenge for better clearness of some aspects of the gameplay. For example, if the player is out of ammo, the **FIRE** button turns into a disable state, and there is text, **Find some ammo**, above it. Or if some function is not available by now, the game does not display a corresponding control on the screen.

It is important to mention that onscreen controls must be adjustable. People may use their fingers differently; so, sometimes they wish to move virtual buttons a little bit (don't forget to include the option to turn the layout into the default state). Another vital point is a layout for left-handed persons. It can be created very easily. You simply need to mirror the positions of control elements on the screen.

Because of the tricky nature of the onscreen virtual controls, you have to spend a lot of time testing it on a device and asking other people about their experience with your game, figuring out the important nuances of comfort controlling.

Remember that the positions of the fingers are not always obvious for players; so, it is a good practice to show a clarifying scheme at the very beginning of the game. It is worth noting that in most cases, virtual controls are perceived as uncomfortable only at the very beginning, but later, the players may successfully adapt to them. So, your goal is to alleviate that phase, for example, through level design. The first game scenes should not include any episodes that required an accurate maneuvering in space. That should be a room upholstered with soft featherbed where the player can learn how to walk without fear of being harmed. The room can have large spaces, large gates, and simple objectives. For example, if you would put a narrow bridge at the very beginning, many players would fall down from it over and over again, thus hating your game more and more. Another good practice is stage-based learning of controls; they are introduced one by one. For example, there are two control pads in a game, one for moving a character on the ground and the second one for free-looking, and there may be several additional buttons such as **FIRE** or **JUMP**. You can give them all to the player at once, hoping that he might figure out how to use them properly, or you can do it in a more smart way. At the very beginning, the player only has to use the first control pad; the other one is disabled. After a period of time, when the player is already familiar with the basic controls, the objective may become a little harder. He is asked to start using the second control pad. To use such tactics correctly, the plot of the game should express these stages in a creative manner. If the player has only one button for a period of time, that should be the best one-button-game experience ever!

Astronaut is Gone uses onscreen controls in a full manner. The normal layout is made up of a virtual joystick to the left, which controls the AMU's directions on the screen, and a throttle slider to the right, letting the player accelerate the unit or break it. There is also a **FIRE** button near the slider. The plot helps to organize a step-by-step learning of controls. It is intended that the computer system of the AMU is broken, but it tries to repair itself on its own by making various self-tests, which is not a fast procedure; so, systems of the Unit come back to life one by one. At the very beginning, only the direction joystick is available; the throttle control is considered out of order. The AMU is moving forward slowly, and the speed cannot be increased or decreased. The player learns how to maneuver in space, avoiding collisions with rocks and space junk. There are also several objectives such as catching some spare parts that are floating in space. The player needs them to fix the Unit. Then, the computer system declares that the throttle is in order. The environment around the protagonist becomes a little more hazardous; so, the player is forced to use the main engine. One of the ideas is to show a space part that is running away from the protagonist because he should increase the speed to catch it. Finally, after a period of time, the **FIRE** button is activated. To present a new feature, the game asks to shoot some rocks that block the way. As you can see, only the tutorial plays a role of the integral part of the game rather than the boring appendage.

Turning space orientation into controls

Onscreen controls are quite good, but they can be considered as a compromise, a way to reconcile two worlds: the one with physical buttons and a brand new one with some new principles where traditional controls are not an option anymore. But what about the truly new approaches that are written from scratch? Is it possible? Sure! Moreover, iOS devices have interesting tiny sensors that might be useful: the accelerometer and the gyroscope. As a rule, beginners are a little bit confused about the exact functions and difference between these sensors. By a general description, they might look pretty similar. They are tiny instruments that measure some orientation parameters of a mobile device. In reality, each sensor has its own features. The accelerometer is a traditional part of the iOS platform. It can gauge the acceleration registering values of forces that disturb the device. Because the sensor has three axes of sensitivity, the orientation relative to the ground surface can be calculated. The simplest example of using an accelerometer is switching between landscape and portrait screen modes while a device is rotating. But the sensor also has a drawback. It is efficient for stationary objects rather than the moving ones. To overcome this point, a backup system should be used. This is why in iPhone 4, the gyroscope was introduced. It is a tiny device that is capable of measuring the exact rotation degree around the roll axis. It is created to be independent of the movement of the system. It is placed inside, playing the role of a constant criterion. It is funny to think that there are tiny rotors, gimbals, and other elements that a traditional mechanical gyroscope has, but that is not true; otherwise, all these mechanical parts would take too much space. In reality, as a rule, some other technological approaches are used in electronic devices, for example, vibrating structure gyroscopes. They are based on principles that are close to the orientation-measuring system that some flying insects have. These creatures use specially modified hind wings known as halters as mechanical constants. They are vibrating permanently during flight (making the distinctive high-pitch noise that humans can perceive). When some force is trying to change a rotation angle of the insect's body, the halters resist (it is hard to change the plane of vibration) involuntarily by pressing some special sensors; thus, the angle is measured by the insect. Microscopic vibrating gyroscopes inside electronic devices have their own halters. They look like solid-state elements of a specific shape. They vibrate with a special frequency.

The idea of a working partnership between the accelerometer and the gyroscope comes from such complex systems such as the orientation device in aircrafts. Working together, they complement each other and provide an accurate measurement of movement within the space of the mobile device in which they are built.

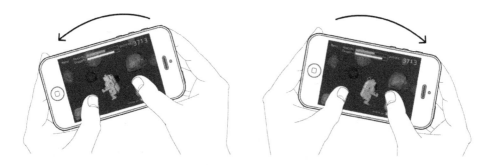

The orientation-based controls try to intercept the angle at which the screen was tilted in a specific direction, and interpret it into commands for characters or other objects. Such an approach became very popular for various arcade simulators; here, players have to control flying vehicles, cars, and so on. The principle is very obvious and natural for the audience. Once the device is turned to the left like a wheel, a vehicle on the screen turns left as well. There is no need for any virtual buttons other than the ones for special actions.

Astronaut is Gone can use such a system too. By rotating a device to the right or left (the first axis), the player defines the horizontal movement of the astronaut. But tilting it forward or backward (the second axis) gives the hero a vertical acceleration. To control weapons and the throttle slider, thumbs are used. The only tricky part is the harsh turn of the device. To exclude unshapely twitches in the trajectory of motion, it is a good practice to provide a special buffer inside the game that would smooth the peaks.

One of the ways to simplify the controls is to automate some operations by shifting the responsibility to the game's **Artificial Intelligence (AI)**. For example, the game may accelerate the character by itself; players only need to rotate the wheel, forgetting about the pedals. Such tactics work fine, but only as simulators for speedy games. It takes away the pauses in a game; so, it is not a walk with a right to stop anywhere, but a rush.

Designing the head-up display

Although there are lots of non-realistic elements on the screen of the game (such as various onscreen menus, texts, and graphical hints), their use can be warranted not only by the suspension of disbelief, but also by the plot itself, especially when it is a question of futuristic vehicles, robotic suits, or exoskeletons. Any onscreen alerts, text messages, graphic hints, and many more can be explained via utilizing a HUD. Such technology is a familiar cockpit element of modern aircrafts or advanced cars. Various useful data is projected on special transparent plates so that pilots (or drivers) see through it, perceiving both the physical space in front of them and additional digital information. It is a form of augmented reality created by combining two types of realities. By saying that an apparatus in the game has an advanced HUD, you may stop to question all the virtual sights, health bars, and other types of vital UI-elements; now, they are realistic.

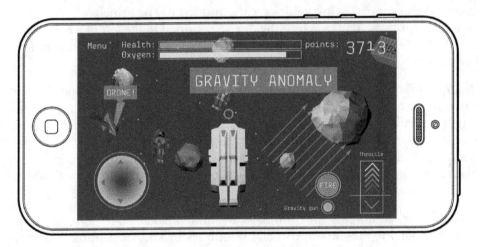

The AMU features the HUD as well; moreover, it is a flying vehicle; so, the virtual display is very good. At the very beginning, it teaches the player by displaying hints and captions. It also highlights the enemies and hazard obstacles. Sometimes, it shows different alerts telling you about the state of the Unit when it is losing energy or oxygen. But the most important thing is that in critical moments, it always tries to cheer up the player via polite commentaries such as: "The Unit is out of oxygen. You will probably die. Sorry" or "The Unit is out of energy, but there are some enemies. I will miss you." To attach the player to it, you should give the machine some portion of personality. So, let it talk more in a different context. In most cases, the phrases should be full of a robot-like sincerity and directness. However, this can be considered as unintentional black humor and even cynicism. AI may sound rude, but there is nothing personal; it is simply doing its job. But for the astronaut, the HUD is the only friend.

Virtual display graphics should be very laconic, featuring simple geometric shapes without any ornamentation and minimalistic angular fonts (such as the **optical character recognition (OCR)** font family, SkyhookMono, and Arame). The basic point is the contrast with the environment; the images must be easy recognizable. It is good to display text messages on semitransparent rectangles. Their color may have a signal function, for example, critical alerts should be in red.

Discussing 3D graphics

An action game is not strictly necessary to utilize a 3D engine. There are a lot of wonderful games based on 2D graphics or isometric perspective. Astronaut is Gone is designed with flat graphics interpretation in mind as well. All elements such as the Unit, enemies, rocks, and meteors can be based on sprites. The movement mechanics in basic gaming modes do not contradict with that. The player does not need to turn the virtual camera because the object may have only one side. More importantly, the game world itself is not flat; each element features three coordinates. The game's universe looks like a long corridor where different objects are suspended on invisible strings. The corridor's walls, floor, and ceiling frame boundaries of the space that the player may reach. If the player gets close to them, he gets an alert, **You are leaving the path**, and the Unit stops. The protagonist can move in two planes: in the longitudinal one by traveling forward and backward and in the corridor's cross-section one by maneuvering in any direction within its limits. When he reaches an object inside the game world, he gets a chance to interact with it. The simple rules of the linear perspective help to determine sizes and coordinates of elements depending on their distance to the viewer. This lets him turn a 3D-described scenery into a natural flat image. Such a concept is very close to classical one-screen arcades; the only exception is the format of levels that are three-dimensional. Nevertheless, the final image that you would work with is flat. Therefore, it is not hard to actualize the idea in 2D graphics, especially if your favorite SDK is not supported by 3D.

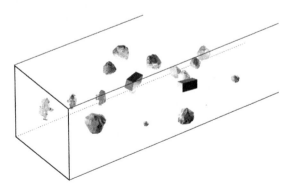

Schematic image of a level's corridor structures

However, an additional dimension may offer many new opportunities as creative as the gameplay ones. First of all, the action genre is generally associated exactly with 3D graphics. This is like a technical vanguard that requires only advanced solutions since 3D engine gives the game the correct touch needed. Then, it lets us organize more spectacular and natural scenes on the screen. The objects may rotate and interact in an interesting manner, the virtual camera can be used for more dramatic angles, and so on. Some moments can be simply impossible or very hard to recreate via 2D graphics. There is a notable story about the animation studio Pixar, which tried to impress Disney with their approach on 3D graphics animation. They simply showed dynamic shadows using venetian blinds falling on an environment across a scene, a job which could not be done by traditional animation. That demonstration was worth a thousand words. You do not need shadow tricks to impress the audience; a character that can be seen from different angles dynamically in real time is already a good start. In Astronaut is Gone, a rock rotating in three-dimensions and demonstrating all elements of its geometry looks much better than a sprite rotating only clockwise or counter-clockwise.

The technology rewards you with more flexibility and freedom, thus letting you control any scene more boldly. In some cases, it also makes the process of porting the game to another platform, such as computers, more comfortable. 3D graphics are vector-based; so, they can be easily scaled by solving the problems about different screen size, aspect ratios, and so on. There would be some issues with textures and the number of polygons, but they can be managed.

Of course, on the other hand, 3D engines may require some additional knowledge. Most importantly, the assets for them are more complex. They need special efforts on modeling, animation, texture creation, and so on. You must be ready for such a challenge. It is also a question of appropriate optimization. Modern mobile devices are pretty powerful, and nevertheless, they are not as talented as desktop computers or gaming consoles yet. You can prove it yourself by looking at compatible tables of GPU tests on special sites such as GFXBench (http://gfxbench.com), which shows that the average desktop video cards have better results by several digits than video chips of popular smartphones. So, the visual complexity can be an issue (keep in mind that a game should be oriented on the average models of mobile devices that the majority of consumers have now rather than on fresh, new devices that are more powerful but not common yet). Usually, it is not a problem of a single object made up of a large number of polygons. But the situation is more complex; materials, textures with alpha-channels, post-processing operations, and the overall number of objects in the scene may overload the GPU, thus decreasing the FPS dramatically.

Additional calculations such as AI or other complex game logics can take their portion of resources. So, it is always about appropriate equilibrium, and usually, the situation is different for each project because the conditions and number of variables can be different in each particular case. It also depends on the gaming context. Sometimes, it is a task to find out the right harmony. For example, most of your scenes are calm. There are few objects on the screen. The high frame rate tempts you to think about extra tris for the models, but then, there is a battle. Suddenly, a big combat begins. A lot of enemies are around; fragments and particles are flying in the air. The system may be stuck. To prevent such bottlenecks, objects need to have less complex visual multiplicity, providing some fund for the new elements on the screen, or some story tricks can be used. The battle plays its part; all irrelevant elements as props can be removed from the scene, but the level design by itself may be simplified for performance sake. In addition, the structure of the battles can be thought up in a way in which it would require fewer resources. The optimization is a very complex process involving not only the geometry, but also all the aspects of the game. Besides the obvious ways, always try to invent a creative way by looking at the problem from another angle. For example, you can turn the disadvantages into a special graphic style by turning the simpler and optimized type of graphics into a visual language that a game can use when talking with its players.

Turning low poly graphics into art

In the early days of 3D games, the number of polygons was a much more critical issue than today, even in such delicate domains as mobile devices. The calculation power of hardware was pretty limited. This means that game developers had to adjust the overall number of polygons in a scene to a specific minimum level. Each game object should have the lowest number of geometric faces for the game to run smooth and fast. For example, a character in the original Quake from id Software, published in 1996, was constructed using 200 polygons (many modern games spend more than ten thousand tris). Game designers always tried to make games as realistic as possible because the craft of 3D modeling was based on two opposite points: an economy of polygons and an ambition to make the 3D model look fine.

To find the correct balance, various tricks in 3D modeling and texture design were used.

Automatic sphere   A more artistic sphere

Nowadays, this intention has successfully transformed into a form of art. The past was reinvented for creative purposes. Low poly graphics are not only a technical need anymore, but additionally, an approach to present 3D models in an interesting visual way, thus brandishing polygons. The most obvious analogy is the 8-bit-like graphics in many indie games that are not about the hardware or screen resolution, but only a question of visual style. The graphics look sharp, minimalistic, and clear, having some pleasant connotations, talking about a past that we are all recalling with some warm feelings. It can be considered as a story fused in artwork. Low poly models, in a similar case, let some players drift back for more than a decade, switching on memories about the night spent playing Quake, Heretic II, Half-Life, and so on. This experience cannot be forgotten because for that period of time, each 3D game was a real breakthrough and the graphics were a symbol of the technical revolution. That is why, from a semantic point of view, low poly graphics are perceived by the audience to be more 3D-ish than any complex 3D model made up of thousands of polygons; simply put, a rough wooden taboret expresses the idea of woodenness better than any elegant cabinet made of redwood.

One of the creative advantages of minimalistic 3D models is their cuteness. Incredibly, but in most cases, low poly characters (if they were done with some style) are perceived as very sweet because they look like laconic toys made of paper or wood. Just for example, try to create the simplest game hero ever made of several cubes and parallelepipeds, and you will see that it looks very cute like an attractive paper craft discovered on the Internet.

Thus, using low poly art in a mobile 3D game, you may catch a few birds with one stone. The game is rendered fast, even on legacy devices. It looks pretty stylish and 3D models are quite easy to produce. But of course, there are disadvantages, such as minimum level of details, a generalized look for all objects, and imperfect curved surfaces.

Here's an improvised receipt of a good low poly model:

- **Faces**: These are shown intentionally. The model has a faceted design. Stealth aircrafts are a pretty good source of inspiration as well as the design of many Lamborghini cars.

- **Simple look**: The design is minimalistic. There are no tiny details and complex surfaces, as if the model should be easily gummed up of paper.

- **A circle has four angles**: In low poly models, there are no circles. They are replaced with rectangles, trapezes, or pentagons (octagons, in this case, look like a real luxury). The idea is that the circle element is fully reinterpreted, not simply surrogated with a more primitive shape.

- **Non-realistic proportions**: Because the style itself is not pretty naturalistic, it is better to use a more creative approach on the character's proportions: bigger heads, short arms, and short legs.

- **Controlled mess**: The faces should not look like they are being placed by a machine, such as automatically created tris in a default sphere created in 3D editors, especially if the model illustrates some natural objects such as rocks or tree crowns. There should be some individuality and manual craft in the order of the vertexes.

- **Large minimalistic textures**: In contrary to low poly modes used in early games, the textures can be larger; they should not be blurry. Their design must be based on laconic geometric shapes, clean colors without gradients, or any photorealistic structures.

- **Sharp animation**: Movement of objects and character should obey the overall tone of the graphics. Any moves must be a little bit sharp and non-linear as in stop-motion animation.

Astronaut is Gone is based on low poly 3D graphics as well. All elements are made up of simple shapes and do not have a large number of tris.

Modeling 3D graphics

Sure enough, if you are going to work with 3D graphics, it is necessary to have a 3D artist in your team. A good specialist may help you prevent many pitfalls. But in some cases, especially if the models are not complicated, you may be the chief cook and bottle washer and create all geometry yourself. It is preferable to prepare for such a task with the help of special literature because I only cover some basic aspects of 3D modeling for games without any specific details.

There is a wide range of different 3D editors in the market including some free ones, but a pretty popular tool is Blender (http://www.blender.org/) from Blender Foundation. It is cross-platformed; so, it can be used both on PC and Mac and has a huge community featuring a lot of tutorials, models, and so on. This is a very good editor to begin with.

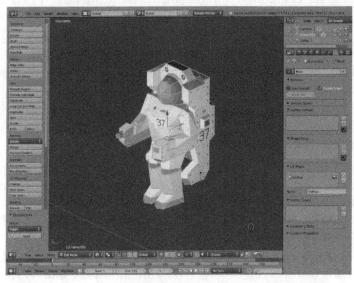

A screenshot of Blender

First of all, you need some sketches and concept of objects that you are going to create. It is good to start on paper. It helps to determine the basic details and principles of the visual look. The process requires some inspiration; so, a little research should be done. For example, for working on the astronaut, you need to find a lot of images of a real astronaut, stills from science-fiction movies of various decades, and even examples of corresponded toys, especially the vintage ones. It is a good practice to create a draft model from clay. It may help figure out many unclear moments in the geometry of the character. Many things cannot be understood only by a drawing on paper and speculative thinking. Therefore, clay might be very useful.

Then, a blueprint must be created—an accurate image of frontal, side, back, and sometimes top projection of the character or object. There is a standard pose for charters; the arms are raised. So, the figure has a shape of the letter T; such a look is known as the T-pose. But now, many modelers choose another version; when arms are raised less, forming a 45-degree angle with the body (the pose can be called an arrow pose), it helps prevent some potential problems with the shoulders after the arms are down. The blueprint must be loaded into a 3D editor, thus becoming a template to begin work with.

One of the ways to create a low poly model is to prepare a collection of cross sections of the object. Place them in the correct position and connect the appropriate vertexes, creating edges and filling surfaces with faces at the end. Such an approach can help to control the edges manually, avoiding the situation where the editors turn polygonal faces into tris automatically, thus creating ugly triangles. Alternatively, a model can be sculptured in a high-poly mode, but then it should be optimized either by using a special modifier controlling the number of faces inside objects (in Blender it is called Decimate) or by doing it manually.

> If you prefer to work with shapes in vector editors such as Adobe Illustrator rather than 3D editors, that is not a problem. Blender may import SVG-documents. Thus, some shapes can be created in Illustrator, saved as an SVG-file, and imported into a 3D scene. To resolve an issue with the anchor point, always place shapes at the very center of the artboard in Illustrator. If you need only paths, remove attributes from them before saving in SVG, for example, fill color so path color and width. Don't forget to turn imported shapes into meshes if you need to.

After the geometry has been completed and is solid, the mesh should be textured. For this operation, you need to learn such non-trivial procedures as UV mapping. It is good to comprehend it with a low poly model. The process becomes very visual and obvious because of the direct analogy with the paper craft. To add an element of texture on a specific surface, you need to tell the 3D engine where to find that graphic fragment in a texture document. For this job, the surface should be figuratively cut out from the 3D object, such as a slice of paper cut by a knife, and then put on a texture as a template. That is the basic idea of 2D-mapping. A principle of projection of 3D geometry on a flat image, three coordinates, X, Y, and Z, are transferred on a flat map which has only two coordinates. For the sake of clarity, these two coordinates are marked as U and V ($U = Xtexture$, $V = Ytexture$), rather than simply X and Y.

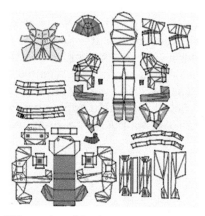

UV mapping of the Astronaut 3D model

Paper toys are not made of individual slices, but of elements connected together. There are lines of seams and lines to fold. The unwrapping has the same principles; some edges of a model must be marked as seams, other ones will be calculated as fold lines. The tricky part is that for the best result, you should define all the seams manually by selecting the appropriate edges one by one. Before that, you should imagine in your head how a 3D element (for example, an arm) can be unwrapped into a series of connected flat images. If the element is complex, it can be split into several separate fragments. Remember that a good UV map is not a conglomeration of abstract geometric shapes, but an image where the elements of the model can be easily perceived and read; this is the head, here are the fragments of the boots, and so on. Such a rule helps to create the texture right. In some cases, several takes are needed to unwrap the 3D model correctly. After each take, you look at the result, notice some error, fix it, and try to wrap the texture again. An unobvious feature of UV-mapping is the visual testing of the mesh geometry. If there are some problems such as double vertexes and sharp edges, the UV-map can demonstrate that; some parts of it will be lacerated.

To create a texture based on a UV-map, the map's layout should be exported as a raster or vector template. Blender has a special menu option for such an operation: **UVs | Export UV Layout**. After that, the layout can be filled with graphics.

3D engines in games required models in specific formats such as OBJ-documents. There should not be any lights, cameras, or incidental geometry in such files; otherwise, an error or visual glitches may occur. Besides the main geometry, there can be several other items in a data folder, such as textures, material files, and normal maps.

Understanding normal mapping

There is an interesting opportunity to add some extra details to your 3D model without adding any excess tris to its geometry. A regular object is wrapped by a special texture that stores some relief information. It is like putting on a dress made of cloth with bulging patterns. That is a very smart technical solution. A bitmap document keeps information about the heights of a specific region of an object. The data can be transferred and compressed as regular raster graphics. There is no need of special file formats. Such a method is known as bump mapping because various elements of 3D relief, called bumps for the sake of simplicity, are projected onto a flat image turning into a map.

Classical bump maps are grayscale maps where heights are coded by a pixel's brightness. A 3D engine wraps such a texture on an object but does not display it in a straight form. It only uses it for simulation of extra geometry (generating both concave and convex elements). All graphic details creating by a bump map are some sort of a fake or technological trick, but the final results are pretty convincing and spectacular, especially if the mapping is done perfectly.

Standard grayscale height mapping is pretty handy, but it has a drawback. Such maps are not carefully optimized, and need some additional post-processing procedures such as calculations of normals. That is why, now, a more popular form of mapping is normal mapping. It uses the same paradigm. The height information is saved as a raster document, but the data is stored in some pre-processing form that is more natural for 3D calculations. Such a result is attained by converting X, Y, and Z coordinates of the surface normals to RGB. Files with normal maps can be easily recognized by a distinctive domination of blue color in their palette. This is because a projected flat surface without any bumps is written as a single RGB color (128, 128, 255), which is a shade of blue.

Normal map

A racing game, Ice Driver, developed by Spooky House Studios UG (haftungsbeschränkt) uses normal mapping to create a shader effect of the bumped ice surface

Bump maps are usually generated via 3D editors using a function that allows you to bake 3D geometry onto a flat texture file. For example, Blender has such an option at the bottom part of the Render panel. But sometimes it is more handy to use some raster editors such as Adobe Photoshop (for example, to create a bump texture from a photo). The simplest case is the regular grayscale height map. It can be created even from scratch using basic drawing tools such as brushes or by converting a photo into a map by some proper color manipulations. A good flair, some tests on 3D models, and proper adjusting of a raster image can help draw the map manually.

A common example is a texture with some text that would be carved onto a 3D surface. But it is practically impossible to apply a similar approach on normal maps because geometry is coded in a less-analogous form, mostly being a source of digital information. Also, it is hard to reproduce it manually. The only exceptions are some minor manipulations with images, such as using a clone stamp tool for cloning some fragments and painting over some elements that are among other things that give an opportunity to create normal mapping textures that are seamless. For more complex operations, third-party tools must be used. For instance, NVIDIA Texture Tools for Adobe Photoshop (`https://developer.nvidia.com/nvidia-texture-tools-adobe-photoshop`), a special plugin for Photoshop that allows converting a grayscale height map into a normal map.

Alternative ideas for the game

Here are some alternative thoughts that may drive the game in another direction:

- The setting can be changed, for instance, to a fantasy one. In this case, the protagonist can be used as a dragon (or have wings, himself being some sort of Icarus) to fly among the clouds where obstacles and enemies can be hidden.

- Instead of space, the deep ocean can be used. The main character can use a diving dress. Shaders can be utilized to create interesting underwater effects.

- A racing mode can be introduced: a circuit in space, few opponents, and some unexpected obstacles on the track.

- Another possible mode can be called maintenance. The protagonist has to repair several modules on a ship deck (the player should hold a special button for a few seconds) while it is assaulted by the pirates. Enemies attack both the main character and the ship's modules. The objective is to maintain as many modules as possible for a fixed period of time (30 seconds, 45 seconds, 60 seconds, and so on). Special friendly turrets can be used as well.

- There can be an alternative and gloomy end to the game. In green containers, the protagonist finds messages from an astronaut lost in space many decades ago. After the last lighthouse, the protagonist will not find his ship but only a new green container. At that moment, he will understand that all these strange messages in containers full of requests for help were written by him. He was in a time loop.

Creating the identity for the game

The game is character-oriented because the best way to illustrate gameplay in the application icon is to display the protagonist. It can be an image of the helmet, for instance, with some enemies reflected on its surface. Or it can be an image of the unit and some deep space around it. A symbol of a cross hair in the game can convince the audience that it is a shooter game.

The following are the links you can refer to for additional information on the topics that are used in this chapter:

- http://en.wikipedia.org/wiki/Magnavox_Odyssey
- http://en.wikipedia.org/wiki/Space_Invaders
- http://en.wikipedia.org/wiki/Duke_Nukem_(1991_video_game)
- http://en.wikipedia.org/wiki/I,_Robot_(video_game)
- http://www.imdb.com/title/tt0082340/trivia
- http://en.wikipedia.org/wiki/Hovertank_3D
- http://en.wikipedia.org/wiki/Catacomb_3D
- http://en.wikipedia.org/wiki/Paratrooper_(video_game)
- http://www.redcross.org.uk/About-us/Who-we-are/The-international-Movement/The-emblem
- http://www.engadget.com/2013/09/19/gamecase-for-ios-7/
- http://store.steampowered.com/livingroom/SteamController/
- http://en.wikipedia.org/wiki/Toy_Story
- http://www.livescience.com/40103-accelerometer-vs-gyroscope.html
- http://gfxbench.com/device.jsp?benchmark=gfx27&D=Apple+iPhone+4S&testgroup=lowlevel
- http://gfxbench.com/device.jsp?benchmark=gfx27&D=NVidia+GeForce+GTX+550+Ti&testgroup=lowlevel
- http://www.rsart.co.uk/2007/08/27/yes-but-how-many-polygons/

Blueprints of the game

Here, you can see the blueprint of the protagonist and some images of the enemies and obstacles. The 3D models are pretty simple and have no moving parts; so, it can be developed even by novice users.

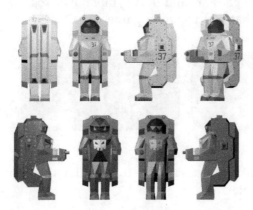

The following blueprint demonstrates the UI flowchart of the game, showing some basic elements of the game's interface including onscreen controls and the main screen layout:

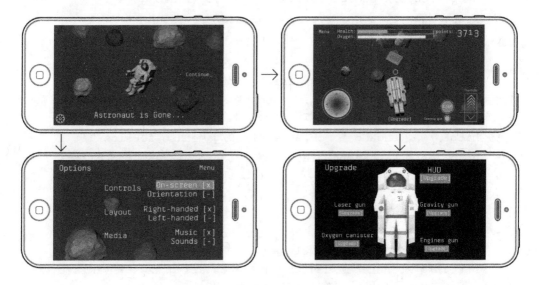

The following blueprint shows several examples of level design and various game situations:

Summary

Action game is very complex and minded genre, a peculiar quintessence of all other types of games since it requires a lot of efforts and skills. Nevertheless, it is not necessary to dread it. You only need to set some reasonable goals; good compromises can always be found. Don't try to develop something big; try to concentrate on a small but interesting project. 3D engines as well as 3D editors are pretty accessible now. It is possible to create simple models of characters and props yourself, especially if the graphic style is minimalistic. Always try to demonstrate the advantages of 3D geometry via game mechanics and story; the player should get maximum experience. There are some issues with controls on touchscreen devices in such types of games, but they can be resolved; you only have to turn on your creativity.

In the next chapter, we will try to expand the boundaries of mobile games, allowing them to interact with real-world objects. The next chapter is dedicated to mixed realities, a situation when boundaries between the virtual and real worlds are almost erased. You will learn what Augmented Reality is, how tracking markers look and operate, and what kinds of games can be created using mixed reality technologies.

9
Games with Reality

Today, video games are an integral part of human leisure. People spend hours in virtual worlds and in most cases, this is a very pleasant experience that makes them glad and sometimes even happy. But what if the games and their principles began to pervade into wider areas of human reality? What do you think about games being an integral part of reality?

Seeing real unreal

The meaning of **augmented reality (AR)** can be derived from the name itself: a reality that is augmented (enriched) by some sort of digital media. The process takes place in real time. It is interactive. The computer-generated elements are tightly connected with fragments of objective physical reality and have some specific reactions to them.

The following figure provides a schematic presentation of AR:

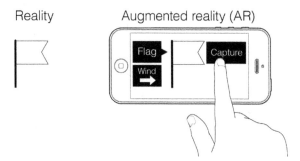

For example, when a system recognizes some landmarks in the game scene, it shows a textual description, plays a video, or displays some sort of 3D content. This information is strongly connected to a specific object, marker, or location.

To interact with AR, special devices are needed such as a computer system with a mounted camera, and some additional sensors may be required. The most advanced example is a heavy, head-mounted display. Most of them are pretty expensive and not easy enough to use everyday, especially outdoors. Fortunately, there is another example, that is, modern mobile devices that feature quite fast chips, good quality cameras, and some special installed software meaning they can easily overlay a representation of reality with some additional information. Moreover, they have given an extra boost to the popularity of AR technology because it is very handy to look at and use AR content on a smartphone rather than a personal computer. Because it is mobile, users have greater freedom to move and tilt the smartphone device to examine objects.

Now, AR is in fashion because so many branches of the modern economy see potential advantages in utilizing this technology. It is used in domains such as engineering, science, medicine, construction, education, commerce, advertising, and of course, entertainment (including games). The number of applications is growing everyday.

The following figure provides a schematic presentation of uugmented virtuality:

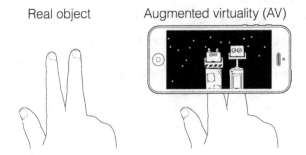

Real object   Augmented virtuality (AV)

In augmented reality, where the real environment plays a major role, some virtual elements are only useful additions, such as **Augmented Virtuality** (**AV**), which can be considered as AR's antipodes. In AV, the virtual space plays the major part, but the real objects are only a minor or functional element. Let's imagine an interactive-surface computer system (something similar to Microsoft PixelSense) that is capable of recognizing real objects placed on it. All computer-generated images displayed on the screen are part of the virtual environment, but a playing dice put on the surface is a real object. If the system would recognize the dice and read the value it would have on its top, since we would see the AV in action. So, the system uses fragments of reality to change virtuality. The usual example of AV is a weather forecast on TV where the background is CGI, but the host is a real human. AR and AV both are part of a space called **Mixed reality** (**MR**), which is an environment where real and virtual elements are blended in various proportions.

Learning augmented reality methods

AR applications need trusted markers to show their tricks, like a magician saying, "See that top hat? There will be a rabbit soon!", where the top hat is the reference point. There are several types of reference points and each of them has their own advantages and spheres of application.

The following figure shows most common forms of markers:

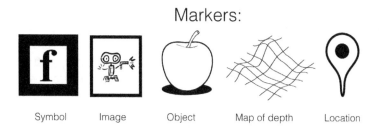

Markers:

Symbol   Image   Object   Map of depth   Location

The following are the short descriptions of these markers:

- **Symbol-based**: This is a basic method. It is the recognition and tracking of special graphic markers that are officially known as **fiducial markers** or fiducials (from the Latin *fiducia*, which means trust), but are sometimes referred to as AR tags, tracking marks, artificial landmarks, and so on. In some cases, slightly modified QR code markers can be used as well.

- **Image-based**: Graphic images such as photos or illustrations are split into reference points (the simplest way is to find a contrast frame around a picture). For instance, some applications use the one-dollar bill as the real-world basis that AR content will be created on, arguing that bills are the most common pieces of paper with graphics on them that an ordinary person can get their hands on. Such practice is used by programs such as Shimmer Augmented Reality Viewer for iOS (`http://ionreality.com/shimmer/`), which allows you to view 3D models in the AR space. In some cases, when very accurate recognition tasks are the goal, the image-based method may require very powerful CPU resources, because graphic images are split into thousands of markers that are being tracked in real time. This is why there is a service called Xloudia (`http://www.lm3labs.com/xloudia/`) that makes such calculations in the cloud computing to recognize complicated images on the server side.

- **Object-based**: Special real objects are used as markers. They can be passive (only their geometry and contrast color will be used as markers) or active (they will emit signals as light ones). Usually, they come in the shape of small cubes or spheres. There are also some applications that track a user's face and use their movements as input data.

- **Map-based**: A 3D map of the surroundings is created and the elements of a landscape are used as references. For instance, AR applications can use **simultaneous localization and mapping (SLAM)** tracking, a technology that is utilized by autonomous, movable robots. This is one of the most advanced methods of orientation and navigation in space. It allows us to use real surroundings, and virtual elements can interact with real-world objects in a more natural way.

- **Location-based**: This algorithm does not require any graphic markers. It uses the advantages of GPS (or its competitors), the compass, and accelerometer to determine the position and tilt of a device. Usually, such technology is used to add some virtual features to AR geo-information about real physical objects, such as city landmarks, in order to give the virtual representation of the information some textual and graphic description, interactive functionality, and so on. There are also some interesting massively multiplayer online game projects based on accurate location detection.

AR is based on three fundamental actions: recognition, tracking, and adaptation. The system analyzes an image that it gets from the camera and tries to recognize some important reference points (usually up to 10 can be used, but advanced AR systems can work with thousands and even tens of thousands of markers). Then it calculates changes of reference point's coordinates over a specific period of time. These parameters are tracking in real time. Then the virtual elements of the scene should be adapted to those changes of the coordinates. Thus general space parameters of the virtual objects, as position variable, rotation angles, and scales must be adapted to the new conditions. Since any shift of a reference point is always compensated by virtual "anti-shift", the subtraction of vectors gives the illusion that the virtual object is physically attached to a point in the real world.

The following image illustrates the process of interpretations of a fiducial marker:

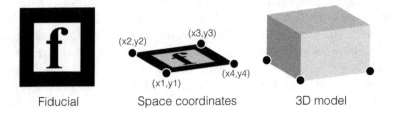

Fiducial   Space coordinates   3D model

The principle is pretty obvious and the mechanics are not so complicated. It centers around the precision of image recognition algorithms, and the smoothness of the illusion depends directly on them. It is not easy to create such algorithms from scratch without being an expert in image-processing theories and practices. Nevertheless, there are some ready-to-use solutions that iOS developers can utilize in their applications. Some people also try to write their own libraries on the basis of a popular AR solution like the open-source program ARToolkit (http://www.hitl.washington.edu/artoolkit/). The following is a brief list of various development platforms for iOS. Many of them can be integrated with popular game development environments such as Unity 3D:

- Metaio SDK (http://www.metaio.com/products/sdk/) from metaio GmbH

- String (http://www.poweredbystring.com/product) by String Labs Ltd

- Vuforia Augmented Reality SDK (https://www.vuforia.com/) by Qualcomm Austria Research Center GmbH

- VYZAR (http://limitlesscomputing.com/SightSpace/custom) from Limitless Computing Inc

- Wikitude SDK (http://www.wikitude.com) from Wikitude GmbH, which has location-based functionality as well

 PrimeSense (http://www.primesense.com/) is the company that created the technology Microsoft Kinect. One of its new innovations is Capri™, a sensor that is capable of creating an accurate 3D map of the depth of surrounding objects. The prototype looks like a tiny device attached to a smartphone or tablet. It scans the environment around in real time, since it draws the 3D map not once, but constantly, and considers any momentary changes in the space. Therefore, it is a real breakthrough for AR applications because it provides a pretty realistic map of surroundings. It is pretty accurate, fast, and graphic-markerless. This would be a great basis for different creative experiments. It is worth noting that PrimeSense was bought by Apple Inc. in November, 2013. So, it is now reasonable to expect that there will be depth sensors in future iOS devices.

Understanding fiducial markers

A graphic marker is both the popular metaphor for AR technology (since people associate it with some mysterious symbols printed on paper) and its weakness (since it means that additional equipment is required for AR applications to operate). The need for additional equipment to operate AR applications is often considered their disadvantage, and hinders the popularity of AR games because players can sometimes be lazy and don't want to print out the markers. Nevertheless, the graphic fiducials have very important advantages: first of all, they require less calculation power, and secondly, they are pretty accurate because fiducials are friendly for computer-vision systems and very accessible to perform digital image scanning.

Engineers have tried to "teach" machines to read some printed data by using optical sensors since the end of 1940s. However, the machines were not good at learning human alphabets because doing so would take a long time. Furthermore, the level of errors could be very high. Thus, a new paradigm was invented, that is, writing systems for machines; machine-readable mediums were introduced. Joseph Woodland and Bernard Silver patented the very first barcode in 1952. It looked like a section of a tree with annual growth rings. For the human eye, such an image was a total abstraction, but not for a machine. So, from the very beginning, machine-readable solutions were totally different from any traditional ways to provide information. The data was coded, so humans were not able to read complete information without an automatic translator.

The title of the book encoded in various data codes. All of them were created with a free barcode generator (http://www.racoindustries.com/barcodegenerator/)

Traditional one-dimensional, rectangular barcodes were standardized and became commercially routine in the 1970s. Since then, barcodes have turned into a symbol of communication between industrial machines and the physical world. However, the barcode was not the only one of its kind. Each industry had its own requirements and tasks, so some alternative solutions were introduced as well. First of all, the optical message got a second dimension, so it could store not only a linear array of information, but a matrix of data.

The approach is used in notable products such as PDF417, Data Matrix, MaxiCode, Aztec Code, and of course, the now famous **quick response (QR)** code, which has become a graphic metaphor of the connection between handheld devices and reality. It's pretty funny because the graphic representation itself is hard to consider beautiful. It looks too pragmatic and foreign, like a robot's fingerprints. The QR code is something that is out. This is because QR code was originally created to track vehicles being manufactured in the automotive factories of Toyota. Nobody had planned for the extra utility of that symbol and only few dreamed about palm-sized computers with cameras and instant Internet connections at the time.

In addition to this, it is interesting to mention that the QR code had a competitor. In 1999, ShotCode was introduced, a data format that was designed for regular cameras that an ordinary consumer might buy, rather than for special industrial systems. It also had a pleasant visual appearance and information inscribed in a circle-based structure; it looked more organic than the traditional barcode. Unfortunately, that was not enough. ShotCode is still in use, but the technology is not so popular. QR codes though, largely through the efforts of the Japanese market, are a sensation now. They are everywhere, in newspapers, magazines, on screens that air TV shows, in video games as hidden secrets, and so on. AR applications are no exception; some of them successfully utilize symbols that look close to QR codes as fiducials. They can be both a source of data (information stored in the data matrix) and a way to display reference points to perform 3D rendering.

Despite the fact that fiducial markers based on simple geometry are very effective, their graphic appearance leaves a lot to be desired. They also reveal all the functional zones of AR gameboards, ruining the magic. To solve this problem, some researchers suggest using invisible markers printed by infrared fluorescent ink, which cannot be perceived by a normal human eye, only by infrared sensitive camera. Thus, infrared fiducial markers can be printed over standard illustrations or text.

The requirements for fiducial markers can be determined very easily. You only need to keep in mind how AR applications work with them in different conditions:

- **Two dimensions**: Contrary to one-dimensional barcodes, which should be placed either horizontally or vertically in order to be read properly, AR markers can be perceived at any angle. Thus, they should be two-dimensional. This is why in most cases, the markers have square placeholders.

- **Lack of rotational symmetry**: This property is pretty obvious. For the vision system to easily determine where the horizontal and vertical parts of a marker are, there should be no hint of rotational symmetry. After being rotated to 90 degrees, the angle of the marker should not be equal to that of its initial state. This is why a plain square cannot be a fiducial marker; it must have some asymmetric elements inside.

- **Contrast with environment**: Markers should be significantly different from the ambiance around them so the image recognition algorithm won't be confused by other patterns or textures. Markers should be like the help symbol in a desert: a triangle with straight lines, which looks very unnatural against the space around it so it cannot be missed by someone looking down at it. As a rule, a contrast-continuous border is required around a marker.

- **Achromatic**: In most cases, this is not about the chromatic colors. Symbols must be made of black-and-white elements (bi-tonal); image scanning algorithms usually transform images turning any shades into their black-and-white representations. Such design also provides very high visual contrast, guaranteeing that the marker will be perceived even in poor lighting conditions.

- **Low density of elements**: Despite the fact that cameras in modern handheld devices have a high resolution, patterns inside markers should not include very small elements. Because of bad lighting, distance, distorted perspective, and other factors, the image-recognition system may lose these patterns.

- **Diversity**: The design should include the opportunity to generate several versions of markers, so the patterns or images inside must be changeable. That will help us use only a few fiducials for a single scene.

One of the major difficulties with fiducial markers is the lack of strong standardization. There is no single format to create geometrical shapes and data coding; each developer of AR platforms tries to invent something unique. Maybe this is quite natural because the technology is pretty young and not that popular yet, so they are only trying to find the right direction. AR technology also gives you some freedom to choose the marker you think is the most effective for your task. Among the popular designs that can be highlighted are as follows:

Fiducials designs

ARToolKit   ARTag marker sheet   SCR   Canon MREAL   IGD   reacTIVision
(fragment)

- **ARToolKit markers**: These are very popular. They look like thick, square frames with simple contrast symbols inside. The system is notable for its use of Japanese Kanji characters as standard patterns (pretty cyberpunk novel, isn't it?), since ARToolKit was originally created by Dr. Hirokazu Kat from Japan. One common marker displays the Kanji symbol: which looks like a letter "A" without a crossbar and means human. Of course, other types of images can be used, including the Latin alphabet, graphic illustrations, and so on. This is an advantage because it can make the design very human friendly.

- **ARTag**: This is a more advanced alternative to the traditional ARToolKit markers, with fewer errors and good overall performance. Our system looks like a grid of matrix barcodes in a small dimension (6 x 6 cells); they cover the screen surface like some sort of digital pattern. Because there are a lot of tiny markers, the accuracy of recognizing something that is displayed on the screen is pretty high. If some of the markers are unreadable to a camera because of the environment conditions or some occlusions, the other ones may ensure the process takes place. In some sense, ARTag markers can be considered a cheap alternative to advanced systems that scan surroundings in depth. If an object in the surrounding environment is extensively covered with markers, AR applications will perceive and include them in the improvised virtual mapping. The disadvantage of ARTags is their machine-friendly look, as the design is too technical.

- **Siemens Corporate Research (SCR) markers**: This system has an attractive simplification as any marker looks like a square array of big dots (4 x 4 elements) and it is very easy to produce, even by drawing them by hand using a marker pen. Besides being logical code, SCR markers look good as dots look pretty harmonic. A similar approach to designing markers is used by the talented indie game developer, int13 (`http://int13.net`), in their AR projects, and they have proved the efficiency of the markers.

- **Canon markers**: These are graphic reference points developed by Canon for its head-mounted display called MREAL. The markers consist of a black frame and hexagonal grid of elements inside the display screen. The design looks pretty elegant and according to developers, has few errors.

- **reacTIVision markers**: One of the most original reference symbol designs is used in an open-source computer vision framework called reacTIVision (`http://reactivision.sourceforge.net/`). It was developed for the fast tracking of fiducials. The markers have a very unusual, bionic appearance, like that of an amoeba. This geometric shape is not accidental; some topological information is stored inside such markers. Unlike the traditional 2D bar codes, the reacTivision markers stores data tree information. The design is so smart and logical that it helps to remove some stages from the digital-vision algorithms. There are some specially coded vertices and edges inmarkers. That is why the design is so organic and don't use any square shapes. The concept is simply genius! The full story is covered in the article *The Design and Evolution of Fiducials for the reacTIVision System* by Ross Bencina and Martin Kaltenbrunner (`http://mtg.upf.edu/node/442`).

The overall list of available marker designs is much longer; for instance, there are fiducials such as the **Hoffman marker system (HOM)**, **Institut für Graphische Datenverarbeitung (IGD)** markers, and some others. In most cases, their structure is very similar: a thick and contrasting outline and a pattern made of square blocks.

The problem with printing fiducial symbols can be resolved in various creative ways. First of all, the product itself should be so exciting and intriguing that the audience will try their best to find a way to print the marker. Moreover, some types of fiducial markers have a graphic structure that is based on simple geometric forms, for example, SCR or reacTIVision markers may be drawn by hand. Only a piece of paper and a black magic marker are needed. The piece of paper should be taken by a player and applied on screen where a PDF document that contains fiducial markers is shown. Because the paper is translucent, all the shapes can be easily traced. Of course, there can be some inaccuracies, but in many cases, they are irrelevant and the AR works successfully.

Note that if your game uses fiducials, a graphic document with a marker must be uploaded on the homepage of your website. It is also good to have a special test page with the marker displayed clearly so players have the chance to test AR in the game without printing anything, for example, you could use a computer monitor or another mobile device (an iPad can be made to act as a marker). Such practice prevails in the cute game *Om Nom: CANDY Flick* from ZeptoLab UK Limited (`http://www.cuttherope.net/ar/`).

The following figure demonstrates concepts of fiducials that don't need a printer and can be done by hand:

Handdrawn fiducial   Origami fiducial

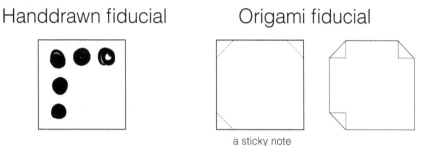

a sticky note

I also think that some research should be done about the idea of turning everyday objects into tracking markers. For instance, several flat-headed tacks spread out in specific positions can be turned into a reference point for an AR application. A more elegant solution can be used: a player turns a square sticky note into a fiducial by folding three of its corners, and such approach can be entitled origami AR marker. Another example is stickers or special branded custom cases for the iPhone/iPad, where to play a game, a player must take the case off and put it on the table. The idea is that the virtual game board is always with you. By the way, the silicone iPhone 5C Case with a distinctive grid of holes in it has an interesting potential as an AR accessory; may be somebody could turn such design into an object-based marker.

Working with graphics in AR games

For a better experience and a smoother perception of AR, all the functional elements should be removed from the screen. The fiducial markers are better kept hidden. This can be done by covering a marker with a virtual model that looks larger than the marker. In the simplest case, a planar image with a pattern or pictures can be used. The smartest way is to imitate a texture of a physical surface by photographing its fragment and reproducing it several times. For instance, the marker is placed on a wooden tabletop, then the game takes of photo of the wooden texture, and covers the marker with fragment of the photo. Of course, such a model is hard to develop and in many cases, the output can be less than ideal, but it looks very interesting.

It is spectacular to utilize 3D models in AR games; they express the idea of a center of a game scene better. If the marker defines a position for a character, the model that hides it is sometimes called a AR 3D puppet, and an inanimate object in turn can be referred to as an AR 3D Tower.

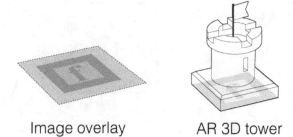

Image overlay   AR 3D tower

In most cases, the concept of 3D models in AR games is similar to that of assets in traditional 3D games; all the principles are the same, that is, rational using of polygons of polygons, simple materials, and good optimization. The only technical claim is a good color and geometrical contrast with its environment, where textures should be bright enough to be noticeable on various types of surfaces, both light or dark and solid or textured. Also, there is no fixed viewpoint for the virtual camera in AR games; players tilt their device very arbitrarily. Hence, 3D models are beneficial from any angle. The drawbacks of geometry or texture mapping cannot be swept under the carpet anymore. Moreover, it is good to think of the design of game elements in such a way that the game can be played comfortably on both horizontal and vertical surfaces.

Among other things, AR games do not necessarily need a 3D engine; they can use flat graphics and spites as well. There should be a good idea behind such a concept. For instance, a game can be created that uses a physical piece of paper as a game board, where tiny characters may interact with the text or printed illustrations. Another good idea is animated pictures in wall frames, in which where actions can take place. Additionally, a wall-projected AR game can be created where all the characters and items are flat and look like animated stencil graffiti—a very stylish approach, especially if the idea behind the game is cool.

Meeting AR games

The number of AR games on iTunes is not that big; they are still a niche product. This can be considered as a form of advantage, since any new title in this domain gets special attention. It is a good way to make a name for yourself. The term augmented reality sounds so great! The funny thing is that although the technology itself can be very complex, some of the game elements may be much easier to produce than traditional games because they require less graphic assets. Many AR games require fewer assets since only general characters are needed; but game scene decorations will be taken by players from the real world.

One of the famous examples of AR games for iOS is the *AR Defender* franchise from *int13* (`http://www.ardefender.com/`) — a smart tower-defense game series that looks especially breathtaking when a player uses outdoor environments as their background or when several people are playing in multiplayer mode, sitting at one desk. The game process is very balanced and addictive (it does not look like a plain technological demo application). AR, in most cases, does not cause frustration and works pretty reliably. The product can be easily considered one of the best demonstrations of fiducial-based AR.

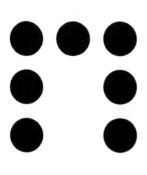 

The fiducial marker used in AR Defender game series and a screenshot of the game

NASA's Spacecraft 3D (`http://www.nasa.gov/connect/apps.html`) is not entirely a game, rather it's an educational tool. However, the process includes some gaming experience. The application is free and allows you to control various spacecrafts, including the Martian Rover. Authors of the application have used a very creative approach to designing the marker; it looks like a photo of a grain of sand taken by the Curiosity rover.

I like the idea implemented into *ARSoccer* (http://labs.laan.com/products/arsoccer/) by *Laan Labs*. The game tracks the motion of the player's feet and adds a virtual soccer ball, so a juggling game can be played in AR. The concept and realization is so brilliant! There should be more games with such mechanics.

One of the most ambitious initiatives is an intriguing game project called *Tabletop Speed* by *Dekko* (http://www.dekko.co/tabletop-racing-out-now-for-ios/). This is a Markerless AR application that tries to develop a 3D landscape of the nearby surroundings using the regular camera included in iOS devices. The standard background for the game is a tabletop that has been made messy with some dispersed magazines, pencils, small boxes, and so on. The application analyzes these objects (apparently some parallax calculations are used) and tries to recreate their 3D geometry in a virtual form. The resulting landscape is used as the track for a race. This sounds very exciting, but the process of 3D map generation may require some patience and attentiveness from the player.

A screenshot from Tabletop Speed by Dekko. The grid system is shown

AR Earth Invasion by *Hoi Yan Mak*, *SKY SIEGE 3D* by *Simbiotics*, and some other titles are examples of the AR fixed shooter, a very popular and viable subgenre. The concept is simple, players get some weapons (the characters are gun-turret operators, fighter pilots, drone operators, and so on), and they need to find and destroy various flying enemies by moving a smartphone or tablet around. Such games do not need any special fiducial markers. They may find some minor reference points around and utilize the advantages of the internal gyroscope. Of course, the space orientation method can be inaccurate, but because of the dynamic nature of such games and because virtual objects on the screen are considered as flying in space and not staying on any fixed surface, this is less evident and can be overlooked by players.

Using real landmarks

Location-based mixed-reality games (also referred to as **pervasive games**) are worth dedicating at least a chapter to, if not a whole book. It is a new and now massively popular class of online entertainment. The concept is simple. Some objectives, events, or items in a game are connected to specific GPS coordinates on a real map. Usually, such a marker is attached to a city or natural landmark in a game to better express it. The introduction of such games was only a matter of time, since they act as handy virtual maps and reliable algorithms of navigation. Sooner or later, it was obvious that developers would implement this in a game.

The general feature of location-based games is the real-world map scaled down for gaming — the story takes place in the physical world; as once stated by one of the characters from Lewis Carroll's books, "We now use the country itself, as its own map". Quests are set in real city streets so players have to step outside their comfort zones by virtually leaving their homes, using their cars or public transportation, and walking on foot to reach the reference points on a map. At specified locations, they must execute some virtual missions such as shooting a virtual antagonist, marking a place, picking up an item for bonus points or special hints, and so on. As a rule, some multiplayer aspects are involved in gameplay. The players can share information, set traps, fight for virtual territories, and so on. It is a truly adventurous experience, usually with some RPG functionality to motivate players more. Sometimes a time limit is involved so players are challenged to finish several game tasks in a predetermined time period. The scale of a game is big, so game matches can last a pretty long time, for example, 30 minutes, 45 minutes, 1 hour, and so on.

Common themes in location-based games are various types of otherworldly and ghoulish mysteries, paraboloidal espionage stories about conspiracy, magical-fantasy challenges, aliens living among us, and so on.

A screenshot of Ingress' official website

A game world can be additionaly supported by other types of media, being much larger than a simple virtual map on the screen. For instance, some portion of narrative can be provided to players via special books, fake piece of advetising, fake articles, and websites which were created by game developers. Because of such element, the game's pervasion in real world is much wider and deeper. The games with such components are known as alternate-reality games.

A notable example is a game that can be considered a world-phenomena — *Ingress*, created by *Niantic Labs* (`http://www.ingress.com/`). Originally, it was Android exclusive, but there are some plans to port it onto iOS as well. Players have to interact with so-called portals attached to public places, which can be built, hacked, upgraded via special mods, attacked, defended, and so on. There are two factions — the enlightened and the resistance — that fight for those portals, since there is a balance of confrontational forces in the game. Players have to use their virtual mobile devices on virtual streets to locate nearby portals, and a special locator provides directions.

The tricky part of developing location-based games is pretty obvious—the lack of universality. Games set in large cities may have better quality game environments as there can be a larger number of markers, a bigger list of challenges, and so on. Smaller towns get less attention from developers because they simply don't have enough time and people to cover all the possible locations. Automatic solutions are not an option since they may accidentally establish reference points at unreadable places, for example, over a water surface, on a roof, and so on. Some human testing and checking of the physical location is always needed to exclude any inaccuracies. The best way is to develop a product that is so attractive that a lot of volunteers will appear and submit candidates for landmarks at the locations where the game will be set. There is also a funny issue caused by such games—players use a real environment and try to interact with it, despite the fact that they might look like tourists taking photo of landmarks. Sometimes, the wider public can get a little bit confused by such strange activities: wondering "Why are so many people running around a statue, staring at their phones?"

Planning an AR game

First of all, let's be honest, the AR technology on mobile devices is very far from its true potential. Because of obvious technical limitations, it takes only baby steps toward the full expression of its talents. In some cases, the name of the technology itself has a greater affect on the audience than the real application's functionality. This means that to provide a truly viable product, rather than a single-purpose, technical gimmick, you should be less-ambitious, and the goals should be chosen very carefully and maturely.

Remember that there is no truly reliable way to generate an accurate model of reality on the screen of a smartphone camera yet. Modern devices can scan and recognize only a small part of the real world, since the screen representation is only an illusion and you have do your best to make it very convincing and attractive. Modern AR solutions should be used on iOS devices only when there's a creative idea and it is clear that a game will gain some advantage if it were to utilize the advantages of the AR environment. In other cases, it is better to skip the idea and use more traditional approaches. Remember that an exciting demonstration of a technology is not yet a game; games are not about an attractive technology, but about interesting playability.

To plan an AR game, it's better to start with the weak points of current technology implementations that are based on graphic-based markers and the standard camera (one the most popular methods today).

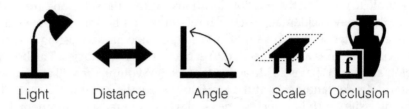

Light   Distance   Angle   Scale   Occlusion

- **Light**: AR systems based on the standard camera and graphical markers are sensitive to the quality of light. Thus, it is harder to play in dark rooms because computer vision begins to lose reference points, and the likelihood of errors is increased. AR activity usually stops when the light is minimal as the markers become unrecognizable. Another aspect is the lack of correlation between the real light source and virtual objects; it is obvious that simple AR systems cannot simulate the effect of real light sources on rendered 3D models as well as imitate real shadows.

- **Distance**: Generally, players' characters should stay at an appropriate distance from the fiducial markers and not too far away. In other cases, the system may lose functional patterns, and the markers will look too small for the camera resolution or be destroyed by distorted perspectives. Therefore, to play from a distance, the markers should be printed or drawn larger.

- **Angle**: This is critical mainly for planar graphic references. These work successfully within the range of the angle between a device and the surface on which a marker is attached, and it's also correlated with the distance. The range is pretty comfortable, although if the camera is tilted to an angle greater than 90 degrees relative to the reference graphics, the AR may be ruined.

- **Environment**: For most AR games, flat and empty spaces are required as the basis for the virtual construction. These may be tabletop surfaces (preferably without a mess!), floors, walls, and so on. There should also be the opportunity to place a marker. It may be hard to get a good background for the game in crowded places such as public transportation, waiting rooms, or even working places, because there a lot of objects around. Therefore, many AR games can be considered as entertainment that is restricted to private zones, such as living rooms. Only in such environments will players get the full experience.

- **Scale**: In some cases, the virtual game world is bigger than its physical counterpart and this cannot be adjusted by players in the game. This is because of some technical issues (for instance, the size of virtual units strongly depends on the dimensions of the graphic marker), or there may be other reasons that developers did not include such functionality.

- **Boundaries**: Ideally, an AR game should track both the fiducial marker as the most trusted reference point, and the boundaries of the surface that it is placed on (for instance, to determine the edges of a tabletop or its distance from walls). However, it is hard not only because of additional technical issues, but also because it raises some big questions about game-level design. For example, what should the application do with some game elements placed outside of the boundaries? The logical answer is not to display them! But that can destroy the total balance of the game! Some sly players begin cheating, whisking some enemies away from a desk or putting them behind walls. A boundaries check creates a more flexible structure in game worlds, AI, and so on, but very often, it is not an option. However, without it game elements may float in the air because a tabletop was over; such a picture is not very realistic and players may become frustrated.

- **Occlusions**: Since games with a single fiducial marker do not scan their surroundings to develop a 3D map, the real-time background through the camera is totally flat. There cannot be an occlusion between a real object in a scene and a virtual one, even if the real one is situated closer to the player.

Markerless AR games are not ideal either. They try to track reference points from the surroundings. This job is not always perfect so virtual elements shift in wrong directions very often, and the process is not smooth enough. The games that generate a 3D landscape of the space around are conceptually interesting, but they require players to make special preparations and adjustments, and some people may be confused or get unsatisfactory results.

You should remember the psychosocial aspects of behavior invoked by AR games. In some cases, a person playing an AR game can look very strange, moving more actively, especially if they are involved in a gameplay of AR shooters. Many games force players to spin around pointing at devices that are on the walls or buildings around. This may be uncomfortable both for the players and the people around them.

Now you see that there are some problems in AR gaming. Many of them cannot be resolved easily without changing some technical paradigms. However, you can try to develop rules and conditions so that players will accept that these disadvantages are not noticeable. The audience should be guided by special directions, showing only the bright side and not the troubles backstage. Primarily, it should be clear that an AR game is not a universal product for the masses as many traditional mobile games are. It is a specific application for a specific gaming experience. This should be explained to future players so they are prepared for this fact.

In the beginning, it is necessary to invite the audience to a proper environment where the game will feel comfortable and can be expressed well. In its name and description, appropriate guidance words may be included, such as top-table fight, table battle, and living room race. Then, photos of ideal spaces to set up games can be included in the promotional materials and the tutorial of the game. It is as though the product is honestly admitting that there are some conditions. The model of proper behavior can be additionally implemented by assigning the game to a reasonable gaming genre and suitable mechanics.

Scheme of pole-based games

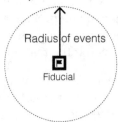

Some of the most popular environments for AR games are horizontal surfaces such as tabletops or floors. A fiducial marker is placed somewhere on them and the game generates virtual fragments around it. The coordinate system of the scene is strongly defined by the marker. Such a paradigm can be referred to as the pole AR game. A game scene has a fixed center and all events take place around this point. In some senses, this concept is very similar to early single-screen arcades and fixed-shooters games. The players cannot leave their specified location and must fight all their battles centered around that spot. It looks like technological postmodernism— classical mechanics rethought using modern principles.

The motion of characters and other game pieces can be organized based on several basic schemes:

- **Towards the center**: All elements try to reach the pole, either to hold this position or defeat a character situated there. Usually, this occurs in assault-based action games. Imagine a game with a fortress or a gun turret at the center and concentric waves of bloodthirsty enemies.

- **Escape the center**: Characters running from the center to the edges of a gameboard. This occurs in "escape-a-prison" type games. There is a dungeon and a lot of prisoners are running out of it and a player has to catch each of them by tapping on their figures on the screen.

- **Running in circles**: This scheme is mostly used by challenges that take place on circuits. It can be various types of races. In such competitions, cars, boats, horses can take part but airplanes look more preferable because you do not need to check interactions with surface of real objects. Additionally the scheme can be used by different race-type board games where players move their game pieces on the circuits.

- **Chaotic**: There is no system or specific location objective for characters. They move in random directions. Since this is seen in games where there are many kinds of arena-based death matches and since it is ideal for multiplayer modes, several people may control the characters fighting in AR.

The pole AR games have a small creative issue; as long as an AR game scene has no strict screen frames and a player may see everything constantly changing in their perspective and vision angle, some procedures cannot be hidden. I'm talking about the spawning of characters. In a traditional game, enemies may be generated out of the current window (behind the back of a player, somewhere around the corner of a 3D map) and then successfully introduced into a main scene. But the AR scene in most cases cannot use such tricks. Therefore, some other tricks should be invented on the fly. Usually, authors simply demonstrate characters that come out of the ground (this is very good for stories about zombies) or dropping down from above (this is suitable for war games). Additionally, doors or hatchways can be used as if they were on a surface. Games with a science-fiction background may utilize a metaphor about space portals.

Another interesting idea is special, flying transportation vehicles that land troops who then disappear from the camera's view so that players cannot easily track where they went.

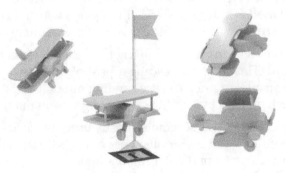

Air race around a fiducial

By its appearance, the concept of the pole AR game is very appropriate for various types of board games. As a rule, they are played sitting at a table, so seasoned players will be familiar with the requirement that a tabletop is needed for the process. In AR, you can create a fully virtual game board or add some additional functionality to traditional game pieces made of paper or plastic. For example, special playing cards can have fiducial markers so by placing them on a game board, players can interact with a virtual elements of the game. Mixed reality is very suitable for various race games, in particular those where flying vehicles are presented, as long as such a concept does not require very accurate tracking of the surface where the game is transpiring. It is better to use aircraft with propellers to animate the scene further. Some strategy-based games are good as well; a tabletop with a lot of tiny units and real-time combat makes a great scene!

You could imagine an AR game concept where some scroll effects are used since the fiducial marker cannot be left behind, the realistic movement of characters in space is replaced with a treadmill-like solution. A character is fixed at one position, but obstacles (or enemies) are moving on a virtual conveyor belt toward him; for instance, in a simple *SteepleChase* game. Such mechanics are called AR-projected scrolling, and are not very realistic since they simulate a moving surface on something that is stood still. Nevertheless, that can be resolved using various creative tricks. For example, the game may use very minimalistic artwork and the obstacles may be designed as simple geometric shapes, so the behavior of such obstacles won't appear that unnatural.

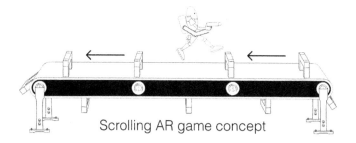

Scrolling AR game concept

A panoramic AR game is another popular type of game mechanics. Its major advantage is its lack of graphic fiducials. A player is in the center of a so-called sphere of events, a space where all game elements are concentrated. AR in such games is not as accurate as models with graphic markers; this disadvantage is usually compensated with faster gameplay and simpler game rules. Usually, this is used in shoot 'em up arcade games or shooting-range games, in which enemies appear around players and they have to move their mobile devices quickly, while aiming and shooting. The most reliable concept is that of fighting flying antagonists, such as alien spaceships or hostile aircrafts, since flying elements look very natural in AR. An interesting concept is to use some ideas from paratrooper-type arcade games, such as tiny airplanes flying above a player's character that may drop some troops, so a lot of angry parachutists are.

A screenshot from AR Earth Invasion shooter game

However, there are some issues with the panoramic games. First of all, the basic concept requires players to spin around to find and fight protagonists; the gaming process looks like simple physical physical jerks and that may sound pretty positive. However, it may become tedious and cause a little dizziness if the gameplay is very fast. Therefore, it is better to include an option that turns the sphere of events into a semisphere, so instead of 360-degree range, a 180-degree range would be used by a game. Another problem deals with the question of game fragments situated outside of the camera frame, for example there can be several enemies which are placed behind the back of the player. They cannot be seen until they do some actions. There must be a signaling system to indicate that an enemy is hidden somewhere. This can be a mini-map or radar on where characters are marked or special red arrows may show the direction of enemy fire so a player can quickly re-orient his mobile device. By the way, the radar can be turned into a general element of the gameplay; a game can hide something in a random position within the sphere of events. The element is very tiny so it cannot be easily noticed from a distance, but the radar can hint at its location by changing the tone of its sonar sound or using special animation. That can be an improvised adventure game.

Remember that for an AR game to be perceived as a reliable product should be very observant and honest. If the system notices any trouble with the AR environment, for instance, the fiducial is lost or it is too dark, it must pause the game and display an alert so a player knows the current conditions are bad and should be adjusted. The interruption of the game process in the case of technical difficulties is necessary; otherwise, it can be very frustrating. The game scene disappears from the screen, but events continue somewhere within the application, causing a loss of game progress. The image-recognition algorithms can report some problems with the light. Additionally, it may track a fiducial and pause the game if a very sharp and dramatic change of values occurs, signaling that the marker is lost. Hence, it is good to have a special support system in a game to avoid misunderstandings with players.

The concept of an AR game

Regarding the concept of a game, I would like to describe a less-common model of using 3D content in AR. As a rule, 3D objects are shown on or above some physical surfaces; figuratively speaking, such AR is convex. However, it is interesting to try to create a concave reality by creating an illusion of a hole in a surface. Fiducials create a boundary for such a virtual recess and players have the chance to look inside the rabbit hole. The idea is manifested in the best way when markers are placed on a wall, since the game creates an AR window where some virtual scene is shown. The illusion is pretty smooth because the virtual image has a real-time response to change the player's point of view and position is space of a camera; there are parallax, real time linear perspective distortions, and so on.

Game content is perceived as a truly and natural addition to the real world. It is like having a window into new dimension in your own room. Of course, a special step is needed to process the final image because a mask should be used to cut off all the faces of the 3D model that have to be invisible, but that should not be a big problem, as long as the marker can provide the exact coordinates of the window.

The following image represent a schematic image of the AR window:

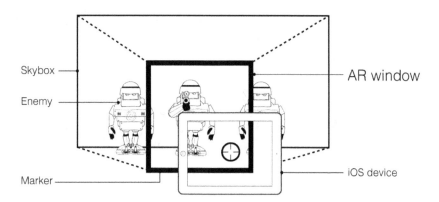

In an ideal scenario, the image recognition system in the game is smart and capable enough to rotate any object in an AR window, that has contrast cadres; so players may use framed pictures on walls or computer monitors. Since rotating objects can be considered unrealizable for some reasons graphical markers can be used instead. It is more efficient to use something similar to the ARtag system when several fiducials are used at once, as such an approach will add some more reliability. For example, the game will continue operating in conditions where only some of the markers are within camera range.

The game scene looks like a diorama: a window-frustum shaped skybox with some decorations inside and of course, a few characters. It is good to make a shooter game. Several enemies are seen behind the AR window; players need to shoot them using their mobile device as a gun.. In the meantime, the enemies have guns, so they can hit the player as well. This means the player has to use strafing, and hide behind the window ledges in the game scene. The ideal plot for using such game mechanics is a story about a fortification defended against hordes of enemies. The AR window demonstrates some avenues to approach a pillbox, it stands on a hill, but a player is a shooter in this improvised tower. There are dozens of angry enemies downhill; who are trying to reach the pillbox. The player has to defeat those enemy waves.

At harder levels, some additional elements can be introduced; enemies may begin to use tanks or other types of armored protagonists may emerge. It would be spectacular to use particle effects to illustrate hits in the pitfalls; some splinters may shoot out the AR window.

The following are the screenshots of various game situations:

This particular game can also have an alternate mode called Sniper duel, for example. The player is a sniper positioned in a building; he has one window for shooting. In front of him is another building with a lot of windows and several holes in the walls. That is the place where the enemy sniper is hidden (maybe a couple of them); the enemy constantly changes his position. The player should be very attentive to be able to catch the small signs that the opponent is about to shoot them. At the same time, he should not be an easy target, his head sticking out a window in the game scene; it is more sane to protrude a little from the corner of the window in the scene. That is a slow, but very alarming type of a shooter game.

Planning game controls

Surprisingly, in most cases, a control system in AR games is not a major issue. Players move the camera over a virtual scene, so there is no need for special controls to maneuver in space. Thereby, many AR shooters only have one major button: **FIRE**. So, it is more interesting to know about a situation when fiducial markers are turned into tools to manipulate a game situation.

There is a difference between AR on mobile devices and some academic experiments that use optical head-mounted displays to produce AR. The latter usually needs a player to hold a gameboard with fiducial markers in his hands, tilting and moving it, since the gameboard is a way to control objects and events in a game.

A very good example is *Marble Game*, designed by *Ohan Oda* and *Steve Feiner* at Columbia University's Computer Graphics and User Interfaces Lab (`http://www.youtube.com/watch?v=6AKgH4On65A`), where players needed to guide a ball through a maze. A special game board with ARTags was used as the physical base for a virtual game scene. Its tilts were transformed into directions and the value of "the speed of the ball". Such a method cannot be applied for handheld devices, as a player cannot hold both the device and the gameboard in his hands for a long period of time. However, some tricks with movable markers can still be done: a player may hold the device with one hand and rotate it, or hold the fiducial marker in the other hand and create a game-like situation. The only issue is that the standard paradigm says that the marker is the center of a game scene, and by rotating it, you rotate the whole scene. Since the game should be oriented towards one item rather than being scene based. For instance, a model of a spherical antenna is used as an AR 3D puppet. The fiducial can be freely rotated on a tabletop by a player, which is followed by the rotation of the antenna on the screen. The main objective of such a game is to catch signals from different directions. It is worth mentioning that these signals should come from the coordinate system of the screen (view orientation) as the local coordinates of the marker are not reliable; they always change their orientation on a surface.

AR Soccer use the player's feet as an input device

A more flexible system can be constructed by using several markers. While a few of them can be used to define the coordinate system of a game scene, one marker can be used for controls. Of course, this can be more problematic in some instances, for example, if players need to print several fiducials and use them efficiently. However, this can be resolved with proper design solutions.

Potentially, markers can be placed on the movable parts of the objects (for example, wheels, legs, and so on) in order to track their motions. For example, special paper rings with fiducial prints can be put on the index and middle fingers and be introduced into the game's reality. This can either be a demonstration of augmented virtuality, where the player's fingers would play unique controls or be a part of the AR experience. This can be imagined as a funny fighting game where the fingers of two players may transform into kickboxers.

Controlling real objects

There is a pretty original and breathtaking initiative that lets mobile devices control small electric toys, turning them into an interesting game experience. All this started with remote control car models and helicopters managed through special iOS applications. This was funny, especially for kids, but also pretty traditional. Except the controller that was new, the process itself was the same and did not require any additional video game background. Later, more advanced models such as AR.Drone, the amazing quadricopter by Parrot (http://ardrone2.parrot.com/) appeared. AR.Drone has an onboard camera, and its native iOS application uses live video images along with virtual controls and other onscreen digital information, since it truly adopts itself to the requisites an AR environment. Moreover, developers also let the quadricopter get involved in some gaming activities. There are special applications that use AR to create a virtual game environment. For example, *AR.Rescue 2* lets players collect items in the air and fight with alien invaders. It even uses fiducial markers to generate virtual decorations for the player's base. The game idea and mechanics are very close to early arcade games; it can even be considered as primitive. However, because of an advanced context involving AR and high-end remote controlled flying vehicles, the immersion effect is simply tremendous!

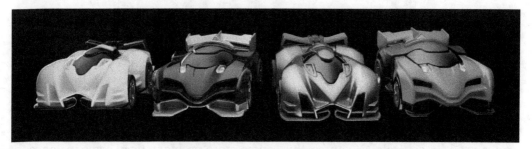

Anki DRIVE's little robotic cars, which use mobile devices as a platform for AI.Image Courtesy: Anki DRIVE

A different approach to mixed reality was made by a company named *Anki, Inc* (`http://anki.com`). They introduced a unique concept of gaming. Their product is known as *Anki DRIVE*; it includes a special mat with track markings on it and a couple of toy cars. These tiny vehicles are not simple remote controlled toys; in reality, they are small robots with sensors that scan the track and send information to an iOS device where calculations and decisions are made in real time and sent back, since the device is the mother computer for these cars. It can control their speed, direction of movement, and so on. Therefore, there are real objects as well as accurate virtual representations of them inside a special iOS application. Any manipulations in the virtual space have a direct effect on the behavior of the real toy, and vice versa.

Primarily, this concept means that the players have a very precious remote control system with advanced feedback algorithms, but that is only a minor part of the idea. Since the application is capable of controlling the tiny cars by itself using artificial intelligence, the machine can take part in race challenges against a human. Therefore, the developers say, "This is a video game in a real world".

From a digital perspective, the system works like a traditional computer racing game: one vehicle is the protagonist and is controlled by a real person, but other participants are NPCs and use AI. The only difference is that the result is shown as real-world installation rather than an image on a screen.

To expose all the advantages of such a paradigm, *Anki DRIVE* provides their robots with some functionalities that can mainly be implemented in a virtual world. The cars can shoot each other, but there are no real bullets; a firefight is taking place inside the application, where virtual calculations of shots are being made. Nevertheless, the consequences are pretty real; the car that is hit loses control.

There is also a system for virtual upgrades, which can either be used for weapons or for racing performance (virtual engine tuning). Thus, ANKI's robotic car can be considered as a shell filled with features available via external programming as the system is very flexible; it only needs to create new code to add new objectives and features. It is even hard to say whether this is a demonstration of augmented virtuality or augmented reality.

The problem with many remote-control toys operated via mobile devices is that there are only a small number of applications which are vanishing quickly. Usually they are created by in-house software divisions and have no SDK for external developers. Another weak point is the lack of universality. The design of vehicles make impact on genres of AR games they are used in. It is hard to turn a tank into a unicorn. The company Orbotix tried to resolve all these disadvantages by introducing a pretty new concept of a mobile-device-controlled toy called Sphero (`http://www.gosphero.com`).

It looks like a simple ball, but special electronic and mechanical systems inside it let it roll in any direction by itself without any external impulse. It gets the direction of its movement from a mobile device. So, at the basic level, the invention looks like a robotic ball that obeys a player's commands and can run around on a floor, a tabletop, and so on. But fortunately, the magic does not stop here.

The Sphero robotic ball. A control interface is seen behind. Image by Obotix

First of all, Sphero has several internal sensors, so it can detect various real-time events and register various types of data. The device has a magnetometer, a three axis gyroscope, and an accelerometer, which can report on collisions with other objects, current position, distance traveled, velocity achieved, and so on. Thereby, the ball can be easily turned into an input device. By holding it in their hand, a person may rotate it, tilt, move in space, and all these actions will be registered and successfully transferred to an iOS device where they will be interpreted and used. Moreover, the ball has multicolor LEDs since a visual feedback is possible that increases the efficiency of the input procedure. Such a functionality may be utilized both in games and other types of applications; developers only have to think of how to use such an opportunity.

It seems that by playing the role of a controller, Sphero brings in some sort of augmented virtuality to the mobile game market (a physical object is used to control computer-generated reality), but that is not all. While it rolls around using its engine, it may be turned into an object-based marker used in AR applications. All the sensors provide pretty accurate positioning information, so the simulation looks smooth enough. In contrary to traditional planar markers, the robotic ball may freely rotate around a vertical axis, changing the angle of the main character (or another type of 3D object attached to the fiducial) rather than whole game scene. This is a much more flexible system, exposing new gameplay opportunities. Another advantage is the universal geometric shape of the marker; a sphere is very handy for putting AR 3D puppets on it or adding digital special effects.

Sphero is widely popularized as a unique gaming system with various functionalities and a lot of interesting features. The technology is very young, but there are a bunch of different games for it, including the ones from third-party developers. Most of the products are for the AV functionality and use Sphero as a handy controller; nevertheless, there are others that experiment with the AR environment. Orbotix did a good job by offering a special SDK (`https://developer.gosphero.com/`) so many more developers might begin use Sphero's talents in their products.

Gamificating reality

Have you noticed that some real-life duties, even very simple ones, are always regarded as boring and exhausting; however, any gaming activity, even very complex ones, in contrary are perceived as very interesting and entertaining? Players may spend hours on video games without losing interest and attention, which means that so much of intellectual energy is concentrated on one particular process and is lost in space! What if it can be turned into something really useful? In such a case, a person may have some pleasant gaming experience and solve some real problems in one full swoop. This initiative became known as gamification. It turns a needful task into a game process by finding the right metaphors and mechanics. For example, it would diversify the meaning of domestic chores: a washing machine in the form of an arcade cabinet or a robotic vacuum cleaner transformed into a rover, exploring some unknown corners of some planets (this illusion is created using the AR technology).

The basic type of a "gamificated" job is a system of various achievements and trophies, so there is no gameplay as such, rather a system of rewards for various ordinary life actions. Did you do something good today? Say helped a colleague, called your parents, read a good book, fed your goldfish, ate some healthy food, or walked a mile? If the answer is yes, introduce some special achievements in each category.

People like prizes, as they have a very strong motivating power, and also like to share them with others. So social networks in this context are very useful.

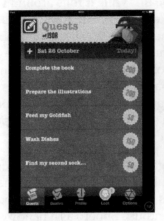

The EpicWin application brings in a reward system from RPG video games into real life

There is an interesting application called EpicWin (`http://www.rexbox.co.uk/ epicwin/`) that can turn any activity into a list of achievements. Moreover, it brings RPG Mechanics into the real world. The application turns any task in the user's sheduler into some sort of a game objective, once a task is complete the user gets some points. Then some special achievements can be attained. That sound funny, but it works, to get some virtual rewards user try to succeed in real world. It is not a surprise that many fitness-oriented applications use such approaches to encourage sportive accomplishments of their users. Another good example is various educational or training software. A system of achievements, which leads to real promotion, can be used in the project's management and, of course, in commerce. Loyal customers can be rewarded with virtual prizes and points that later can be transformed into a discount. Retail networks have been publicizing such promotions for years, motivating customers to buy specific products to collect special promotional stickers, and so on; however, now it can be demonstrated visually via a mobile application with game-like mechanics.

Remember that many non-entertainment applications can be "gamificated" to express functionality better and to have some effect on a user's behavior. There is also a term, **serious game**, that defines this wide class of applications. A very good example is the hybrid vehicle, Honda Insight, introduced in 2010. It had an Ecological Drive Assist System created to stimulate a more ecological style of driving a car. To attain such an objective, the system used a kind of mini game. By driving economically, a driver gets special points, which are displayed as leaves on virtual plants since the goal is to let them grow.

All the examples in this section are a little bit about selfishness. Users make some useful things for themselves, but there is a class of "gamificated" applications referred to as games with a purpose, dedicated to certain public interests. For example, some products help scientists resolve problems by splitting them up into a bunch of small and simple pieces that an ordinary person can deal with. This sounds similar to volunteer computing when people provided the calculating powers of their computers to a third party (the most famous example is the *SETI@home* project), but there is an important difference. The games with a purpose intend that gaming skills of real people are used rather than CPU time. There are some tasks where creative thinking of humans is required to solve problems or generate ideas. It is no secret that humans have better imagination than machines. This is a type of crowdsourcing where thousands of people all over the world work on one project or in one domain; the only difference is that an interface in the form of a game and objectives turn into abstract metaphors that can be used as the elements of a gameplay. As a rule, the goal looks like an unusual puzzle, requiring the player to search for some consistent patterns, recombining elements, and so on. A strong emphasis is made on unique human abilities such as intuition, a thing that none of the computers have.

The best example is the unique online puzzle, *Foldit* (`http://fold.it/portal/`), dedicated to protein folding. Players operate with the structure of proteins; the goal and virtual representation of elements are abstract enough, so a lot of people without a specific scientific background can take part in puzzle solving. The purpose of the project itself is to collect all the solutions that users can provide and to analyze them. In 2011, The Huffington Post wrote that it just took three weeks for Foldit to solve a protein problem of a monkey virus, a process which could not be solved by traditional methods for 15 years in a row. This is simply incredible!

The following screenshot is from a game with a purpose called EteRNA (`http://eterna.cmu.edu/web/`) where the process of designing RNA sequences turn into an elegant connection puzzle:

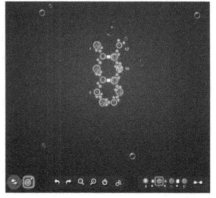

Various natural science tasks are usually presented in the form of puzzles. The game pieces are simple and in many cases have minimalistic design, and the rules are pretty tricky, an ideal mix! Archivist type of duties usually deal with an adventure genre when it comes into the picture; players can be pushed to click photos of a particular location to update an image bank, add tags to improve some search engines, test some digital solutions, and so on.

Of course, there are some disadvantages of gamification. First of all, not every activity can be easily split into abstract pieces and turned into a game. Some compromises should be made that can distort the reality giving inaccurate results. Another weak point can be derived from the main conceptual part of the method—I'm talking about people. The user community may be disappointing. There will be a lot of participants, but only a small number of active ones, so the overall activity can be ineffective. Finally, there are some moral and legal aspects. Are you playing the game with a purpose, is it a form of entertainment, or is it a form of work? In the case of scientific projects this, undoubtedly, is some kind of volunteering. But what if in the near future, an evil corporation creates a pretty attractive and addictive game, hiding its true meaning? In this case, thousands of players would solve the various puzzles without guessing that in reality, they provide employment to this evil corporation. This could be reckoned as some form of virtual exploitation of other people's efforts and ideas. Apparently this is a very good concept for a cyberpunk or dystopian novel. Nevertheless, there is a strong hope that such scenarios would appear only in fiction, but our everyday routine will become more vivid because of gamification. For example, I end this particular chapter with an achievement saying, "Congratulations, you have completed writing this book!"

The following are the links you can refer to for additional information on topics that are used in this chapter:

- http://en.wikipedia.org/wiki/Fiducial_marker
- http://en.wikipedia.org/wiki/PrimeSense
- http://www.youtube.com/watch?v=ORfNNYCgtzI
- http://en.wikipedia.org/wiki/Bar_code
- http://inventors.about.com/od/bstartinventions/a/Bar-Codes.htm
- http://en.wikipedia.org/wiki/QR_Code
- http://en.wikipedia.org/wiki/ShotCode
- http://www.researchgate.net/publication/220302586_Invisible_Marker-Based_Augmented_Reality
- http://www.hitl.washington.edu/artoolkit/documentation/vision.htm
- http://www.hitl.washington.edu/artoolkit/

- http://en.wiktionary.org/wiki/%E4%BA%BA
- http://www.artag.net/
- http://campar.in.tum.de/twiki/pub/ISMAR/IarAbstractARTag/
  IarDetailsFialaSlides.pdf
- http://www.telepresenceoptions.com/2012/07/trying_out_canons_
  mixed-realit/
- http://citeseerx.ist.psu.edu/viewdoc/download?doi=10.1.1.134.27
  19&rep=rep1&type=pdf
- http://en.wikipedia.org/wiki/On_Exactitude_in_Science
- http://news.cnet.com/8301-1035_3-57605616-94/google-augmented-
  reality-game-ingress-to-expand-to-ios-in-2014/
- http://youtu.be/QnsR-kZUx6o?t=3m35s
- http://orbotixinc.github.io/Sphero-Docs/docs/sphero-api/index.
  html
- http://orbotixinc.github.io/Sphero-Docs/docs/collision-
  detection/index.html
- http://orbotixinc.github.io/Sphero-Docs/docs/sphero-locator/
  index.html
- http://jalopnik.com/5094111/2010-honda-insight-ecological-
  drive-assist-system-grows-leaves-gets-other-features
- http://www.huffingtonpost.com/2011/09/19/aids-protein-decoded-
  gamers_n_970113.html

Summary

AR games are at once ambitious and a very young class of digital entertainment. They have a very high potential and bright conceptual base, but very few really good examples exist. Many games look like a good presentation of some aspect of the technology, rather than a product with an addictive gameplay and interesting plot. AR is a capricious thing; there are dozens of factors that can ruin the illusion of an additional layer of reality. Nevertheless, it is worth to dream and design such games, especially if there is an interesting idea at hand. Some technical issues can be minimized by various creative tricks. The concept should be so good and intriguing that players should not be lazy to print out some fiducial markers or simply trace them by hand. It will help them to open a window into a new reality that can only be seen through a mobile device. Maybe someday we will be surrounded by games, and all our duties and even the physical reality will be "gamificated". Boredom will be totally overcome and this will make us a little bit happier!

Index

augmented reality. *See* **AR**
Augmented Virtuality. *See* **AV**
AV 296

B

board game components
board 101
bonus 101
cards 101
game pieces 101
pitfalls (force majeure) 101
random number generator 101
rules 101
board games
basic components 101
history 99-102
objects 102-106
unpredictability level, changing 105
board game squares
door (or Container) squares 112
empty squares 112
spares squares 112
Bog 153
bonus
about 186
earning 186, 187
types 186
bonus types
accumulator 186
color bubble 186
bump maps
about 289
drawback 289
Button game idea
advantages 90
disadvantages 90
buttons
functionality 57, 58
receipt 56
states 56
using 55
buttons states
disable 56
focus 56
normal 56
pressed 56

C

canvases 24
card decks
containers 113
doors 113
spares 113
card games 101
Catch the sequence mode 148
CCG 108
collectible card game. *See* **CCG**
color blindness
about 66, 67
red-green blindness 68, 69
color bubble
about 186
one-off 186
renewable 186
color gun 171
color vision deficiencies
achromatopsia (monochromacy) 67
deuteranopia 66
protanopia 67
tritanopia 67
controlled falling 199
conversation tree
about 238
constructing 238-241

D

design and idea concept
advantages 89
disadvantages 89
device orientation
about 85, 86
one finger 85
two thumbs 85
dialogues
using, in adventure games 236-238
digital board game
alternative ideas 125
application icon 125
blueprints 126, 128
character restrictions 115
elements 110, 111
goals 110, 111

Metaio SDK 299
Mixed reality. *See* **MR**
Mixed shooters
   about 257
   examples 257
monologues
   main domain 235, 236
   using, in adventure games 234
motion tween 25, 198
Moving columns mode 147
MR 296

N

negative feedback 150

O

offline positive feedback 150
onscreen controls
   advantage 276
   disadvantage 275, 276
   working with 274-277
optical character recognition (OCR) 281
orientation-based controls
   about 278
   working 278, 279

P

parallax
   about 188, 189
   example 188
   scrolling parallax 189-192
photography light box 42, 43
Photosensitive epilepsy. *See* **PSE**
phrases
   working with 241-244
physics-based puzzles
   about 135, 204
   examples 135
pitfall
   about 186
platformer characters
   brutality, creating 180, 181
   creating 184, 185
   cuteness feature, adding 177, 178

scary factor, creating 178-180
   uncanny valley, avoiding 181-183
platformers
   about 165
   animation, starting 192-195
   application icon 205
   characters, creating 184, 185
   character's look, planning 176
   game controls 173, 174
   objectives 167
   planning 170
   plot 171, 172
   screen layout, setting 174, 176
   types 167-170
platformer scaffolding 165-167
platformer triggers
   about 187
   On-floor trigger 187
   Specific color trigger 187
   Universal color trigger 187
platformer types
   scrolling setup 169, 170
   single-screen setup 167, 168
player
   portraying 46
plot squares chart 11
positive feedback 150
PowerVR Texture Compression. *See* **PVRTC**
programming animation
   creating 203, 204
protagonist walking cycle
   about 197
   additional phases 200
   intermediate phases 201, 202
   main phases 199
   main phases, basic principles 199, 200
   planning 197, 198
   working 198
PSE
   about 71, 72
   flashing elements, checking 72
Purr game idea
   advantages 91
   disadvantages 91
puzzle
   about 129

About Packt Publishing

Packt, pronounced 'packed', published its first book "*Mastering phpMyAdmin for Effective MySQL Management*" in April 2004 and subsequently continued to specialize in publishing highly focused books on specific technologies and solutions.

Our books and publications share the experiences of your fellow IT professionals in adapting and customizing today's systems, applications, and frameworks. Our solution based books give you the knowledge and power to customize the software and technologies you're using to get the job done. Packt books are more specific and less general than the IT books you have seen in the past. Our unique business model allows us to bring you more focused information, giving you more of what you need to know, and less of what you don't.

Packt is a modern, yet unique publishing company, which focuses on producing quality, cutting-edge books for communities of developers, administrators, and newbies alike. For more information, please visit our website: www.packtpub.com.

Writing for Packt

We welcome all inquiries from people who are interested in authoring. Book proposals should be sent to author@packtpub.com. If your book idea is still at an early stage and you would like to discuss it first before writing a formal book proposal, contact us; one of our commissioning editors will get in touch with you.

We're not just looking for published authors; if you have strong technical skills but no writing experience, our experienced editors can help you develop a writing career, or simply get some additional reward for your expertise.

Unity iOS Game Development Beginner's Guide

ISBN: 978-1-84969-040-9   Paperback: 314 pages

Develop iOS games from concepts to cash flow using Unity

1. Dive straight into game development with no previous Unity or iOS experience

2. Work through the entire life cycle of developing games for iOS

3. Add multiplayer, input controls, debugging, in app and micro payments to your game

Cocos2d for iPhone 1 Game Development Cookbook

ISBN: 978-1-84951-400-2   Paperback: 446 pages

Over 90 recipes for iOS 2D game development using cocos2d

1. Discover advanced Cocos2d, OpenGL ES, and iOS techniques spanning all areas of the game development process

2. Learn how to create top-down isometric games, side-scrolling platformers, and games with realistic lighting

3. Full of fun and engaging recipes with modular libraries that can be plugged into your project

Please check **www.PacktPub.com** for information on our titles

UDK iOS Game Development Beginner's Guide

ISBN: 978-1-84969-190-1   Paperback: 280 pages

Create your own third-person shooter game using the Unreal Development Kit to create your own game on Apple's iOS devices, such as the iPhone, iPad, and iPod Touch

1. Learn the fundamentals of the Unreal Editor to create gameplay environments and interactive elements

2. Create a third person shooter intended for the iOS and optimize any game with special considerations for the target platform

3. Take your completed game to Apple's App Store with a detailed walkthrough on how to do it

SDL Game Development

ISBN: 978-1-84969-682-1   Paperback: 256 pages

Discover how to leverage the power of SDL 2.0 to create awesome games in C++

1. Create 2D reusable games using the new SDL 2.0 and C++ frameworks

2. Become proficient in speeding up development time

3. Create two fully-featured games with C++ which include a platform game and a 2D side scrolling shooter

4. An engaging and structured guide to develop your own game

Please check **www.PacktPub.com** for information on our titles

www.ingramcontent.com/pod-product-compliance
Lightning Source LLC
LaVergne TN
LVHW062304060326
832902LV00013B/2037